JACK WELCH
and the
GE WAY

JACK
WELCH
and the
GE WAY

Management Insights and Leadership
Secrets of the Legendary CEO

ROBERT SLATER

Best-selling author of *Get Better or Get Beaten! 31 Leadership Secrets from GE's Jack Welch*

McGraw-Hill

New York   San Francisco   Washington, D.C.   Auckland   Bogotá
Caracas   Lisbon   London   Madrid   Mexico City   Milan
Montreal   New Delhi   San Juan   Singapore
Sidney   Tokyo   Toronto

Library of Congress Cataloging-in-Publication Data
Slater, Robert
    Jack Welch and the GE way / by Robert Slater.
        p.   cm.
    Includes bibliographical references.
    ISBN 0-07-058104-5
    1. Welch, Jack (John Francis), 1935–   .   2. General Electric
Company—Management.   3. Chief executive officers—United States—
Biography.   4. Industrial management—United States.
5. Leadership—United States.   I. Title.
HD9697.A3 U5   IN PROCESS
338.7'62138'092—dc21
[B]   98-22053
                                                                    CIP

McGraw-Hill

A Division of The **McGraw·Hill** Companies

    2 3 4 5 6 7 8 9 0 DOC/DOC 9 0 3 2 1 0 9 8

ISBN 0-07-058104-5

The sponsoring editor for this book was *Jeffrey Krames*, the editing supervisor was
John M. Morriss, and the production supervisor was *Suzanne W. B. Rapcavage*.
It was set in Janson by *North Market Street Graphics*.

Printed and bound by R. R. Donnelley & Sons Company.

McGraw-Hill books are available at special quantity discounts to use as premiums and
sales promotions, or for use in corporate training programs. For more information,
please write to the Director of Special Sales, McGraw-Hill, 11 West 19th Street, New
York, NY 10011. Or contact your local bookstore.

This book is printed on recycled, acid-free paper containing a minimum of
50% recycled de-inked fiber.

Contents

Jack Welch Launches His Revolution

"Business is simple."

AUGUST 1997.

It's a perfect day for golf.

There isn't a cloud in the sky on this glorious summer day at Martha's Vineyard, and as the two men tool around the freshly manicured course, soaking up the sunshine and the easy conversation, they can't help but reflect on how lucky they are just to be out of their offices, away from the usual, frenetic grind. And it isn't only the fresh air and sunshine that help them forget their worries—it is also the satisfying victory they have just chalked up against the other half of their foursome. After all, these are men who hate to lose—at anything.

To an onlooker, the scene seems ordinary enough: two middle-aged men out for a day on the links: one tall and graying, with a slight paunch; the other shorter and at least a decade older. They could be friends or colleagues, or perhaps a couple of salesmen playing hooky from the job.

But to a discerning eye, the scene conveys much more. Muscular, crew-cut figures clad in bulky business suits stand incongruously at the ready, speaking softly into walkie-talkies. Set against the smooth, contoured green of the course, they seem wildly out of place, like some bit-part actors who have wandered onto the wrong movie set. But their presence makes it abundantly clear that this is no ordinary golfing duo. In fact, these are two of the most powerful men on earth. The older of the two men is John Francis Welch Jr., chairman and chief executive officer of the General Electric Company; and the taller figure is William Jefferson Clinton, the forty-second president of the United States.

Golf is Welch's favorite form of recreation. In May 1995 he had open-heart surgery and recovered quickly from the ordeal. Now he's out on the links every chance he gets, often playing as many as thirty-six holes a day. (In the summer of 1996 he broke 70 for the first time; his 69 helped him win his club championship at the Sankaty Head Health Club in Nantucket.)

Though Welch and Clinton have knocked off eighteen holes already, the two men agree to play another round. It's a rare moment of relaxation and freedom for both of them, and they're not yet ready to quit. In fact, no one wants the day to end. Completing the foursome are Ben Heineman Jr., GE's general counsel, and attorney Vernon Jordan, one of Clinton's closest friends. Pleased that Welch and the president are getting along so well, Heineman silently congratulates himself for proposing to Jordan that the two men, who happen to be vacationing at the Vineyard at the same time, get together for a round of golf.

The foursome plays another nine holes. This time Clinton and Welch lose, but even that doesn't put a damper on their day. They are prepared to carry on, but Heineman has to catch a ferry, so the group finally breaks up. Two days later, a photo of a relaxed Welch and Clinton, smiling in their golf cart, appears in *The New York Times*.

Welch has a lot to smile about.

He is the head of the most valuable business enterprise on the face of the earth, the most admired and powerful business executive in the United States. Sure, the media pays far more attention to the Bill Gateses (Microsoft) and Andy Groves (Intel) of the world, but Jack Welch doesn't mind others grabbing the limelight. He is indisputably the most successful chief executive on the American scene, and he doesn't need a newspaper or magazine article to validate his achievements. Gates, Grove, and company may be flashier, but Welch has the distinction of presiding over a business that has few rivals in size and none in complexity. And although Welch may not admit it, he takes great pride in the fact that GE is the envy of every one of its worldwide competitors.

Although Welch has much to crow about, he is not the boasting kind. What other figure, having attained so much in business, would say, as he did in December 1997, "I take absolutely no comfort in where we are today"? Doesn't he care that he has revived GE and turned it into the most dynamic company in the United States? Is this just false modesty? Not at all. What he really means is this: *I cannot afford to rest on my laurels. If I do, I'm dead!*

Earlier in the summer, Welch's General Electric led the *Business Week* list of Top 100 Companies in Market Value for the second year in a row, with $198.09 billion. This was not just a list of American companies, but a list of *all* companies. In second place was Coca-Cola ($169 billion), followed by Royal Dutch/Shell of the Netherlands and Britain ($168 billion), NTT of Japan ($151 billion), and Bill Gates's Microsoft ($148 billion).

GE, which had been number one in U.S. market value since 1993, had a market value of $240 billion by December 31, 1997, $50 billion more than the next highest in the world, Royal Dutch/Shell. By March 1998, GE's market value had risen to $250 billion.

What was more, General Electric ranked near the top of the list of the most profitable companies in the United States. Its first-quarter profits in 1996 reached $1.67 billion, more than the company earned ($1.65 billion) during all of 1981, the year Welch took over as chairman and chief executive officer. Its third-quarter profits of $2.01 billion led all American companies, ahead of Exxon ($1.82 billion) and Intel ($1.574 billion). (In 1996, GE had its best year ever. Its revenues rose to a record $79.2 billion, a 13 percent increase over the previous year's revenues, and its profits increased 11 percent, to a record $7.28 billion.)

Back at work in September, Welch carefully monitors his latest initiative, a companywide program designed to improve the quality of GE's processes and products and save billions of dollars. He is proud of the initiative, proud that his 270,000 employees have embraced the program so enthusiastically, proud that the early indications of the program's value are far better than he expected. He didn't invent the concept of business quality, but listening to him, one would have thought he had. That's Jack Welch. If he likes an idea, he embraces it with the ardor of a fiery preacher delivering a favorite sermon. If Welch likes an idea, it becomes *his* idea.

In late October, Welch dines at the White House, a guest at the State dinner for China's president, Jiang Zemin. Spotting Welch in the receiving line, Bill Clinton introduces him to Jiang as "My favorite golf teacher." Clinton and Welch enjoy a warm laugh. Both silently recall their relaxed golf outing that August day at the Vineyard. But the president's purpose in inviting the GE chairman to the White House this night is not merely social. It is Clinton's way of recognizing General Electric's growing business role in China; and of acknowledging Jack Welch as one of the country's most successful—and most powerful—individuals. (A *Time* magazine survey in June 1996 selected Welch as the sixth most influential figure in the United States. Clinton topped the survey.)

On November 19, 1997, Welch turns sixty-two years old, and he makes it clear that in three years he will step down as GE's chairman and CEO.

How could this be? How could the man who golfs with presidents, who runs the most powerful business enterprise on earth, who seems so fit despite his years, contemplate quitting in the year 2000? The answer has to do with GE's practice of retiring its CEOs at age sixty-five. Yet, anyone meeting Jack Welch that fall would conclude, just by looking at the spring in his step and listening to the lilt in his voice, that the chairman of General Electric is just revving up, that he is years away from walking away from it all. Though he had been through open-heart surgery two years earlier, the GE CEO is bursting with energy.

Yes, his face has a few more lines, and his receding hairline gives away his true age. Yet, with his squat, muscular build, and his solid five-foot eight-inch frame, he still looks like the hard-checking hockey player he once was. If a film were to be made of Jack Welch's life, one might choose to cast Hollywood actor Robert Duvall in the lead role. Welch's face shifts from one expression to another: There is the warm, eager smile when he likes what he hears, and the stern, steely-eyed countenance when someone has said something silly (a favorite Welch phrase). The childhood stutter is almost gone; it surfaces only occasionally, usually in an emotional burst. Despite the earlier heart surgery, Welch continues to put in long business hours, making endless phone calls to employees, visiting GE businesses around the world, sitting down with financial analysts, board members, and journalists (and this author). He is, one could argue, the proverbial last person at GE headquarters in Fairfield, Connecticut, to turn the lights off (a GE-manufactured light, of course!).

Great business leaders, Welch believes, have to possess large doses of energy. More important, great business leaders have to know how to use that energy to re-energize others. Like a football coach, Welch moves from meeting to meeting, conveying that message—and a host of other ones as well, some of which have become his trademark:

- Business is simple.
- Don't make it overly complicated.
- Face reality.
- Don't be afraid of change.
- Fight bureaucracy.
- Use the brains of your workers.
- Discover who has the best ideas, and put those ideas into practice.

Learn, Learn, Learn

It is that last management secret—Discover where the best ideas are, and implement them—that captivates Jack Welch the most today.

Keep learning. Don't be arrogant by assuming that you know it all, that you have a monopoly on the truth.

If there is one feature of American business that eats at Jack Welch, it's the all-too-frequent and pervasive arrogance of senior managers who insist that they know it all—that there is nothing new for them to learn.

Welch thinks differently.

Always assume, he argues, that you can learn something from someone else. Or from another GE business. Or even from a competitor. *Especially* a competitor.

Welch today is caught up in creating, nourishing, building what he calls a learning culture at GE. He likes that phrase, and never stops talking about it.

Creating a learning culture at GE is, in Welch's view, the best way to eradicate one of the least attractive features of the old GE.

The "not invented here" syndrome: Unless a GE employee thought of the idea, it was simply not worth pursuing.

The CEO of General Electric has no qualms about urging his "troops" to scour the corporate landscape, searching for good ideas, studying them, and then incorporating them into GE's business life.

Any idea, if it's a good one, says Welch, is worth pursuing and adopting—no matter where it comes from—inside GE or at Wal-Mart, Motorola, Mitsubishi, wherever. Welch has a neat phrase for adopting an idea. He calls it "legitimate plagiarism."

On the surface, it may seem odd that Jack Welch encourages his GE colleagues to search elsewhere for the best ways to run a business. After all, GE is the strongest company in the United States, and for decades other business leaders looked to GE for original ideas and strategies. Many GE alum are now leading other *Fortune* 500 companies, and GE is widely regarded as a virtual training ground for corporate leaders. Shouldn't GE be the one to teach others what business is all about?

Nope. Not at all, the GE CEO would say. That would be the silliest thing in the world. Why should it be assumed that I, Jack Welch, know all there is to know about business? I don't. Believe me, I don't.

Still, it needs to be said that Jack Welch *does* have lots of ideas on how business should work, and many of them make great sense. And he is constantly imploring his employees to inculcate them into GE's business activities.

Communicate, Then Communicate Again

But it is Welch's ability to get others excited about those good ideas that truly explains his phenomenal results.

He is a communicator par excellence. Of all his management secrets, his uncanny ability to communicate, to engender an enthusiasm in employees, may well be his greatest. He knows that it is not enough to simply raise an idea with employees. He's not naive enough to believe that all 270,000 of his workers will absorb his ideas the first time around. He knows that he will have to keep repeating an idea until it finally sinks in with everyone at the company.

To be sure, it's becoming easier for Welch to get his ideas across to people in the company: reviving GE has earned him enormous respect, so the mere fact that Jack Welch endorses an idea gives it a significance it did not have before. As W. James McNerney Jr., head of GE Aircraft Engines, notes: "The excitement comes from within him and is extremely contagious. He's a tremendous motivator. He's excited and he gets you excited and you're always moving forward. He keeps it simple. The differentiator between GE and many other companies is that there are more people moving in the same direction and with the same enthusiasm. Jack might like this on his tombstone. 'I wasn't smarter than anyone else, but I helped 270,000 people make me look smarter than most.' "

Others at GE have been good at their jobs, and have been able to motivate and to explain, but no one has Welch's ardor. He remains GE's number one cheerleader. No wonder he calls himself "the advertising manager of our company."

He has the zeal and the optimism and the lexicon of a winning football coach:

"Exciting."

"Remarkable."

"Staggering."

"Incredible."

These are the words Welch employs to describe one of the most powerful enterprises in the world. General Electric's employees are scattered all over the country, indeed all around the world. To get his messages across, Welch places himself in front of General Electric employees in Paris, Tokyo, Croton-on-Hudson, Cleveland, and dozens of other places year after year. He yearns to teach, to communicate, to energize, to summon the best from his troops. He presides over these meetings mostly to learn, however.

To ask.

To probe.

To get a "take-away" (another favorite Welchism).

The Revolution That Began at the Top

By late 1997, General Electric is a far different company from the GE of a decade ago, or two decades ago. And that is largely due to Jack Welch. Revenues for 1997 reached a record $90.84 billion, making it the fifth-largest American company in revenues (after General Motors, Ford Motor, Exxon, and Wal-Mart Stores); its net earnings increased to more than $8.2 billion, another record figure, making GE the second most profitable American enterprise (after Exxon). GE's first-quarter earnings in 1998 showed revenues at $22.62 billion and profits at $1.89 billion, significantly ahead of 1997 first-quarter figures. The figures are a testament to the resounding success of the Welch revolution launched in the early 1980s.

It was clear from the day he took over the company that he planned to launch a revolution at GE. He wasted no time in executing his plan. No one tinkered with a basically healthy major company as much as Jack Welch did. No one in American business had the vision to fix something that wasn't broken. No one was as successful in making the repairs as GE's then-new CEO.

It was an odd revolution that he fought, but it was still a revolution. Frequently, revolutions start at the bottom. Welch's began at the top. He made General Electric leaner, tougher, more competitive—with fewer people, fewer business units, and fewer managers. To many, GE had been an icon, a sacred institution that could not be tampered with. But Welch had no such notions. He applied a kind of "survival of the fittest" rule of thumb to his businesses and to his personnel; those who survived were the ones who were needed. All others were discarded. He sold $10 billion and purchased $19 billion worth of businesses. And he pared the 1981 workforce from 412,000 to 229,000.

For seventeen years, quietly yet meticulously, he led a series of revolutions at GE, seeking to recast a highly bureaucratic, labor-intensive corporate giant into a highly productive machine that would function with the speed and simplicity of a small entrepreneurial company. Given GE's size and complexity, it was a Herculean task. Yet throughout the 1980s, he wrought enormous change at GE. Others accused Welch of creating turmoil. He remained unfazed. He knew that, to turn GE around, to make it the world's most competitive enterprise, change was essential.

Not surprisingly, GE personnel responded to Jack Welch and his unsettling plans with wariness, even suspicion. After all, change, to them, usually meant a turn for the worse. Change was just a sugarcoated word for a plant closing or dismissal.

By the late 1980s, when Welch was satisfied that he had restructured General Electric sufficiently, that the company was positioned to become a world-class competitor, he shifted ground and turned his attention to GE's employees. He knew all too well how discomfiting and unnerving the earlier part of the 1980s had been for these, the survivors. While they had not lost their jobs, many of their friends had, and they themselves had spent the past decade fretting over their futures.

He decided that the best way to give his employees a sense of stability was to let them take part in company decision making. One major side benefit of this new plan was to make employees more productive as well.

When, in 1989, Welch decided to empower GE's employees, he used a companywide vehicle called "Work-Out." This was a program that was designed to give everyone down to the factory floor level a chance to propose ways of improving GE's day-to-day operations. Not surprisingly, it took time for the chairman's ideas to sink in.

By the late 1990s, Jack Welch could have stood still. He could have said to himself, We've done it. We've made GE the most competitive enterprise on earth, let's ease up, let's sit back and enjoy things for a while. But Welch is not about to tread water. He enjoys the game of business too much and yearns to be in the middle of it. He is too passionate about his work; he wants to be the very best at what he does, and he wants GE to be the very best.

Coupled with that unremitting zest for business is his belief that GE can only suffer if it stands still. He believes in change. He believes in remaking things. He believes in taking a hard look at what he and the company have done in the past few years, and making decisive, bold changes, sometimes in the blink of an eye.

And he is far more self-confident today than he was when he took over the company Thomas Edison founded over a century earlier. Then, in 1981, Welch had ideas, plenty of them, but they were simply that, ideas. He could have no way of knowing whether his ideas, once implemented, would produce the kind of financial results he wanted. Now, seventeen years later, Welch knows that his business strategies have worked, that he was right all along. And he relishes the fact that his troops now exhibit deep respect for him and for those strategies. Example: When he proposed, as he did in 1995, that GE undertake a new initiative to improve the quality of its products and processes, the program was adopted with religious zeal around the company.

Anyone traveling around GE facilities during 1997, as the author did, could sense an almost revivalist atmosphere coursing through the offices and corridors. In his "Letter to Share Owners" (Welch's phrase) in the company's 1996 Annual Report, he described that atmosphere as "monomania," and indeed it was. Slogan-filled banners hung on walls.

GE businesses held "tournaments" as project teams competed to see who could achieve the best results in improving quality. Nearly every conversation with a GE employee, senior or junior, contained a positive reference to the quality initiative, a far cry from the early dismissive noises heard when Work-Out was first introduced.

The Past? Never Heard of It!

Jack Welch rarely talks about the past. He's constantly talking about the present—and the future. He cares passionately about where GE stands today, but, above all else, he wants to figure out how to make the company improve itself over the next year, the next two years, the next five years; how to make sure that GE employees adapt themselves to GE's values—to the GE Way.

So he is simply not interested in the past.

He sees no point in reliving old experiences. There's nothing he can do to change the past, so, he suggests, why dwell on it? He's just the opposite of the war veteran who can't wait to recount the glory days to anyone who will listen.

To Welch, there are no glory days of yesteryear. At least none that are worth retelling. The past is not a pleasant road to travel for Jack Welch. It's a road strewn with tough decisions and controversial changes that helped to make GE what it is today. It's a road littered with the people he laid off, the business units that were shut down or sold off. It's a road that has its own malodorous lexicon.

"Downsizing."

"Restructuring."

"Rationalization."

This was the "hard stuff," as he calls it, the stuff that Jack Welch felt he had to do to revive GE.

Well, he did it, he downsized, restructured, and rationalized, and has little appetite for talking about how he did it now. Welch, the tomorrow-driven man, would much rather talk about the future.

There's a bit of irony in Welch's disenchantment with the old days. For it was in the past—the past seventeen years, that is—that Jack Welch earned his stripes and made his name as America's most impressive business leader.

Yet, he never gloats.

Ask him to compare GE with other companies and he'll wince.

Don't ask me that. "No comment" is the phrase he throws at you, as if you've tossed him a hot potato he doesn't want to handle. He just doesn't want to be known as someone who critiques and criticizes rivals.

Sure, at times he'll talk about another company. But he'll never accuse a company of being slothful or stupid, or of not doing things the GE Way. It's as if he knows how hypocritical it would be to bad-mouth other companies while at the same time adopting some of their "best practices." It's also not his nature to stand on Mount Olympus and pontificate. He insists he's got too much to do.

In some noteworthy ways, General Electric is still the same company that Welch took over in 1981. It's the company that has for years been making:

- Power generators
- Lightbulbs
- Locomotives
- Dishwashers
- Refrigerators
- Aircraft engines

Yet, there's a new GE as well. The new GE of the late 1990s is increasingly a service-oriented business. More than 60 percent of the company's revenues now comes from its traditional services businesses (GE Capital and NBC, two of the company's most prized assets) and the service components of its equipment businesses (such as aircraft engines, power generation, and locomotives).

Once the symbol of GE was a lightbulb. Lately it has been Jerry Seinfeld or Tom Brokaw or the First Colony Insurance Company.

Even the sign outside company headquarters says GE, not General Electric.

Yet, even as Jack Welch is shifting the emphasis of the company away from manufacturing and toward service, he constantly warns outsiders against jumping to the conclusion that one day General Electric will abandon its manufacturing side. The opposite is true, he insists.

For GE to grow in the late 1990s, it needs a strong manufacturing base, if only to convince the public that the company possesses the skills and resources to handle the service end.

The chairman's goal—in pushing for a learning culture, in driving quality, in transforming GE into a more service-oriented enterprise—is to demonstrate that a multibusiness company can endure and flourish. He's been fighting that battle for years. He's still waging it. Unlike what CEOs at other multibusiness enterprises have been doing, Welch has no plans to spin off parts of the company. He acknowledges that a number of GE's major businesses, especially GE Capital, would function beautifully on their own. But he sees no benefit to the company in spinning off any of GE's twelve major businesses. He knows all of the side effects of getting too big—the bloated bureaucracy, the difficulty of controlling so big a place, the layers of managers—but he thinks he has a handle on all those issues. And he's not afraid of GE's employment rolls getting larger. Indeed, GE's workforce has increased from 229,000 in the 1980s to 270,000 in the late 1990s, partly because the big drive to downsize is over and partly because of some new acquisitions.

Welch is not afraid to throw fresh human resources at projects that he wants to promote—like quality and service.

To those who still cling to the notion that GE is merely a conglomerate (a word that Welch hates), he retorts that, unlike other conglomerates, at General Electric, the sum is greater than its parts. The benefits of having so many varied businesses far outweigh the disadvantages, and GE's twelve major businesses really do learn from one another and help one another out when necessary.

GE is steeped in a learning culture and it is this fact—and this fact alone—that makes General Electric a unique company. Not because it has so many market-leading businesses. Not because those businesses are so diverse. But because it is the only major American enterprise with such a diverse group of huge businesses that possesses a learning culture. As Welch puts it:

> **What sets [GE] apart is a culture that uses this wide diversity as a limitless source of learning opportunities, a storehouse of ideas whose breadth and richness is unmatched in world business. At the heart of this culture is an understanding that an organization's ability to learn, and translate that learning into action rapidly, is the ultimate competitive business advantage.**

Jack Welch's track record is the envy of every executive in the United States—and, for that matter, around the world, so we can do no better than to take a good, hard look at the strategies and management insights of this enigmatic business leader. As we do, it is worth keeping this in mind: The techniques and ideas that Welch has employed to move GE forward are applicable to any size corporation, small, medium, or large.

So it's worth paying attention to Jack Welch's business philosophy. His track record is the most compelling evidence that his ideas work. Undoubtedly, there's a great deal to be learned from him. What follows, then, are the leadership lessons that Jack Welch, America's most successful CEO, used to transform GE from a $25 billion company steeped in bureaucracy and tradition into a $90 billion corporate juggernaut.

Thomas Edison would hardly recognize the place.

PART I

Act Like a Leader, Not a Manager

"Find great ideas,
exaggerate them,
and spread them like hell
around the business
with the speed of light."

Embrace Change, Don't Fear It

"Change was occurring at a much faster pace than business was reacting to it."

TOO MANY MANAGERS are afraid to change.

Too many managers believe that standing still is the best business strategy—probably because it's the safest.

Jack Welch says it's nonsense to fear change.

Welch, the tomorrow-driven leader, loves change.

He finds it exciting, daring, imaginative. Thinking about change, he argues, keeps everyone alert and on their toes.

Change, he notes, is a big part of the reality of business. Take the business environment—it is constantly changing. New competitors. New products. Any business that ignores these facts is doomed to collapse.

Because he doesn't fear it, change is one of the great constants at Jack Welch's General Electric.

The place is constantly being reinvented.

From Welch's restructuring initiative of the early 1980s to the companywide quality initiative of the mid to late 1990s, Welch never stops rearranging the GE agenda. The goal may be the same, never-ending growth, but the tools and methods are constantly evolving.

Welch encourages colleagues to never stop thinking about the need for change.

Start each day as if it were your first day on the job, he tells his managers. Make whatever changes are necessary to improve things. Re-examine your agenda constantly. Rewrite it, if necessary. In that way, you avoid falling back on old habits.

Make decisions yourselves, he tells employees at the factory level. If you're confident that you are right about something, don't just sit back and give in: you can change things, and urge change upon your boss.

Don't Be Afraid of Change—and Don't Let Your Boss Avoid Change

W. James McNerney Jr., is one of those GE business leaders who has watched Welch in action for years. From mid-1995 to mid-1997 McNerney was president and CEO of GE Lighting. Then he was appointed head of GE Aircraft Engines.

Welch implores McNerney and everyone else at GE to reexamine their agendas all the time. To face the reality of each morning. It might be a competitive reality, or a marketing reality, but each morning is different. What was important yesterday may no longer be important today. "As a result, you are forced to adapt," says McNerney. "We might make a completely different decision about a deal we agreed on yesterday, or a program we started, in light of the changing environment of the last twenty-four hours. Jack is one of the few guys who's not afraid to do that. In many organizations, the temptation is to drink your own bath water. In many organizations, the leader is afraid of going back on something, of giving the troops a direction that is different from what he said yesterday."

Yet, observes McNerney, Welch sees that willingness to change as a strength, even if it means plunging part of the company into total confusion for a while. All of Welch's values say "Confront what the reality is today." It is a management style that forces people to change. The decision to make a change happens so fast that most people have little time to dwell upon their actions. All they know is that keeping an eye out for change is both exhilarating and fun.

"Jack is quick to sense when ideas or activities are out of focus or out of style or less valuable than they used to be," says Robert Wright, the president of the GE-owned NBC television network. "His ability to figure when an organization has run out of gas with an idea is pretty good. He always has the strength to pioneer another idea on the heels of ideas that have been mined as far as you can go."

Jack Welch's very first change at General Electric was revolutionary.

In 1980, the year before Welch took over GE, the company had been doing very well—or so most people thought. It had sales of $25 billion, with profits of $1.5 billion, and was hailed as a model organization by many of the popular management textbooks used by business schools across the country.

Still, the chairman of GE was worried. Perhaps he didn't believe the textbooks.

He worried that without some major changes in its structure, its products, and its size, GE would falter.

He knew that the business environment was becoming more competitive. He believed that these changes could spell big trouble for GE, and that the most effective way for a company to deal with a constantly evolving business environment was to adjust and adapt as required.

His task would not be easy, for, as he liked to point out, change has no constituency. He would find it difficult to rally huge numbers of employees behind his plans. Few people in business find change enjoyable.

The very idea of tweaking a tradition-bound company like General Electric seemed absurd to many people.

But not to Jack Welch.

In contrast to almost everyone else, he understood the perils that confronted large corporations like GE during the 1970s and 1980s.

Others preferred to dismiss those perils as minor blips on the screen. And why not? By ignoring the warning signals they could keep their heads in the sand and they wouldn't have to change their ways.

Nonetheless, high-tech industries and global competitors were popping up, challenging GE for sales and market share. They were producing products of ever-improving quality at higher standards of productivity.

And all of these changes were occurring at a more and more rapid pace.

Jack Welch not only recognized that such changes could not be avoided; he embraced them with his usual intensity. The changes gave him the chance to create a new General Electric, to forge a company that was more in tune with the evolving business environment.

As he studied the company, one thing became abundantly clear: the kind of change that GE required was not a Band-Aid–type quick fix. No, in order to make General Electric truly competitive, he would have to put it through more dramatic and far-reaching changes than any major American business enterprise had ever undertaken. And nothing intimidated him—not even the screaming and hollering of junior GE executives, who argued that the company was in fine shape. He was sure he was right—and that was enough.

Explaining what the situation had been like when he took GE in 1981, Welch focused on two dominant trends: the high inflation of the late 1970s, and the Asian threat that confronted every GE business.

> It was a reminder that we'd better get a lot better, faster. So I guess my message in our company was, "The game is going to change, and change drastically." And we had to get a plan, a program together, to deal with a decade that was totally different. The Japanese had moved since the late sixties and early seventies from poor quality and low prices to low price and high quality. And their plants and their quality and their discipline were overwhelming us in some businesses.

A Process That Had No Name

No one had tried to make such monumental changes before. No one had dared. The changes that Jack Welch pioneered in the early 1980s were so new that the process had no name.

Today we call it "restructuring."

Welch saw the crisis coming when no one else did.

Only a handful of General Electric's 350 business units were leaders in their markets:

- Lighting
- Power Systems
- Motors

Only three GE products had a reasonably good share of the export market:

- Plastics
- Gas Turbines
- Aircraft Engines

Of these, only gas turbines enjoyed market leadership overseas. Still, deceptively, GE's balance sheets in the 1970s seemed to glow with health.

Welch sensed a different truth. A different reality.

He knew all too well that manufacturing in the United States was becoming less and less profitable. Yet, as late as 1970 fully 80 percent of General Electric's earnings came from its traditional electrical and electronic manufacturing businesses.

The company had financial achievements to be sure, especially in plastics, medical systems, and financial services. But these businesses contributed only one-third of GE's total 1981 earnings. In addition, a number of GE's businesses (aircraft engines was the best example) often consumed more cash than they generated.

For decades, the United States had dominated the most important markets of the world economy:

- Steel
- Textiles
- Shipbuilding
- Television
- Calculators
- Automobiles

So, few American business leaders noticed when others, especially the Japanese, began to steal customers by seducing them with higher-quality products bearing cheaper price tags.

Smokestack America was deteriorating. The most telling sign came in 1982, when the steel industry lost $3.2 billion. Meanwhile, the Japanese had gobbled up 20 percent of the American steel market. And what was occurring in steel was happening in the car industry as well.

The American economy looked increasingly unhealthy by the early 1980s. Inflation, for example, which had been only 3.4 percent in 1971, soared to 18 percent in March 1980. And while the United States still led the world in productivity, its lead had been deteriorating steadily since the 1960s.

By the summer of 1981, the country was on the brink of recession.

To meet competition around the world, the United States had to become more productive, more aggressive—and fast. Yet few American companies were exporting their products. Only 1 percent of American companies accounted for 80 percent of the nation's exports.

Why Not Just Stand Pat?

Jack Welch could have made do.

He could have gambled that GE, the 115-year-old icon of business, would continue to sell its products no matter how much the market environment shifted ground.

He could have argued that General Electric was so strong that it could withstand the economic ups and downs.

But Welch knew better, and it wasn't in him to ignore the truth.

GE executives scoffed at Welch and insisted that no change was needed. GE employees greeted Welch with disdain, disbelief, often with outright fear. Why tamper with a good thing? Why play with fire? Why was he intent on fixing something that wasn't broke? General Electric was doing just fine. After all, it had generated enormous sales and profits.

Yet Welch followed his gut instinct:

> **I could see a lot of [GE] businesses becoming . . . lethargic. American business was inwardly focused on the bureaucracy, [which] was right for its time, but the times were changing rapidly. Change was occurring at a much faster pace than business was reacting to it.**

An important building block of Welch's new strategy was weeding out certain businesses, keeping only those that could dominate their markets. From now on, a GE business would have to be first or second in its market. If the company could not bring flagging businesses up to speed, it would close or sell them.

That new policy positioned GE for solid growth throughout the 1980s and early 1990s. There were many other changes as well, and they marked only the beginning of what Welch would do to improve the company.

Throughout his seventeen years in the job, Jack Welch has embraced change as a fruitful, and necessary, business strategy.

It's OK to Acquire!

GE had traditionally advocated that it was better to nurture one's own business than to acquire from outside. In the mid-1980s Welch took a dramatic step, reversing this time-honored tradition.

On December 12, 1985, General Electric purchased RCA, the communications giant, which included the NBC Television Network, its jewel in the crown, for $6.28 billion. At the time General Electric was the ninth largest U.S. industrial firm. RCA was second among the nation's service firms.

Together, GE and RCA formed a new corporate power with sales of $40 billion, placing it seventh on the *Fortune* 500.

James Baughman, then head of Crotonville, GE's leadership development institute, called the merger the biggest countercultural step Jack Welch's GE had ever taken. Welch took that as a compliment. He wanted to develop General Electric's highest-growth businesses, and he intended to do whatever it took.

If buying outside businesses helped the company, he would do it. After the GE-RCA merger, General Electric expected to obtain 80 percent of its earnings from service and technology businesses, helping to fulfill one of Welch's original goals from the early 1980s.

Two years later, in 1987, Welch, the driver of change, took another countercultural step: he discarded one of GE's most cherished businesses and acquired a company in the medical diagnostics field.

For some time, GE's $3 billion-a-year Consumer Electronics division, the leading maker of television sets and video recording equipment in the United States, had been in trouble. Welch understood that it would be "mission impossible" to turn the business, then ranked fourth in the world market, into a first- or second-rank player. GE had to get out of consumer electronics and to place its resources behind something that had the potential to become a market leader.

So in June 1987 GE turned the division over to Thomson S.A., the largest of the electronics companies. In return, GE acquired the

Thomson-CGR medical-imaging unit, which had been selling about $750 million of x-ray and other diagnostic machines in Europe each year. This gave GE an entrée into the European medical diagnostic market.

The media attacked Welch ferociously for selling a business that had seemed so quintessentially American, like apple pie or baseball, and for exporting manufacturing jobs. Welch thought the criticism made little sense. GE simply had to change. It had to strive to make its businesses market leaders if it was ever going to beat the competition.

Two years later, in 1989, the chairman embraced change once again; taking a whole new look at the way GE dealt with its workers. Having witnessed massive layoffs in the 1980s, and still fearing for their jobs and their futures, they were in desperate need of a confidence booster. Welch came up with just what they needed.

Until 1989, Welch and his colleagues had doubted there was much to learn from their employees, believing instead that the workers, like drones, were just supposed to carry out management's decisions. They were not supposed to show initiative; after all, they were workers, not managers.

But eventually the chairman began to realize that GE's employees were a vital and unending source of new and imaginative ideas. Allowing them to have input into the day-to-day operations of the company could improve business and dramatically increase productivity. This approach had one more giant benefit: it could make workers, survivors of the Great Corporate Downsizing, feel more satisfied in their jobs.

Using the brain power of employees was a major change for Jack Welch and General Electric.

Welch launched his Work-Out program, designed to use those brains, putting them to work to effectively expand the level of debate throughout every corridor of the company. In doing so, GE became the first company to implement a program of this kind on such a large scale.

The Proof Lies in the Pudding

Change worked—whether it was the change that made GE businesses leaders in their markets, or that added profitable, productive businesses to GE's family, or that tapped the brains of knowledgeable employees.

Welch knew that it worked because GE's numbers were improving.

He knew that it worked because by the mid-1990s GE had become the strongest company in the nation and the most valuable company in the world, as measured in market capitalization. Even that record of achievement did not keep Welch from searching for the next major change to bring to his organization.

In 1995, he took a bold new step, launching a companywide initiative to improve the quality of General Electric's products and processes.

It was bold because it tacitly admitted that GE's products and processes could stand some improvement.

Once again, Welch was facing reality—and embarking on change.

He could have resisted change. After all, as he likes to say, "GE today *is* a quality company. It has always been a quality company." So why not stand pat? Welch's answer?

We want to be more than that. We want to change the competitive landscape by being not just better than our competitors, but by taking quality to a whole new level. We want to make our quality so special, so valuable to our customers, so important to their success that our products become their only real value choice.

Change: It may seem easy to do. All it takes is one decision from the boss, then getting employees to alter their patterns of behavior. But it sounds simpler than it is. It's not easy to discard old ways and habits and adopt new ones. In fact, it just might well be the hardest thing for anyone in business to do. Jack Welch understood how difficult change could be. But he was not dissuaded, for he viewed change as his only real chance to transform GE into the competitive enterprise he hungered for. Only through change—massive change—could GE win, and Jack Welch firmly believed in winning. He loved the way winners acted, like John Wayne heros who weren't afraid to take on foes that made others quake in their boots. He knew that winners won because they never flinched.

He felt sorry for the losers, the ones who always stuck their heads in the sand.

But he wanted to be a winner. And winners weren't afraid to make changes.

CHAPTER 2

Stop Managing, Start Leading

"Weak managers are the killers of business;
they are the job killers."

For a long time, the conventional wisdom in American business was that managers should do little else but keep a close eye on what their subordinates were doing.

Monitor.

Supervise.

Control.

A whole bureaucracy of junior and senior managers were talking only to one another. Shooting memos to one another. Holding high-level meetings left and right. Making sure that things below—on the factory floor and everywhere else—were proceeding properly.

That's all that managers were supposed to do.

Not to inspire. Not to give junior managers the chance to do things on their own. Not to have direct contact with the men and women who actually *produced* the company's products.

Who could argue? American corporations appeared to be doing well—or so it seemed.

But Jack Welch despises these bureaucrats. He regards them as relics of the past. And Jack Welch hates the past.

What is the right way to manage a huge company? More specifically, in the case of multibusiness General Electric, how does one manage numerous business units and hundreds of thousands of employees? How does one manage those employees effectively so that they are as productive as possible? Is it better to be a hands-on manager—or a hands-off one? Jack Welch has given a great deal of thought to these questions. And he has come to a seemingly paradoxical view. The *less* managing someone does, the better off the company.

He dislikes the very notion of "management." Most managers, in his view, *over*manage. Those who overmanage help to create the bureaucratic sloth and sluggishness that kills large companies.

From the very moment that he took over as head of General Electric, Welch regarded the place as a bureaucratic dinosaur. Management did too much controlling and monitoring. He decided that its leaders had to change their management styles.

If he was going to get GE to successfully compete in an increasingly complex and competitive business environment, he would have to significantly alter the way the managers did their jobs. He certainly had his work cut out for him. After all, in those days the concept of managing less by managing more was anathema to the folks in the corner offices, who were accustomed to working through the old boys' hierarchy.

Welch wants to discard the term *manager* altogether because it has come to mean someone who "controls rather than facilitates, complicates rather than simplifies, acts more like a governor than an accelerator."

Some managers, Welch says, muddle business decisions with pointless complexity and detail:

> **They equate [managing] with sophistication, with sounding smarter than anyone else. They inspire no one. I dislike the traits that have come to be associated with "managing"—controlling, stifling people, keeping them in the dark, wasting their time on trivia and reports. Breathing down their necks. You can't manage self-confidence into people.**

If it were up to him, no one would be called a manager. Instead, he much prefers the term *leader.*

Leaders are people who "inspire with clear vision of how things can be done better."

Managers Muddle—Leaders Inspire

Managers slow things down. Leaders spark the business to run smoothly, quickly.

Managers talk to one another, write memos to one another. Leaders talk to their employees, talk *with* their employees, filling them with vision, getting them to perform at levels the employees themselves didn't think possible. Then (and to Welch this is a critical ingredient) they simply get out of the way.

Above all else, Welch wants his business leaders to keep things simple.

Managing need not be overly complicated, he stresses, because business is actually quite uncomplicated:

> **We've chosen one of the world's most simple professions. Most global businesses have three or four critical competitors, and you know who they are. And there aren't that many things you can do with a business. It's not as if you're choosing among two thousand options.**

To Welch, the secret of running a successful business is to make sure that all key decision makers in that business have access to the same set of facts. If they have, they will all reach roughly the same conclusion about how to handle a business issue.

The problem, says Welch, is that they don't get the same information; they get different pieces of the information pie and are cut off from other vital pieces of information.

But, even with the same information, might people still come to different conclusions? "Very rarely on a quantitative point," says Welch. "Very rarely on a business situation. I'm not talking about the color of a house or the beauty of a chair. I'm talking about *business decisions*."

But even in business, how is it possible to quantify everything?

> **You can quantify it sufficiently to arrive at a strategic direction. I mean, you can clearly define enough parameters for a debate on**

**strategy. And when you conclude something, the team will gener-
ally have wrestled it through.**

David L. Calhoun, head of GE Lighting, has taken Welch's cue on leading, as opposed to managing. "Managing," explains Calhoun, "is knowing a little bit more than anyone who works for you and holding that
pretty close to your chest. It totally constrains your organization. We all
have only a certain amount of personal capacity to do our jobs and
implement change. If I use half my capacity memorizing thoughts and
details, I've got very little left to look for things to change and drive.
That goes for everyone in the organization."

Calhoun finds too much of the old management style around the
industry, and too much of it still around GE. "We need to eliminate the
insecurity in those folks who need to know more than anyone else.
Once you do that, you can encourage employees to get out of their
world; no longer are they constricted by the boundaries erected around
their business. That's when the world opens up. Getting them out of
that box to one that's bigger—one that has more toys, is more fun—
that's what it's all about."

Ask the Right Questions

To Jack Welch, the business leader who is good at keeping things simple, knows just what questions to ask of his subordinates:

1. What does your global competitive environment look like?
2. In the last three years, what have your competitors done?
3. In the same period, what have you done to them?
4. How might they attack you in the future?
5. What are your plans to leapfrog over them?

That's all managing is, says the chairman and CEO of General Electric: just coming up with the right questions and getting the right answers.

Superleader

Running the mighty General Electric enterprise, with its twelve major
businesses, Jack Welch does not seem like a manager in the normal
sense of the word. He seems more like a superleader.

And what is the main task of a superleader, who supervises an array of major businesses? "My job is to put the best people on the biggest opportunities and the best allocation of dollars in the right places. That's about it. Transfer ideas and allocate resources and get out of the way."

He doesn't get involved in deciding on the style of a refrigerator. He leaves that to the experts:

> **I have no idea how to produce a good [television] program and just as little about how to build an engine. . . . But I do know who the boss at NBC is. And that is what matters. It is my job to choose the best people and to provide them with the dollars. That's how the game is played.**

To Welch, having the right kind of managers in place is essential for a business's success. A successful leader can shock an organization and lead its recovery. An unsuccessful leader will shock an organization and paralyze it. Weak managers kill businesses:

> **They are the job killers. . . . So organizations constantly need to be regenerated. There's a constant flow of ideas, excitement, and energy that has to be put into an organization.**

> **And it has to keep getting better. The bar has to keep going up. . . . My job is to find great ideas, exaggerate them, and spread them like hell around the business with the speed of light. . . . And to put resources in to support them. Keep finding ideas. That's the job of just about all of our CEOs.**

He is emphatic that a good manager doesn't run a business. *Run* is not the right word. "I don't *run* GE. I *lead* GE."

He can't micromanage such multibillion-dollar corporations as GE Capital and NBC:

> **It's silly. I can't. But I do know my job, and my job is to understand the strategic issues within each of those businesses where they're going around [the above] five questions. I know the talent they need to win in those markets and the amount of capital they**

need. I make bets. But I know I've got enough coverage over here to bet on that.

What kind of goals does he set for his business leaders?

I don't set them. In the old days, they'd set a goal and I'd set one and then we'd negotiate. Now, we don't reward them according to whether or not they reach their objectives. They're all going to get paid on their improvement, and they know that. In bureaucratic companies, they waste a lot of time on making budgets. They waste energy. The world is changing quickly. We can't afford to waste time in bureaucracy. GE is an informal company. We trust each other.

Nobody wears a tie at our quarterly two-day meetings. We take coffee breaks for almost an hour sometimes so people can swap ideas. We bring in an outside speaker to every meeting—the heads of Wal-Mart, Pepsi-Cola, and Compaq. We have dinner together and drinks after eating. We run this place like a family grocery store.

Being a business leader in the late 1990s has become far more demanding, Welch asserts, than in earlier years:

The thing I've noticed is that the intensity level and the global understanding and the facing reality and the seeing the world as it is, is so much more pronounced in December 1997 than it was ten years ago, and certainly fifteen years ago, where form was very important. Today form isn't allowed. Global battles don't allow form. It's all substance. Form means somebody is not intensely interested in the company. Somebody on umpteen boards. Somebody off giving speeches all the time. Somebody that doesn't have their eye on the ball. Somebody who has reached the position of chairman as the culmination of a career, rather than the beginning of a career. See, my career starts again next January. What I did until now is meaningless. Meaningless. It's just the beginning.

Jack Welch has given American business leaders a whole new outlook on how to manage. Or, more aptly, how *not* to manage. In insisting that managing less is managing better, Welch has set an entire new style for the management of large corporations. Of course, the "managing less is managing better" notion is a paradox. And no one appreciates that more than the chairman of GE. Yet, Jack Welch would never say that managers should *not* manage at all. What he's really saying to managers is this: Don't get bogged down in overmanaging. Manage by creating a vision—and then make sure that your employees run with that vision. That's all there is to it. After all, business isn't really complicated. So lead, don't manage—and don't forget to get out of the way.

Cultivate Managers Who Share Your Vision

"What we are looking for . . . are leaders . . .
who can energize, excite, and control
rather than enervate, depress, and control."

IF JACK WELCH has little use for autocratic managers who over-manage, overmonitor, oversupervise, just what kind of managers does he actually like?

First of all, they should be bursting with energy. Second, they should be able to develop and implement a vision—not just talk incessantly about those visions. And, perhaps most important, they must know how to spread enthusiasm like wildfire by firing up the entire company.

Getting employees excited about their work—that is key to being a great business leader. The way to engender enthusiasm, says Welch, is to allow employees far more freedom and far more responsibility.

In 1987 Welch requested a meeting with the head of a particular GE business. The business had produced profits, but it certainly was not setting any records, and Welch had a strong feeling that it could do much better. He hoped that the meeting would lead to improved performance.

But Welch's message was lost on the manager. He had no idea what Welch wanted. "Well, help me with that," he pleaded. "Look at my earnings. Look at my return on investment. All the things I'm doing, all the people I've taken on. What the hell do you want me to do?"

"I don't know," Welch told him in all honesty. "I just know your business could be doing better." Welch wanted the man to get some vision. To get some enthusiasm for his work and re-energize his employees. Finally, Welch had a proposal for the perplexed manager.

"What I'd like you to do is take a month off and just go away. When you come back, act as if you were just assigned to the business and you hadn't been running it for four years. Just come in brand new, hold all the reviews, and start slicing everything in a different way."

The man still didn't get it. He did not understand that Welch wanted him to rewrite his agenda, take a new look at the business plan, and see things with a fresh eye. The CEO of General Electric didn't think that was asking too much of the man. But the junior executive was clueless. He didn't get Welch's insistence that he become excited about his work, and that he figure out how to energize his troops.

Six months later the executive no longer worked for GE.

Get on Board

As far as Jack Welch is concerned, middle managers have to be team members and coaches. They have to facilitate more than control. They should be able to excite and praise people and know when to celebrate. Managers should be energizers, not enervators. Welch gives a hypothetical example. Assume there is a multifunctional business consisting of engineering, marketing, and manufacturing components. And the business has the best manufacturing person it has ever had—someone with excellent numbers, who produces high-quality goods on time:

> **But this person won't talk with people in engineering and manufacturing. He won't share ideas with them, and won't behave in a boundaryless way with them. We used to reward this type of person with a bonus because of the good figures. But now we're replacing that person with someone who may not be quite as perfect but who is a good team player and lifts the team's performance.**

> Maybe the predecessor was working at 100 percent or 120 percent, but that person didn't talk with team members, didn't swap ideas. As a result, the whole team was operating at 65 percent. But the new manager is getting 90 percent or 100 percent from the whole total. That was a discovery.

In 1993, Welch began to talk openly about taking steps against those managers who couldn't learn to become team players. He acknowledged that it wouldn't be easy to change the way GE managers think and behave. The compulsion to control and direct was powerful, he noted in the company's Annual Report; it was supported by GE's century-old tradition of measuring self-worth by how many people one employed and whether or not one was a manager:

> What we are looking for today at GE are leaders at every level who can energize, excite, and control rather than enervate, depress, and control. . . . The kind of people we need in this company are those unwilling to "put in their time" in the bowels of the bureaucracy, or grunt along under the heel of some autocrat for years, before they get a chance to make decisions, try something and be rewarded in their souls as well as their wallets.

> In some difficult cases this means parting company with some impressive people—Heisman Trophy candidates, to use an American football expression—who won't block for others or play as part of a team. Their debilitating effect on the team can outweigh the benefits of their individual talent. . . . To be blunt, the two quickest ways to part company with GE are, one, to commit an integrity violation, or, two, to be a controlling, turf-defending, oppressive manager who can't change and who saps and squeezes people rather than excites and draws out their energy and creativity.

My Type of Manager

In describing the four types of GE managers and assessing which ones will ultimately succeed—and which ones won't—Jack Welch is essentially suggesting that the *only* way to last at General Electric is to get on board, to become a team player, to adapt oneself to the company's values and culture.

The first type delivers on commitments—financial or otherwise—and shares GE's values. Welch likes such leaders and will make sure they stick around. Their futures are an easy call: "Onward and upward."

The second type does not meet commitments (read "bring in a healthy balance sheet") and does not share GE's values. They are not Jack Welch's type of leader. Out the door they go: "Not as pleasant a call but equally easy."

The third type misses commitments but shares the values. Though many business leaders would find such a person totally unacceptable, Welch is not so unforgiving of this type. He cares more that a manager adheres to company values than meets the numbers—and will give this person every chance to succeed: "They usually get a second chance, preferably in a different environment."

The fourth type delivers on commitments but does not subscribe to GE's values. This person created the greatest quandary for the chairman: "They're the most difficult to deal with."

By the late 1990s, Welch talked less of these four kinds of managers and more of managers who would or would not do well at GE. While there was no one definition, the fate of each type was clear: type A was to be kept and promoted; type B was to be nurtured in the hope that they might improve; and type C was to be fired.

At the January 1997 operating managers' meeting, attended by the company's 500 top managers, Welch made a heart-felt plea, urging his colleagues to keep the type A's, the team players who subscribe to the company's values. He made an equally compelling plea to get rid of the type C's, those managers who have no business hanging around GE because they don't buy into the company's value system. As for the type B's, he wants to make sure they remain productive and continue to grow:

> **Too many of you work too hard to make C's [into] B's. It is a wheel-spinning exercise. Push C's on to B companies or C companies, and they'll do just fine. . . . We're an A plus company. We want only A players. We can get anyone we want. Shame on any of you who aren't facing into your less than the best. Take care of your best. Reward them. Promote them. Pay them well. Give**

them a lot of [stock] options and don't spend all that time trying work plans to get C's to be B's. Move them on out early. It's a contribution.

Later that year, in September 1997, during a talk at Crotonville, Welch spoke at length about the characteristics of A, B, and C managers. He asked junior executives from GE, seated in the audience, to suggest what defines an A.

Trust, said someone enthusiastically. Impact on decisions, shouted another. Leaders who seek to develop high value in other leaders below them, said a third.

Welch began to sketch each of the features on a white board, a signal that he liked what he heard.

What defined C's? More suggestions from the audience: They don't know they are C's. They're afraid of A's. They're blah, neutral.

Then Welch said that all he wanted them to do was to demand more of the A's, to cultivate them, to nourish them. As for the C's, the best thing to do was to get rid of them. It wasn't nice, he said, but it had to be done.

When someone in the audience said, apologetically, that she had recently been forced to let go of a few people, Welch urged her not to feel guilty or sorry.

Can I Watch My Kid Play Little League?

Patrick Dupuis, the vice president who heads the GE audit staff, makes the point that Welch's less dictatorial approach to management sits well with the generation in their twenties and thirties who, by their nature, want more freedom over their lives. "The younger people really want a more balanced life. It's true for both Europeans and Asians. They can be more ambitious, but they want a more balanced life. What this means is that they want to be successful in their family as much as they want success in business. They want a social life; they want to help educate their children. That tension fits well with the GE culture. You still have a lot of hours, a lot of intensity and stress, but you also have a lot of control compared to our predecessors. Pressure used to come from the top and you didn't have a lot of control."

That was Patrick Dupuis's perspective. Jack Welch's view was somewhat different. Uppermost in his mind is GE's performance. He offers no opinion on how his employees should balance their personal and family lives with work at GE. He simply notes that if they don't work hard at General Electric, his employees won't be able to enjoy the high living standards to which Americans have become accustomed:

> We have in the U.S. more than most countries have, and most countries want what we have. We care about the delivery of results. We have a high work ethic. We have more than most countries have, and most companies want what we have, and therefore people have to have a culture of delivery, of hard work, because we can't have two cars in every garage, a boat in the yard, while people are eating in the streets of developing countries. We can't have it without productivity, without innovation, without all these things.
>
> God didn't decide to grant two hundred and fifty million people in this country exclusive status in the perks of life. It didn't happen. Now we have a lot of things going for us. We have a large country, natural resources, an open society that brought in all kinds of people, all races and creeds. . . . So there is in our culture wonderful things for achievement. We as business people have to maximize the opportunity for this country to provide great jobs and great lives and great educations for people. But in the end we can't be in the business of dictating (when and for how long you should take a vacation, or take a few hours off, etc.). Individuals have to make those kinds of decisions. These are individual personal trade-offs.

If someone left work at 3 P.M. to attend a child's Little League game, would that person go from a type A to a type B? No, he replied, adding:

> That is a total personal relationship between the person and the manager. . . . If the results aren't good, we'll ask, "Why aren't the results good?" We won't ask him, "How many hours did you work and what was your shift? Did you obey policy 17.11?"

What counsel does Welch give to junior executives to help them become future great leaders?

The biggest advice I give people is you cannot do these jobs alone. You've got to be very comfortable with the brightest human beings alive on your team. And if you do that, you get the world by the tail. . . . It's too bad that we can't define people in business as easily as you can on a basketball court or a hockey rink. If the guy couldn't skate, you wouldn't have him at left wing. If the guy couldn't shoot, he wouldn't be the forward. He wouldn't be on the team. And it's no different in the business team you have to build. . . . Always get the best people. If you haven't got one who's good, you're short-changing yourself.

But isn't it hard to convince young people who want to make a name for themselves that the main thing is to become a team player?

Very hard, Welch acknowledges. "A lot of them don't get it. That's why I always talk self-confidence, because you've got to have the self-confidence to hire brilliant people, many times smarter than you are sometimes. You've got to feel very comfortable with that situation."

An intriguing question arises: If GE has such stringent entrance requirements, how was it that people arrived at General Electric who were only C managers? Welch explains:

What happens is, it's a bureaucracy. And some very bright people get in here. And they decide: I like the amount of resources that are here; I like the pension plan. I like the atmosphere. And before you know it, they stay. And before you know it, they've been there twenty years. And they got a track record and they got a history that's OK, and they're not good enough to play in the world the way the world is.

They started off with the right credentials, the right potential. And the potential may not have developed for any number of reasons, some very valid. "I want to be the best parent that God ever made and I want enough money so I can bring up my kid perfectly, and I'm going to be the parent of the year. I'm going to be the best artist in my art class that I go to two nights a week." There are any number of interests that might envelop them, all perfectly good interests—but they don't make them A's sometimes in this company.

Live Action All Day

So much for the junior managers. What does Jack Welch think it takes to become a great CEO?

The current business environment, the CEO of General Electric believes, requires an energized, energizing CEO. It is not a job for the faint of heart.

Twenty years ago, being named chairman and CEO was the culmination of a career; today, for the CEO who wants to keep that top job, it is merely the beginning:

> **Today's CEO . . . knows it's the beginning of a career, that the battles are just beginning. No one can come to work and sit, no one can go off and think of just policy, no one can do any of these things. You've got to be live action all day. And you've got to be able to energize others. You cannot be this thoughtful, in-the-corner-office guru. You cannot be a moderate, balanced, thoughtful, careful articulator of policy. You've got to be on the lunatic fringe.**

Welch understands that the nurturing of his managerial talent is one of the main keys to GE's success. And he feels that the talent he has amassed in the late 1990s—especially at the senior management levels—is of a higher quality than in years past. "I've got all A's in the Corporate Executive Council [a forum of thirty or so senior GE executives who meet for two days at Crotonville four times a year]. It wasn't like that before. I'm really pleased about that."

This is quite an admission for the chairman: Among his most senior advisers in earlier years were people whom he regarded as less than the best.

He pays special attention to shifting around that talent, particularly at the higher levels. His involvement in these hiring decisions is testament to the importance Welch places on decisions affecting people. He makes a point of getting to know every one of the 500 top GE managers, and he personally signs off on their promotions. He also interviews anyone who is hired from the outside for one of those top 500 posts.

The kind of manager Jack Welch likes bears little resemblance to the type found so often in American business. The kind who feel they've been given the title of manager in order to do just that—manage. The kind who feel they've got to stick out in the crowd—and not merge their identity in "the team." Welch is a revolutionary in defining a new type of manager for the twenty-first century. He wants managers who can swallow their egos, blur their identities, and work for the good of the company.

Has Welch got something there? Judging by an August 11, 1997, article in *Business Week*, it would certainly seem to be the case. *Business Week* conducted a survey of the top twenty-five general management recruiters, asking them for a list of executives likely to become CEOs at major corporations within five years. Out of the 133 candidates named, *Business Week* compiled a Top 20 all-star list. Five of the top twenty were from GE: David L. Calhoun, W. James McNerney Jr., Robert L. Nardelli, Gary L. Rogers, and Robert C. Wright. The top vote-getter of all 133 candidates was McNerney.

Face Reality, Then Act Decisively

"In the twenty-first century would you rather be in toasters or CAT scanners?"

Face reality.

Look reality in the eye and don't flinch.

What could be more straightforward than that? Yet Jack Welch thinks facing reality is one of his most important business rules.

Whether in business or in life, those who are able to acknowledge truth are usually successful. To Welch, it's really that simple.

Yet for all sorts of reasons, it is difficult to face reality.

It often seems so much easier to avoid the truth. The truth hurts. The truth is painful. The truth is embarrassing. The truth can be self-deflating.

Yet, facing that truth is what makes business so simple to Jack Welch.

Facing the truth in business is a large part of the ball game. Do that, and the chances are that your business will turn out all right.

The art of leading (he prefers "leading" to "managing") comes down to one simple thing: Determining and facing reality—about situations, products, and people—and then acting quickly and decisively on that reality. Most mistakes that business leaders make, says Welch, arise from not being willing to face reality and then acting on it.

Most of Welch's business philosophy is based on the simple premise that it is better to own up to reality than to bury one's head in the sand:

- Face the reality that the world is becoming increasingly competitive.
- Face the reality that no job is guaranteed for life.
- Face the reality that managing a business by erecting huge bureaucracies is ineffective.
- Face the reality that business is really simple.

In October 1981, six months after he became chairman and CEO, Welch wasted no time in spelling out his revolutionary plans for a new GE to 120 corporate officers of the company. He said there would be no more bureaucratic waste and no more deceptive budgets and plans. And no one would be able to hide from hard decisions.

In short, from then on, General Electric's employees were going to stare reality in the face—and acknowledge it. And if they needed help acknowledging reality, Jack Welch would be there to point them in the right direction.

Better to Be in Toasters or in CAT Scanners?

The first reality Welch observed was the rising peril of foreign competition. It was he—and he alone—who discerned that peril.

To combat the increasing competitiveness from abroad, it would be critical, he believed, to restructure the company in a revolutionary way.

It would be critical to reduce the size of GE's workforce and get rid of businesses that had long been a burden to the company.

Scrapping GE's housewares business in 1983 was an early example of Jack Welch facing reality. For General Electric employees it was the most anguishing divestiture. Giving up on toasters and irons and fans was like selling off the company's heritage. Housewares had been a mainstream GE business for generations. People questioned Welch's decision: How can you exit housewares? They're a GE tradition! These products had made the company a household name across the land. The business was a core part of GE's portfolio; anytime a housewife put a GE toaster, coffee pot, or steam iron in her home, the General Electric name was there, garnering publicity and brand-name recognition for the company.

Welch had a great one-liner in retort: "In the twenty-first century, would you rather be in toasters or in CAT scanners?"

GE's housewares business had been good for the company in the past, but Welch felt that it had no role in the GE of the future. GE's strengths could not be applied easily or effectively in housewares.

"Our strengths were lost in a business like Housewares," says Joyce Hergenhan, GE's vice president for corporate public relations. "You come up with some great new hair dryer, and within two months, all over the Middle East people would be coming up with a lower-priced knockoff of the same thing. GE's strengths are technology, its technological resources, its financial resources. . . . We have the ability to take the hundreds of millions of dollars and the years that are required to come up with a new generation of jet engines, a new generation of gas turbines, a new-generation plastic, or a new-generation medical diagnostic imaging machine. These businesses have certain common things: high technological content, high development costs, staying power."

Through the years Welch continued to stare reality in the face.

In 1986, he steered GE toward one of its most revolutionary undertakings—the merger with RCA.

The GE-RCA deal was very much in keeping with Welch's view that in order to succeed in the late eighties and nineties, GE would have to develop a serious service-oriented dimension.

RCA, owners of the NBC Television Network, fit the bill beautifully.

By the late 1980s, Welch began to realize that he faced a new reality, this time in connection with his efforts to make GE more productive—a major goal of the company. The reality was that every truth or facet of wisdom about how to run a business did not reside with GE's senior management. The factory workers and junior executives—the men and women who were really closest to GE's products and customers—had as good a sense of GE's operations as senior management, maybe better. By tapping these workers' potential, by tapping their brains, senior managers would enable them to make a major contribution to GE's productivity. So Welch faced reality and began the companywide Work-Out program.

By the mid-1990s, Welch began to face yet another reality. This had to do with the quality of GE's products and processes.

For years Welch had not been a great believer in programs designed to boost the quality of GE's products. Nearly everyone proclaimed GE's products to be of a superior quality to their competitors, so Welch felt no need to focus on this area.

But GE employees began to complain to Welch that there was still much that could be done to improve GE products and processes.

In effect, those employees were urging the chairman to face reality. Welch responded, and in 1995, GE began its companywide quality initiative.

In the late 1990s, Welch faced another reality—about the company as a whole. Welch's goal for GE never wavered: it was, and always will be, ever-increasing growth. Yet he was aware that the manufacturing side was not going to deliver the double-digit growth that Welch had always demanded. Accordingly, he mounted a new campaign to increase GE's role in providing service.

In All Candor

Facing reality also means being candid, in Welch's view, so on occasion he admits to making mistakes. For instance, he regrets not buying a food company in the early days. That would have paid off, he believes. But he was too slow to make a decision.

In the early 1990s, Welch acknowledged that while he had made some progress toward his goal of removing bureaucracy, much more remained to be done:

> **Unfortunately, it is still possible to find documents around GE businesses that look like something out of the National Archives, with five, ten, or even more signatures necessary before action can be taken. In some businesses, you might still encounter many layers of management in a small area—boiler operators reporting to the supervisor of boilers, who reports to the utility manager, who reports to the manager of plant services, who reports to the plant manager, and so on.**

His biggest mistake of all, he feels, was not moving more quickly to implement major changes at GE. When asked if he had any regrets when he looked back in his career, Welch replied:

I would have liked to have done things a lot faster. I've been here for seventeen years. Imagine if I'd taken four, three, or even one year too long in making my decisions. I would have had a rude awakening. I would very much have liked, for example, to get all my divisions working together ten years ago.

It's refreshing to listen to a chief executive acknowledge that he's not infallible. Dennis Dammerman, the chief financial officer at GE, a man who knows Welch as well as most, notes: "One of the truly distinguishing characteristics of Jack Welch is, whether it's six seconds later, six months later, or six years later, his absolute ability to say, 'I know that I made that decision, but it was the dumbest idea anyone ever had,' his ability to look at a changing set of circumstances or facts and have no inhibitions at all about saying, 'That was a dumb idea, let's do it this way.'"

In Welch's case, such admissions come easy if only because he's been so successful. His track record speaks for itself.

Other chief executives, reading that Welch admits to past mistakes, are probably saying: 'Well, sure, the guy can afford to admit to committing errors. No one's going to fire him for making such a confession. But if I were to admit such mistakes, what with my company's mediocre record, I'd be out on my ear."

Still (and this is the message that Welch is trying to get across) a little candor, a little honesty, a little bit of facing reality just might make chief executives seem less hostile, less distant, less arrogant.

And the more those CEOs face reality, the more likely it is that they will learn from their mistakes—and eventually bring their businesses success.

Be Simple, Be Consistent, and Hammer Your Message Home

"The only way to change people's minds is with consistency."

RELENTLESS CONSISTENCY.

That's what Jack Welch calls one of his business tenets. Welch is almost a fanatic when it comes to consistency. He believes in relentless consistency in everything: in checking a factory's plans, in determining whether training programs are working, in making sure that the company values are alive and well at every level of the organization.

Put another way, *follow up on everything.*

Follow-up, to Welch, is one key measure of success for a business.

GE's chairman has little use for managers who call a meeting, set goals, but never follow up to see if the goals are achieved:

Somebody runs the January meeting and they leave and say, "Nice going," and they thank the person that ran it. "It was a great meeting." Then they have a March meeting. Somebody else runs that. And he brings in somebody else. Then they have a long-

range planning session, and there's no relationship to the meeting they ran in January.

At GE executive meetings, he points out, there's a "relentless consistency, a pounding, a drumming, over and over. We don't change our mind. We don't jump around. We don't give them a new flavor of the month."

A Few Themes, a Few Phrases

Follow-up to Welch also means harping on a few key themes and repeating them over and over. These key themes reverberate endlessly at General Electric. Add them up and they amount to an effort to be consistent, to follow up.

In the early days of the Welch era, these were the key phrases:

- Number one, number two.
- Fix, close, or sell.
- Speed, simplicity, and self-confidence.

In the late 1990s, the key phrases are different. But Welch and GE pursue them just as doggedly as in the past:

- Boundarylessness
- Work-Out
- Stretch
- Quality
- Service
- Learning Culture

My Handy Little Values Guide

The key words and phrases pop up in all sorts of places—in Jack Welch's annual Letter to Share Owners, in his speeches to the GE board, in talks with financial analysts. Nowhere, however, do these words take on greater importance than on a small, wallet-size card that GE employees now carry with them. GE's values are so important to the chairman that he had them inscribed and distributed to all GE employees, at every level of the company.

But before the cards were furnished to the staff, GE had to come to some consensus on which core values it wanted to cultivate in its employees. Countless hours were spent at Crotonville and elsewhere deciding on exactly what those values should be. It became a badge of honor not only to carry the card but also to uphold the values. As Welch notes:

> There isn't a human being in GE that wouldn't have the Values Guide with them. In their wallet, in their purse. It means everything and we live it. And we remove people who don't have those values, even when they post great results.

What are the GE values inscribed on that wallet-size card?

GE Leaders . . . Always with Unyielding Integrity:

- **Have a Passion for Excellence and Hate Bureaucracy**
- **Are Open to Ideas from Anywhere . . . and Committed to Work-Out**
- **Live Quality . . . and Drive Cost and Speed for Competitive Advantage**
- **Have the Self-Confidence to Involve Everyone and Behave in a Boundaryless Fashion**
- **Create a Clear, Simple, Reality-Based Vision . . . and Communicate It to All Constituencies**
- **Have Enormous Energy and the Ability to Energize Others**
- **Stretch . . . Set Aggressive Goals . . . Reward Progress . . . Yet Understand Accountability and Commitment**
- **See Change as Opportunity . . . Not Threat**
- **Have Global Brains . . . and Build Diverse and Global Teams**

A business leader is obligated, according to Welch, not only to create a vision, but to make sure employees are living that vision at every level of the organization. As Jeffrey R. Immelt, the head of GE Medical Systems, points out, "If a leader wants to drive change, he or she must intervene. For example, when Jack says we're going to be a Six Sigma quality business by the year 2000, he doesn't just throw it over the transom and say, 'Now do it.' It's on the agenda of every meeting. It's half of the Session C [the annual review of personnel]. Jack is kind of an icon of leadership in that regard that all of us get to see firsthand. If you want to drive change, it's not a passive event." (Six sigma is the statistical measurement which expresses how closely a product has come to high-level quality.)

Be Consistent—Consistently!

To Welch, one of the most crucial aspects of being consistent and following up is making sure that he delivers the identical no-nonsense message to every audience. The CEO of General Electric boasts that his message never waivers, whether he's talking to the GE board, the financial analysts, the labor unions, or GE's employees: "I don't say one thing to outsiders and another to insiders."

He credits the follow-up business strategy with paving the way for GE's success:

> **It's not that I changed. We just expanded the reach of our communication. We refined it, got better at it, and it began to snowball. If you have a simple, consistent message, and you keep on repeating it, eventually that's what happens. Simplicity, consistency, and repetition—that's how you get through. It's a steady continuum that finally reaches a critical mass.**

Welch was offended when it was suggested that he changed direction over the years:

> **I haven't changed a thing! . . . The ideas were always the same. We've been talking about reality, agility, ownership, and candor since the beginning. We just got it simpler and more carefully articulated over time. . . .**
>
> **You don't get anywhere if you keep changing your ideas. The only way to change people's minds is with consistency. Once you get the ideas, you keep refining and improving them; the more simply**

your idea is defined, the better it is. You communicate, you communicate, and then you communicate some more. Consistency, simplicity, and repetition is what it's all about. . . .

David Calhoun, head of GE Lighting, talks about Welch's unwavering interest in being focused and consistent. "The most remarkable thing about Jack Welch is how few differences I see in him over the years. In the beginning, I saw someone who was superintense, supercharged, and always asking us to look for new and better and more exciting ways to do things. He's even more intense now on this set of issues. He's always thinking about tomorrow. He takes more time now in looking at other companies. He'll ask, 'Why can't we do it like so-and-so?' He hasn't lost a beat on that. That consistency has allowed us to keep looking forward and changing our game."

Welch's consistency has indeed helped to revive GE and remake it into one of the world's most competitive companies. It certainly didn't hurt that so much of what he predicted about the business world actually came true. As his legend grew with every correct prediction, so did the respect of the GE workforce. However, as Welch recalls, the journey was often arduous, and at times downright painful. Welch recalls how difficult it was for GE employees to swallow what he calls his "change ideas." But he takes great pride in the fact that so many of his calls have been correct—that the world has become more global, more service-oriented, and far more competitive. And as he pounded his message home over the years, he won the hearts and minds of the GE workforce and converted critics into believers. By accomplishing this, he created a far more fertile environment for change, which made his task of transforming GE that much easier.

**PART
II**

Building the Market-Leading Company

"What can I do to make one of my businesses dominant in its market?"

Be Number 1 or Number 2, But Don't Narrow Your Market

"When you're number four or five in a market, you get pneumonia when number one sneezes."

I N   B U S I N E S S, Jack Welch asserts, the strong survive, the weak do not. The big, fast ones get to play, the small, slow ones are left behind.

Those who succeed in business do so by becoming more competitive. And it is much easier to be competitive if a business is a market leader.

To make GE more competitive, Jack Welch developed a strategy that required all GE businesses to be either first or second in their fields. He saw the competitive advantage of being the best—or the second best—in a market and he wanted to exploit that advantage.

But more than that, Welch simply believed in exacting the highest standards and making sure that everyone in his company met those standards. Welch was convinced that mediocre players would eventually lose out:

I had the luxury of being an insider who ran high-growth businesses like plastics, or saw opportunities in wonderful things, like

> **GE Capital, and then had big, bureaucratic, hundred-year-old businesses reporting to me. I saw businesses that were number five in the marketplace, not even number three, that we were holding onto as a shrine to our past. GE trained me with good businesses and bad ones.**
>
> **I always felt sorry for the people in the bad ones because they never saw a good one. All they really did was work in the vineyard they were sent to toil in. They always compared themselves with their direct competitor. So if their returns were nine and their competitor's seven, they were doing very well. The fact that they should be getting fifteen was difficult to comprehend.**

He evolved a game plan, a business strategy he called "number one, number two."

He was convinced that inflation would become the most prominent enemy confronting American business in the 1980s, leading to slower worldwide growth. That meant there would be no room for the mediocre supplier of products and services—the company in the middle of the pack. He argued that "the winners would be those who insisted upon being the number one or number two leanest, lowest-cost, worldwide producers of quality goods and services or those who had a clear technological edge or a clear advantage in their chosen niche."

Why Pick on Us? What Have We Done Wrong?

Welch remembered being in some GE businesses that were first or second rank—and some that were fourth or fifth. It was clear to him that being number one in the market was far easier and better than being in weaker businesses. The weaker businesses lacked the resources, muscle, and power to compete on a global scale.

If General Electric found itself in a business that was not number one or number two, and that didn't have a technological edge, tough questions would be asked, including this one, originally posed by management theorist Peter Drucker: "If you weren't already in the business, would you enter it today?"

If the answer was no, then swift action had to be taken. Welch predicted that corporations in the 1980s that hung on to losers, whether out of tradition or sentiment or their own management weakness, would not be around by 1990.

GE's business leaders were expected to ask themselves this critical question: "What can I do to make one of my businesses dominant in its market?" Then they were required to make tough decisions, asking which businesses were worth nurturing, which were not. What was crucial for a GE business leader was to create a vision and make sure that everyone working with that executive shared that vision.

None of this sat well with GE executives, who resented the chairman's vision of keeping only the best-performing businesses and discarding the others.

In the early 1980s, GE had quite a number of profitable businesses that were third or fourth in their fields. Leaders of those businesses didn't understand why their businesses had to be dismantled.

They thought little of Welch's decision to make performance the main criterion at GE. Yet the new chairman felt he had no choice, no matter how painful those decisions were. He knew the company simply had to be reshaped.

When others asked, "Why sell off a business that's making money?" Welch countered that there was simply no choice:

When you're number four or five in a market, when number one sneezes, you get pneumonia. When you're number one, you control your destiny. The number fours keep merging; they have difficult times. That's not the same if you're number four, and that's your only business. Then you have to find strategic ways to get stronger. But GE had a lot of number ones."

No Untidy Conglomerate

To Welch and others, GE appeared to lack a central focus.

He presided over a large, diversified portfolio of businesses—350 in all, clustered in 43 strategic business units.

Few American corporations boasted such a large portfolio of businesses. GE was not only large, it was diverse.

In the early 1980s it was producing nuclear reactors and microwave ovens, robots and silicon chips; it had businesses in time-sharing services and Australian coking coal.

While that diversity had given General Electric earnings protection from economic downturns, investors had trouble understanding what GE produced—and how it would perform in the future.

Welch wanted to send a message to Wall Street, that General Electric was not some untidy conglomerate with all kinds of scattered and unrelated businesses.

The company had a purpose and a focus.

It was determined to become the most competitive enterprise on earth.

And it would reach that goal by making sure all of its businesses were first or second in their markets.

To his credit, Welch never allowed any of the criticism to get to him. When he was asked how he would determine which GE businesses would survive and which would not, he took a pad and pencil and sketched three circles. One circle contained GE's core businesses; the second circle contained GE's high-technology businesses; and the third circle contained GE's service businesses.

"These are the businesses that we really want to nourish," he said. "These are the businesses that will take us into the twenty-first century. They are inside the circles. Outside the circles you have businesses that we would prefer not to pursue any further."

How Can I Get into That Circle?

Welch's vision was becoming more concrete, more focused. Anyone interested in how Welch planned to operate simply had to look at the circles. Businesses inside the circles would receive the company's resources; those outside would not.

Fifteen businesses, which when taken in aggregate produced 90 percent of 1984 corporate earnings, went into those circles.

Those businesses outside the circle were not automatically doomed to purgatory. Adopting the motto, Fix, close, or sell, Welch made it clear that if a business outside the circle could be fixed, he would bring it back inside the circle.

Part of the chairman's realism, however, was in acknowledging when it was time to get rid of struggling businesses. He liked to say that there was no real virtue in simply looking for a fight. If someone was in a fight—that is, in a competitive battle to dominate the marketplace—your job was to win. But if you couldn't win, it was best to find a way out, to jettison your weak businesses so you could live to fight another day.

The three-circles concept, Jack Welch's compass during the early 1980s, was designed to instill clarity into an organization that outsiders had described as a confusing conglomerate. Here's how the three circles broke down:

1. *Core circle:* Lighting, Major Appliance, Motor, Transportation, Turbine, Contractor Equipment
2. *Technology circle:* Industrial Electronics, Medical Systems, Materials, Aerospace, Aircraft Engines
3. *Services circle:* General Electric Credit Corporation, Information, Construction and Engineering, Nuclear Services

Outside the circle were these GE businesses: Housewares, Central Air Conditioning, TV and Audio, Cable, Mobile Communications, Power Delivery, Radio Stations, Ladd Petroleum, Semiconductor, Trading, Utah International, and Calma.

One-fifth of General Electric's businesses, valued at $9 billion, did not make the grade. GE let go of 117 businesses and product sectors, including coal mines, semiconductors, toasters, hair dryers, and clocks. Meanwhile, GE purchased assets that totaled $16 billion.

Winning was what mattered to Welch, not tradition. During a one-year period he got rid of both Housewares and Utah International, a mining subsidiary that former CEO Reg Jones had bought only eight years earlier. In another twelve-month period Welch bought RCA, which included NBC, the television network, and Kidder Peabody, an investment bank.

Welch did not keep the number one, number two strategy a tightly held secret. He might have, in order to avoid embarrassing the businesses outside the circle—and angering their bosses. To keep everyone guessing about his intentions. To wait and see whether his assessment of GE's businesses was on the mark.

Instead, he disclosed his intentions throughout GE. And sent shivers throughout the organization.

I Hate That Name!

Welch's early restructuring efforts won the new chairman sharp criticism. He was often described in the media as "Neutron Jack," an allusion to the neutron bomb that eliminates people but leaves the buildings standing. He hated the name because it suggested that he had been unfair to his employees, that he had pushed them into the streets without a way to make a living. That wasn't the case, he argued:

> **I have never laid off anyone. Even when selling businesses, I have set aside twice as much as retirement money for employees and have given them as good a safety net as possible before they have left. Fifteen years later, managers in the United States are doing what I did. But nobody calls them "Neutron." The businesses I eliminated were not simply in the red for two or three years; they had been depressed for thirty or fifty years in the long history of GE. And their employees had consciously become underdogs.**

Welch felt he was a caring person, yet he believed he had no choice. To have behaved differently would have turned General Electric into a welfare society, not the lean, agile enterprise he intended to build.

By the late 1980s, Welch's number one, number two strategy had evolved: now the chairman wanted his businesses to dominate not simply the American market, but the world market as well.

Welch's strategy was alive and well in the fall of 1997. GE's businesses have retained dominance or near-dominance in their markets:

- *Number one in the world:* Industrial motors (manufacturers of electric motors); medical systems (imaging and diagnostic equipment); plastics (plastics for various sectors); financial services (credit, credit cards, leasing); transport (locomotives and rail equipment); power generation (turbines for power stations); information services (company networks, electronic commerce, etc.); aircraft engines (aircraft jet and other engines); and electric distribution equipment (control systems for industry). NBC, which includes general interest programming and CNBC (business news), is ranked the number one American network.

- *Number two in the world:* Lighting (makers of lightbulbs and neon strips) and Household Appliances (stoves, refrigerators, washing machines, etc.).

The number one, number two strategy has been less applicable in GE's nonmanufacturing activities.

Ironically, when it comes to the business that would eventually become GE's most important revenue driver, GE Capital, the number one, number two strategy really didn't apply. "Jack," notes GE Capital's CEO Gary C. Wendt, "never tried to force [the strategy] on us, because the financial service business is so broad. Citibank is the biggest and has only 1 percent of the market. It's less important for our twenty-seven businesses at GE Capital to be number one. But we can be very good—and significant—by focusing on very narrow customer groups. In railcar leasing we are the biggest provider of cars as a lessor. So we're number one in that. But in our bank card business we're probably fourteen or fifteen."

A Flaw in the Strategy

While the strategy worked for General Electric during the 1980s, by the mid-1990s GE began to review its usefulness and discovered that it had a built-in flaw:

Over time, the strategy tended to be limited. After a while, the natural tendency of GE managers in search of market dominance was to define those markets in a way that virtually guaranteed that they were number one or number two.

Businesses wound up defining their own markets too narrowly when it was far better for them to define their markets more broadly. One example was GE's power generation business, which produced products for the big utilities. In focusing its energies on the huge power plants—and defining the market as such—GE neglected the smaller, but burgeoning, distributed-power market that had developed all over the world. GE wasn't making products in that area at all, because when it defined its market, that end of it was conveniently outside GE's purview. When customers required smaller units, the power generation business simply decided that producing such products was not worthwhile.

In late 1995 Welch met members of a business management course at Crotonville. The class urged Welch to refine his strategy so that GE businesses would not define their markets so narrowly, as no more than 10 percent of the total market. The mandate of GE's businesses would be to pursue a larger part of the newly defined market. Welch liked what he heard and the recommendation was implemented in early 1996.

The refinement dovetailed nicely with GE's plans to infuse more of a service dimension into its businesses. This service shift forced GE to reexamine its basic approach to many of its target markets. For example, while historically GE had provided service and parts for GE engines only, in 1997 it began offering repair and parts for GE, Pratt & Whitney, and Rolls Royce aircraft engines. In short, GE was defining the aircraft engine market far more broadly in order to capture more service-oriented business.

Could redefining markets make it harder for GE to remain in its number one or two position?

GE executives did not think so. They were confident that GE would figure out how to remain on top, by working more aggressively to capture a larger share of the newly defined market.

Asked how he would feel if he learned that power generation turned out to be number three in this redefined market, Jack Welch replied confidently that he would stay the course. "We wouldn't even think about [dropping] it because I'd see the opportunity to be number one— if we're building off of our strength."

Still, some GE insiders worried. One was Steven Kerr, the head of GE's Crotonville Leadership Development Center: "The notion behind being number one or number two is right. You end up setting price, and setting market standards, and you don't wind up being walked over and bullied. And in most of the markets today that we are in, we continue to live it and believe it. And the strategy gives us the ability to dominate the market. But if you define the market more broadly, it may mean you will end up third or fourth. I don't know any way to prevent that and it may well be desirable."

For anyone who imagined that Jack Welch had rested on his laurels, the evolving business strategy of "Number One, Number Two" should dispel any such notion. The embracer of change, the man who insisted on facing reality, was at it again. He had taken a 1980s strategy and reinvented it so that it applied to today's fiercely competitive markets. Jack Welch had shaken things up once again, forcing his leaders to look at their businesses anew, giving them yet another challenge to grapple with: the challenge of staying number one or number two under wholly new and more competitive conditions.

He liked that. He liked setting the bar a bit higher. He liked forcing his people to think anew about their business situations. It was healthy. It was invigorating. It was a must.

Look for the Quantum Leap!

"I don't think I've moved fast enough or incisively enough."

J ACK WELCH BELIEVED in the surprise move.

The bold play.

Shocking his rivals.

He loved the idea that he could shake things up while others looked on from the sidelines, sitting idly by while he knocked his competitors for a loop.

Surprise.

Boldness.

Shock.

These were the crucial ingredients of the quantum leap. This was what Jack Welch had in mind when he began reshaping General Electric. It's what he had in mind when he began thinking about his conquest of RCA.

Acquiring RCA was a revolutionary move for General Electric. Throughout most of its history, GE has grown from within. It simply did not believe in growing by acquisition.

But that was part of the old GE mentality.

Jack Welch believed that adhering to outdated traditions was not facing reality. To him, facing reality meant acquiring businesses that could bolster GE's earnings.

Although he was concerned about criticism that GE was just one of those unfocused conglomerates that bought and sold businesses by the seat of its pants, Welch remained confident that he could acquire and divest and remain focused. He knew that the right big purchase, the right quantum leap, could add to the company's earnings and value.

By 1985, four years after he took over as chairman and CEO, Jack Welch's revolution was well in stride.

Annual sales at GE had increased from $27.24 billion in 1981 to $28.29 billion in 1985 and GE was the tenth largest of the *Fortune* 500 companies, up a notch from the year before. Even more important, its earnings had risen 2 percent in 1985, to $2.33 billion, which made GE the fifth most profitable company in the United States. Contributing immeasurably to those improved earnings was the $5.6 billion worth of businesses that Welch had sold since taking over as CEO.

Welch made clear that he was not averse to grabbing a large company if the fit and price were right.

He was not averse to a quantum leap.

He cast his eyes on the Radio Corporation of America, one of America's most famous corporate names. In 1984, RCA's sales had topped $10 billion.

Striking a Deal for the Peacock

Until the early 1980s, the notion that a General Electric would even consider buying an NBC, or one of the two other major television networks, was ridiculous.

The owners of these television monoliths could not fathom parting with these highly visible, highly profitable properties.

But if the NBC acquisition seemed like a strange one to many, it did not seem strange to Jack Welch.

To him it made perfect sense.

After all, he needed a cash flow stream that would compensate for his manufacturing businesses, which were coming under increasing pressure. He viewed service businesses as the solution to any possible future cash flow problems.

When the Big Three TV networks changed hands in the mid-1980s, there was a widespread belief that NBC got the worst deal.

ABC had been sold to Capital Cities, a broadcasting company. CBS was now in the hands of Laurence Tisch, who had the resources to turn the network around. But NBC? Why, it got the lightbulb people. What did they know about developing a television network?

At NBC, the reaction to having GE as a new parent was mixed at best. NBC News executives were concerned that General Electric would interfere with the news operation. Welch assured them that such was not the case—that the traditional independence of NBC News would be maintained.

Tom Brokaw, the NBC News anchor, admits that his heart sank when he heard the news. "GE people were engineers and accountants. They came from a different gene pool. It was not a traditional communications company. Even though I knew that Jack Welch had brought new energy and vitality and direction to GE, I had grown up with [General Electric] as a stolid manufacturing company that was mostly associated with appliances, boring products. I knew that when you have a change of this magnitude there are going to be consequences that you're not going to be personally happy with.

"A change of that kind brings about some pain. I kind of forewarned everyone around here: 'This is a guy who really believes in efficiencies.' I also knew that there was still a fair amount of financial chaos in this company. We were doing well, but I knew there was a lot of excess."

And What about Nipper?

The NBC television network, which had faltered some years earlier, was on an upswing in the mid-1980s, making it more attractive to Welch.

Grant Tinker, the head of NBC, had performed miracles in the early 1980s, improving the network's ratings with a series of highly popular shows, including *Hill Street Blues, Cheers, St. Elsewhere*, and *Family Ties*.

It was on the verge of winning the prime-time ratings race for the first time with such hits as *Golden Girls, Alf, Matlock, L.A. Law*, and *Amen*. Its biggest hit was *The Cosby Show*, which sometimes won its time slot with a whopping 50 share of the market.

In 1984, the network's earnings of $248 million formed fully 43 percent of RCA's $567 million total; a year later, the network's earnings had risen to $376 million. NBC was truly the jewel in RCA's crown.

As Welch pursued negotiations, RCA staffers found it hard to swallow the idea that GE would soon become their boss. Would the brand-name of RCA, David Sarnoff's baby, the home of RCA's mascot Nipper, be subsumed under the General Electric logo?

Such a question didn't faze Jack Welch one bit.

Though the purchase was certainly the largest counterculture step GE had ever taken, purchasing the communications giant for $6.28 billion (or $66.50 a share) made wonderful sense to Welch. Some analysts felt RCA was worth $90 a share. Welch promised that he would create a fantastic company.

Curbing the Big Spenders

Now that he had his quantum leap, the chairman of General Electric wanted to impose the GE culture on the new acquisition. Nowhere were Jack Welch's business ideas tested more than at the NBC television network.

GE had its own business culture, and so did NBC. The battle of corporate culture, long entrenched in these two giants, might prove to be a bloody and protracted one. Which one would triumph?

Welch wanted NBC to face the reality that times were tough. The free-spending network could no longer function without budgetary constraints. He would not permit this to be his Waterloo. At the heart of the issue was one vital question: How much money should NBC be permitted to spend?

For years the three major television networks had functioned without having to be concerned about costs. But when Welch came along in the mid-1980s he expected the same response from NBC as from his aircraft engines or lighting business:

- To be profitable
- To be careful with expenses
- To fit into the General Electric culture

Unhappy network staffers were not eager to face reality.

They feared that the venerable Peacock Network, famous for Milton Berle, Huntley-Brinkley, and *Bonanza*, would simply become another cog in the GE machine.

One early GE decision seemed to confirm their greatest fears. Welch announced that he was changing the name of the landmark RCA building at 30 Rockefeller Center to the GE Building. NBC employees were appalled.

The network's employees were certainly not going to make it easy for the new Welch-appointed CEO at NBC, Bob Wright.

He had been a product of GE and a close friend of Welch. Welch had brought Wright back to GE in the early 1970s after Wright had left briefly to practice law.

Wright had worked in GE's Plastics and Housewares divisions, but then left again to become president of Atlanta-based Cox Cable in the early 1980s. In the mid-1980s he returned to run one of GE's treasured businesses, GE Capital.

Wright was bound to face resistance in asking the NBC troops to face a new reality. For one thing, Wright had big shoes to fill. He was replacing the classy, well-liked producer, Grant Tinker. In comparison to the elegant, ebullient Grant Tinker, Wright seemed stiff and colorless. Worst of all, he was an outsider.

And NBC seemed to be doing just fine, enjoying its best ratings in years, thanks to prime-time programming genius Brandon Tartikoff. The powerhouse Cosby-led Thursday-night lineup had been Tartikoff's creation.

NBC's employees thought they deserved applause. Wright had a different, more sober message for them. His message was completely in keeping with Welch's philosophy. The ratings were great, of course, but the costs were just too high. He told NBC employees that the network was well positioned for the short term, but would face problems in the long run.

Let's Opt for Cable

On Wright's very first day on the job, he observed: "We ought to figure out how to get into the cable business quickly. We're not in it. But it will be around forever. We're going to have smaller network audiences."

But to traditionalists at NBC, cable was the enemy—and no one wanted to get in bed with the enemy. Wright's message was not welcomed. Still he remained determined.

To his regret, NBC could not just go out and purchase cable networks. Those valuable properties simply were not up for sale. So Wright had to start from scratch, a far more difficult task than out and out acquisition.

While Wright focused on expanding the network's reach, Welch was eyeing those exorbitant costs. He had a hard time fathoming how the network that had the highest ratings also had the lowest profits. And he could not understand how NBC could justify its huge budget.

The NBC News budget had mushroomed from $207.3 million in 1983 to $282.5 million in 1984. And because advertising on NBC's news program never equaled the news division's expenses, NBC News lost millions of dollars. In 1988, the year Michael Gartner was hired to replace Lawrence K. Grossman as NBC News president, the operation lost $126 million.

Welch had truly been stymied by Larry Grossman's attitude. When Grossman said to him that because the network was a public trust, NBC News should not have to confront the type of bottom-line pressures that other GE business units had to endure, Welch went ballistic.

He believed he too had a public trust, which had to do with making sure that refrigerators did not explode and airplanes did not crash. Welch's customers put their lives in his hands.

In short, NBC did not deserve an exemption from GE's Face reality credo.

Working in tandem, Welch and Wright were able to turn the network around quickly. In 1985, NBC had profits of $333 million. The following year profits rose to $350 million, while revenues soared past the $3 billion mark for the first time, buoyed by the network's first-place ratings. The *Today* show was ranked first, as was *NBC Nightly News with Tom Brokaw*.

The network's financial picture brightened further in the late 1980s. NBC's profits grew to $410 million in 1987; $500 million in 1988; and ballooned to $750 million in 1989.

As NBC moved into the more competitive 1990s, the competitive pressures increased, and NBC found it difficult to maintain the huge audiences and the heady profits of the preceding decade.

When advertisers turned from the networks toward other ways of reaching consumers, among them cable television and direct mail, NBC's profits began to drop. Throughout 1990, NBC was rated the number one network, but by that summer, its financial picture darkened. NBC's revenues fell by 4.6 percent to $3.2 billion, and profits fell to $477 million.

In 1991, NBC's profits plummeted to $209 million.

One reason: The Persian Gulf war had eaten up $60 million in additional news costs and lost advertising revenue. Ratings fell too, leading some to speculate that GE was prepared to sell NBC for the right price.

Even Bob Wright acknowledged that the network was in play.

In the 1990–1991 television season, NBC had managed to log its sixth straight triumph in the ratings competition, but it was the closest race in almost three decades. And for the first time, NBC was no longer the number one choice of advertisers trying to reach the premier demographic group: men and women aged 18 to 49. NBC had surrendered that honor to ABC.

What did Welch think of NBC in 1991? He found it the most exciting of GE's thirteen businesses, its most intriguing, but also the costliest, the most resistant to change.

I've Moved Too Slowly

In October of that year Bob Wright felt he had moved too slowly and that NBC was not well positioned to deal with the changing marketplace. "We are very much in danger of being eradicated," he said, "and after five years here I still have not been able to convince people enough that that's a fact. We are suffering essentially the same fate as the Big Three automotives. We can be a big participant [in broadcasting], but we will be an unprofitable big participant. We can either try to structure ourselves as a business going forward, and be a much more modest business than we have been; or we can remain enormously visible, probably at a very unacceptable level of profitability."

The early 1990s were tough years for NBC. After several years as the number one network, NBC slipped to third place by the end of 1992. To make matters worse, the collapse came just as the television advertising market fell into its worst slump in twenty years. NBC's profits slipped to just $204 million in 1992.

While GE had encouraged its business leaders to find the strongest person possible for each job, Wright chose Michael Gartner, a respected newspaper editor, as president of NBC News. Gartner had an unhappy ride at NBC. Though he managed to curb losses in the news division by cutting costs, critics blamed him for a variety of inept behavior—from bungling *The Today Show*'s transition from coanchor Jane Pauley to Deborah Norville to offering the tabloid TV show, *I Witness Video*.

On the entertainment side, when Brandon Tartikoff left NBC to run Paramount in 1991, Wright turned prime time over to Tartikoff's deputy, Warren Littlefield, a great programmer with limited business skills. Also that year, after a much heralded negotiation that inspired a book and an HBO movie, popular talk-show host David Letterman jumped ship, moving from NBC to CBS.

So Jack Welch had his quantum leap. He also had a new business strikingly different from the traditional GE businesses of yesteryear—lighting, power generation, major appliances. It was much easier to bring these manufacturing divisions into line with GE's emerging corporate culture, but far more difficult to tame the folks at NBC. None of this diminished the value of making the bold ploy, however, of surprising one's competitors and grabbing the initiative. And that's precisely what Welch had achieved in acquiring NBC.

Fix, Close, or Sell: Reviving NBC

"Getting great talent, giving them all the support in the world, and letting them run is the whole management philosophy of GE."

THE EARLY 1990s had been difficult years for NBC and there was constant buzz that Jack Welch would sell the network. Most of those who prophesied an eventual NBC sale failed to take into account one of Welch's key business strategies: Fix, close, or sell.

Welch had a special affection for the network. There was, after all, a lot more glamour in owning NBC—home of *Seinfeld, ER,* and *The Tonight Show*—than in owning a lightbulb business. Coaxed along by NBC president Bob Wright, who had great faith in his own ability to turn the network around, Welch decided to "fix" NBC with a series of quick, clever maneuvers.

Having lost patience with their own division heads in the early 1990s, Welch and Wright decided that NBC needed to replace current managers with more business-minded, entrepreneurial leaders. To head entertainment, they chose Don Ohlmeyer; for news, they chose Andy

Lack; and for sports, Dick Ebersol. Once this trio was in place, Welch and Wright were confident that the NBC could indeed be "fixed."

Putting the NBC Fix-It Team Together

Early in 1993 Bob Wright turned to Don Ohlmeyer, a sports and entertainment producer who had run his own production company, hiring him to take over as president of NBC West Coast. Ohlmeyer demanded full control over entertainment along with more freedom to spend money on programming. Wright concurred.

Ohlmeyer produced the best results of all the aggressive managers Wright had appointed, carrying out one of Welch's favorite business strategies. By holding a daily 2:30 P.M. "war room" meeting of department heads for brainstorming, Ohlmeyer tore down internal barriers in the division.

Under Ohlmeyer, NBC devised new promotion stunts that worked wonders: its "Must-See TV" became part of the lexicon. NBC was the first network to eliminate commercial breaks between programs; this kept viewers who had tuned in to one show tuned to the next as well. After a rocky start, *The Tonight Show with Jay Leno* overtook CBS's *Late Show with David Letterman* by corralling such news-making guests as Hollywood actor Hugh Grant and NBA basketball star Magic Johnson.

Still trailing its broadcast rivals in daytime television—always an NBC weak spot—the network made some important strides in the profits and ratings side under Ohlmeyer.

Very much in the mold of Jack Welch, Ohlmeyer explained the secret of his success: "People try to mythologize this business. They talk about 'the men with the golden guts.' But it's no different than any other business. You pay attention to detail. You have good taste. You know what you're doing. You get in business with the right people. You support them with the right assets. And you succeed."

Ohlmeyer provided three years of steady ratings growth in prime-time television programming and attracted the youthful demographics that sponsors wanted. Within eighteen months of his arrival at NBC, megahits *Frasier, Friends,* and *ER* were launched.

His record at NBC was sensational, including the fifteen Emmys he won for his work. He moved NBC Entertainment from number three to number one in the ratings; annual network profits increased from

$264 million in 1993 to $738 million in 1995. Ohlmeyer was not at all inhibited about saying what was on his mind. He compared Rupert Murdoch with Hitler, and labeled Michael Ovitz the Antichrist. He described major league baseball owners as "brain-damaged" and argued that his close friend O. J. Simpson was not a double murderer. Wright and Welch were largely forgiving of Ohlmeyer. Wright admitted to cringing at times over Ohlmeyer's outbursts, but then insisted: "He's generally, if not always, pretty accurate in his portrayals."

"There's a lot of Don in every one of us," said Welch. "Most of us don't have the guts to be Don. Our suits constrain us."

On the news side, Wright knew that a bright new face was needed. Tom Brokaw knew it as well. Brokaw sought Welch out: "I talked about the integrity of the news division and the reputation of GE that was entangled in the perceptions. In all that, Welch got it exactly. He was well ahead of me in understanding the problem. He said, 'We're going to do something about it.' And that's when we found Andy Lack."

Wright hired Lack, an innovative CBS news producer, to run NBC News. Lack, like Don Ohlmeyer, had that entrepreneurial spirit; he had worked in advertising, produced a television movie, and created the CBS news magazine *West 57th*.

Since Lack was hired, the *Today* show has taken a dominant lead in the mornings. *Dateline* has grown into a commercial, even though not a critical, success. And the *Nightly News with Tom Brokaw* has mounted the first serious challenge since the late 1980s to ABC's *World News Tonight*, anchored by Peter Jennings.

Pursuing the Olympics

To run NBC Sports, Wright hired Dick Ebersol. Both Ebersol and Ohlmeyer had worked for Roone Arledge at ABC Sports. Ebersol had produced *Saturday Night Live*, a professional wrestling show, and Bob Costa's late-night NBC talk show.

It was Wright's idea to have executives like Ohlmeyer, Lack, and Ebersol, who had an instinctive sense for TV production—something Bob Wright lacked.

Adapting one of Jack Welch's favorite managerial precepts, Wright in effect was creating the vision and letting his three top executives run with it, all the while demanding that they move fast—another Welch strategy.

The Welch strategy of stressing speed was in evidence when Bob Wright summoned Dick Ebersol and Randy Falco, who were responsible for NBC's Olympic coverage, to an August 1995 meeting soon after the Disney-ABC and Westinghouse-CBS mergers. NBC had covered three Olympics since Welch had became CEO and Dick Ebersol wanted to get one more, Sydney in 2000. Wright told Welch that Ebersol wanted to bid on Sydney, not as a purely NBC project, however, but rather as a joint venture with the ABC television network, to minimize the risk. Wright was lukewarm about participating in the joint venture, and Welch shared his feelings. Ebersol also wanted to bid on the Salt Lake City Winter Olympics for the year 2002, but bids were not being accepted yet. Wright was concerned about putting all of his Olympic investment in Sydney. Perhaps NBC could bid on Sydney and Salt Lake City together? It had never been done, but why not? The idea had one big advantage: It could commit the same advertisers to both projects at the same time.

Wright spoke to Welch, vacationing in Nantucket. Welch gave the go-ahead on the spot, providing a GE jet to fly Wright and Falco to present their plan to International Olympic Committee officials, first in Montreal, then later in Sweden. The deal was sewn up, a $1.25 billion package.

Later, Dick Ebersol and the IOC worked out an even larger deal, a $2.3 billion package that gave NBC the rights to cover all Olympics through 2008. By the time ABC, CBS, and Fox woke up, the battle for the Olympic rights was at an end: NBC had secured American television rights to five of the next six Olympics at a cost of $3.55 billion. (CBS had previously bought the right to the 1998 winter games.) When Welch and Wright told the tale of that triumph, they both made the point that acting swiftly was the key factor in landing the deal.

Jack Welch's willingness to make decisions quickly on large amounts of money was not easy for him. He acknowledged that, after the decision to dismiss someone, decisions to make large GE investments were the second most difficult to make:

> **Making small calls . . . is the easiest job in the world because I've got a big company. "Small" means investments of a hundred million, fifty million, thirty, seventy million. Making two-billion-dollar swings or five-billion-dollar swings or four-billion-dollar**

swings . . . where you change the game [is a huge challenge].
Where you risk the image of the company. Where you can tip it
upside down.

What's the hardest big-money decision he's ever had to make? "They're all tough," he answers. "They're all tough."

In the 1995–1996 television season, NBC Sports presented the strongest lineup in television history, airing the World Series, Super Bowl XXX, the NBA Finals, the Olympic Games in Atlanta, U.S. Open golf, and Notre Dame college football. NBC's coverage of the Olympic Games reached a record-breaking audience of 209 million viewers. The Olympics also were the most profitable in history for both the NBC television network and NBC's affiliates.

The Virtues of Cable

Overall, the network enjoyed its most profitable year in 1995 ($738 million); it was the third straight year of double-digit earning increases, 7.6 percent of all GE profits. Revenue that year was also a record-breaking $3.9 billion, 5.6 percent of GE's overall revenues.

Providing the success were the television network, NBC's owned and operated stations, and CNBC, its business and financial news network. NBC also captured every prime-time ratings "sweeps" and was the only broadcast network to show ratings growth in 1995. Two first-year series, *The Single Guy* and *Caroline in the City*, joined *Friends, ER,* and *Seinfeld* as regular Top 10 shows (although *The Single Guy* was later canceled).

Internationally, NBC continued to expand, offering four overseas channels, two in Europe and two in Asia, which together reached 70 million households on a full-time basis. Its international operations in Europe and Asia cost the company $65 million in 1996.

The year 1996 was the most profitable year in the seventy-year history of NBC. It was also the fourth straight year of double-digit earnings increases. NBC also dominated the prime-time ratings that year as it expanded its services around the world.

But NBC's greatest victory was the joint-venture deal that Bob Wright negotiated with Bill Gates of Microsoft that enabled NBC to create a news channel with no cash outlay. Thus it was in July 1996 that MSNBC Cable, a 24-hour news-and-information channel, and MSNBC on the Internet, a comprehensive, interactive, on-line news service, debuted. MSNBC got under way with 22 million subscribers, the largest subscriber base ever for a new cable service; it had commitments to reach more than 55 million households by 1999. Fox News Network had stalled by February 1997; it reached only 19 million homes. Wright had made his fledgling network, MSNBC, the clear number two after CNN.

NBC expected to contribute $250 million to MSNBC until the new venture broke even. While MSNBC's ratings have been small, it does reach 35 million homes, and therefore has an asset value of around $1 billion.

Cleverly expanding NBC beyond broadcasting into cable, new media, and global television, Bob Wright drove NBC to its fourth consecutive year of record revenues and earnings, with more than $5 billion in revenues and an estimated $960 million in operating profits for 1996. NBC's profits from the network alone were at $500 million. Nearly $500 million more came from cable and television station operations.

By 1997, NBC had become one of General Electric's most lucrative businesses. Wright had cut NBC's bloated workforce from 8,000 to fewer than 5,000 full-time jobs, at a savings of $120 million in overhead.

A Show about Nothing

One of the major reasons for NBC's prosperity in 1997 was the weekly sitcom *Seinfeld*, a program that has made television history. While some, including the cast, joked that *Seinfeld* was essentially a "show about nothing," its fast pace, clever lines, and well-constructed plots made it a fixture in nearly every American family's television-viewing week.

While NBC had to pay $120 million to bring *Seinfeld* back for its ninth season in the fall of 1997 (over 10 percent of NBC's entire prime-time budget), the investment paid off: NBC was raking in $180 million from advertising on the program alone. *Seinfeld* became the first television series to command more than $1 million a minute for advertising.

Thanks to *Seinfeld* and the demographics it delivered to advertisers, the network in 1996 was seven times as profitable as the only other network in the black, ABC.

Up until a few days before May 12, 1997, when NBC planned to unveil its fall lineup, it was not clear that *Seinfeld* would be back. Jerry Seinfeld and his supporting cast played hardball with NBC, threatening not to return to the show unless their whopping salary demands were met. Seinfeld negotiated an unprecedented deal, for himself, $22 million for acting, writing, and producing the show, and an additional cut of the profits. The three supporting characters, Jason Alexander (George), Michael Richards (Kramer), and Julia Louis-Dreyfus (Elaine) also played hard to get. NBC gave them a handsome package as well: they would be paid $13 million for each one of the three per season.

Ironically, *Seinfeld* got off to a shaky start when it first aired in 1989, and for the first four years its ratings were only so-so. It became a hit in 1993 only when NBC scheduled it after the highly popular *Cheers* on Thursday nights.

The *Seinfeld* effect on the business side of television has been startling. Reruns, shown at 11 P.M. in the New York City area, have pulled in higher ratings than the news shows of network affiliates, even NBC's. Sitcoms slotted in before and after *Seinfeld* add millions of viewers. "You could read the phone book after *Seinfeld*, and get a 25 [percent] share," said one advertising man.

In late December 1997, Jerry Seinfeld let it be known that he wanted to discontinue the show at the end of the 1997–1998 season. So crucial was *Seinfeld* to NBC that Welch himself intervened—in vain, as it turned out. Seinfeld's argument—that he wanted to end the show when the crowds were still applauding—undoubtedly made little sense to Welch. Would he have "retired" an aircraft engine or a lightbulb that was dominating its market and gave every indication of continuing to dominate it for the next few years?

Spreading the Culture

How did Jack Welch and Bob Wright turn NBC around? They did it by choosing the right people to run the place. Welch loves what Wright did for NBC:

Bob Wright is like an orchestra conductor in that he's able to take extreme egos and he's very self-effacing. He doesn't need a

> lot of stroking. He's very self-confident, very capable. He gives [his team] room. The idea of taking three producers, all well known, all big-leaguers, and giving them big platforms, and letting them go—that was a courageous and brilliant move.

Welch and Wright turned NBC around by doing just what critics told them not to do, importing GE's hard-driving culture to NBC. And they did it after confronting—and ultimately winning over—people both inside and outside NBC who argued forcefully that because television was a uniquely creative business, the traditional rules that applied to all other businesses didn't apply, and wouldn't work, at NBC.

One traditional rule was Keep costs down. Welch and Wright were zealous, however. NBC news executives thought the idea of saving money irrelevant to the news business. The two men disagreed—and won—paring $400 million from the operation over the years.

It was often heard around NBC that Welch and Wright knew nothing about how to run a television network. Jack Welch addressed this point:

> People say, "Jack, how can you be at NBC? You don't know anything about dramas or comedies." Well, I can't build a jet engine, either. I can't build a turbine. Our job at GE is to deal with resources—human and financial. The idea of getting great talent, giving them all the support in the world, and letting them run is the whole management philosophy of GE, whether it's in turbines, engines, or a network.

So Bob Wright and his senior executive run NBC "the GE Way," thinking strategically, globally, long-run.

The people who are hired at NBC are expected to be strong and self-confident. They are expected to encourage speed and simplicity, to have no love of bureaucracy. This helps to explain why NBC has done so well. Why it owns the rights to the Olympics through 2008. Why it has mounted a successful cable news network at a time when its rivals, Disney and Rupert Murdoch, were unable to. And why it beat its competitors to the Internet and expects to become a major programming force in Europe and Asia.

Bob Wright knew that remaining within the broadcasting category at NBC was a nonstarter. He knew traditional network broadcasting was in decline, so he moved into new businesses to create a hedge against that decline. In February 1997 broadcasting still represented the bulk of NBC's revenues and profits, but it was in decline and bound to get worse. In 1992, 60 percent of the viewers tuned in to one of the three networks in prime time; by 1997, that figure had dropped to only 49 percent. Viewers were defecting to such cable networks as Fox, WB, and UPN.

Wright had seemed foolish to many for limiting spending on profitable broadcast operations so that he could invest in seemingly risky cable deals. But unlike his CBS counterparts, Wright was a strong advocate of cable. (CBS had sold cable assets, including a sports channel, and ABC had passed up the chance to take sole ownership of ESPN.)

But Wright pressed on with expanding into a dozen cable networks, purchasing stakes in regional sports channels and such networks as Court TV, Bravo, American Movie Classics, and Arts & Entertainment Television. Most of them by early 1997 were making money. NBC has also taken a 25 percent stake in Madison Square Garden, the National Basketball Association's New York Knicks, and the National Hockey League's New York Rangers.

Wright's largest cable gamble was CNBC, which NBC had created as a business news channel in 1989; it later ensured its survival when it outbid Dow Jones and Westinghouse to purchase a money-losing rival, Financial News Network, for $155 million, far more than FNN was worth.

But since then CNBC, with a worth perhaps as high as $2 billion, has moved into 61 million homes even though its ratings are modest and its programming is considered lackluster. (Its prime-time fare has included a sex call-in show, Geraldo Rivera's talk show, and Conan O'Brien reruns.) Its operating profits have grown fast, from $85 million in 1996 to $125 million for 1997.

Early in 1997 Wright worried about keeping the prime-time TV hits coming; already NBC blockbusters like *ER* and *Friends* were starting to show their age. Then, too, Wright was concerned about NBC's top programmer, Don Ohlmeyer, who over the past few years had turned NBC's prime-time lineup around. Ohlmeyer spent February

1997 in the Betty Ford Clinic seeking treatment for alcoholism even as Wright was counting on him to keep the prime-time hits coming.

Having pushed cable ten years ago, Wright in early 1997 was making a risky, long-term investment in Europe and Asia. There NBC lagged behind Rupert Murdoch, CNN, and ESPN. NBC is distributing four networks: CNBC Asia, CNBC Europe, NBC Europe, and NBC Asia. All four are losing money, but NBC's strategy is to gain a toehold in markets that will one day take off.

That same thinking permeates NBC's investment in new media like NBC Desktop, an on-line financial service.

Jack Welch and Bob Wright, facing a reality that others preferred to ignore, tamed the NBC network. "There was no one," insisted Tom Brokaw in mid-1997, "really addressing the long-range future. They [Welch and Wright] knew from the moment they came in that NBC could not survive the challenges coming from all angles if it relied solely on the core business of an over-the-air network. I honestly believe that they saved the company. Now we're perfectly positioned. I'm confident that with the cables and the investment in Asia and the owned and operated stations, they have really spread the risk and strengthened the [network]."

In October 1997 *Entertainment Weekly* published its list of the 101 most powerful people in entertainment. Number eight on the list was Bob Wright, Don Ohlmeyer, and Warren Littlefield, the president of NBC Entertainment.

Toward the end of 1997, when it became clear that NBC had racked up a record $1 billion in operating profits, Jack Welch proudly gazed at NBC's accomplishments and happily acknowledged that GE's sometimes-bitter struggle with NBC executives over cost cutting and the like was a thing of the past:

> **Don't forget, after a decade, you end up with a team that's *your* team. We don't have people around there who thought being capable was stupid. I remember people who said that, "Why are we doing this?" Eventually an organization becomes a group of bright people who buy into the values. The naysayers sort of look silly in an organization after time. If the organization fails, then they say, "We told you so." But cable was right. Bob [Wright] was right. Hiring Andy [Lack], Dick Ebersol, and Don Ohlmeyer was**

right. So all those things worked out. When you look at the company, we've created a lot of wealth. A lot of people have lived off this success.

When Jack Welch bought NBC in the mid-1980s, people wondered why he chose a business that seemed so unlike all the other GE businesses. When NBC seemed to flounder in the early 1990s, there were a lot of "I told you so's," and reports surfaced repeatedly that Welch wanted to sell the network. But many people did not understand a simple truth: Jack Welch had no desire to part with the network. From the day GE took it on, he believed that he had done the right thing. And he kind of liked NBC, with all the public attention its people and products attracted. He liked the idea that GE could produce turbines and lightbulbs, locomotives and power-generating equipment, but it could also produce *ER* and *Seinfeld*, the *Today* show and the Olympics.

Jack Welch was confident that GE's way was a winning way—that it would be possible to turn NBC around by putting the right people in the right jobs and giving them the space and resources to do their thing.

It didn't hurt that a Jerry Seinfeld came along, or that the network's sports lineup was masterfully crafted, or that the news division was picking up viewers. But Jack Welch prefers to think that GE turned NBC around, because the network had begun to follow the GE Way. And the rest is television history.

Don't Focus on the Numbers

"Numbers aren't the vision;
numbers are the product.
I never talk about numbers."

HOW OFTEN HAVE YOU HEARD one of your bosses say, "We've got to produce better numbers. We've just got to."

That's the extent of the boss's management philosophy—egging on his troops to produce larger revenues, larger profits.

Don't blame your numbers-fixated boss too much for having such a clear-cut goal—and for repeating it so often to his employees.

The trouble is, after a while, "numbers-speak" gets boring, not to mention unnerving, for the troops being asked to make good on those lofty financial goals.

But the worst thing about all this numbers talk is that numbers have little to do with creating a vision or fulfilling a mission; they don't instill values into the hearts and minds of the employees, and they don't provide much help in living up to those values or carrying out the vision. In short, it's not management philosophy, it's just a lot of cheerleading.

And cheerleading doesn't turn a company around.

Jack Welch has figured all of this out—and that's why he's so down on talking numbers all the time.

Oh, he mentions the numbers—in every speech, in every Letter to Share Owners, in every talk to financial analysts. And why shouldn't he? He's proud of how much he's accomplished in his seventeen years as chairman and CEO of General Electric.

Numbers Aren't the Vision

But he won't dwell on the numbers. He refuses to get bogged down in them. That's not what leaders do. Leaders lead. And the only way to lead, as far as Welch is concerned, is to teach a clear-cut, consistent, well-thought-out management philosophy. The only way to lead is to talk about the company's values. So that's what he does, almost all the time:

Numbers aren't the vision; numbers are the product. We always say that if you had three measurements to live by, they'd be employee satisfaction, customer satisfaction, and cash flow. If you've got cash in the till at the end, the rest is all going to work, because if you've got high customer satisfaction, you're going to get a share. If you've got high employee satisfaction, you're going to get productivity. And if you've got cash, you know it's all working.

When Welch talks to financial analysts, to the GE board, or to GE's junior executives at the Crotonville Leadership Development Center, Welch talks values, not numbers. Even his handwritten notes to employees refer to those values. But nowhere is Welch's dislike of numbers more plain than in his annual Letter to Share Owners.

Every year Welch spends the latter half of January laboring over the letter, which appears in GE's Annual Report, a letter that affords him the perfect platform to discuss GE's prior-year performance as well as his management philosophies and business strategies.

Since the elusive chairman rarely gives interviews or speeches, Welch's letter has become one of the primary vehicles for him to transmit his business strategies to GE—and to the business world at large. Welch himself considers this letter one of the most important events of his year.

He knows the letter will be carefully scrutinized by both business executives and the media, so Welch spares little effort in crafting this important document. He truly puts his heart and soul into it and takes great pride in the finished product. Welch takes the first stab at drafting his all-important letter when what he heard and learned at the just-completed operating managers meeting in Florida is still fresh in his mind.

Seated comfortably at his desk at company headquarters in Fairfield, Connecticut, Welch dictates his first draft into a dictating machine. (Of course he has a computer, but the chairman prefers to dictate.) Once the first draft is complete, a secretary transcribes the recording. Welch then begins the process of editing and redrafting. Like a master artist guarding his unfinished canvas, Welch does not allow anyone to see the work-in-progress. Once it is refined and polished, he gives the letter to ten senior GE executives for their input.

In the early years of his chairmanship, Welch's Letter to Share Owners was fairly straightforward and to the point; he would discuss GE's performance over the past year, and that was usually about it. But by the late 1980s the letter had undergone a major transformation; it had become a major platform for disseminating Welch's business ideas and management strategies. The numbers—that is, the company's financial position—had been relegated to a few sentences at the start of each letter. The Letter to Share Owners has now emerged as an important communication tool, for it is through these letters that GE personnel read for the first time about such concepts as "number one, number two," "boundarylessness," and "speed, simplicity, and self-confidence."

Let's Get On to the Important Stuff

Most of the Letters to Share Owners begin with a nod to the numbers: "In 1996, your company had its best year ever." Or, "Your company had a terrific 1995." Or, "GE had a great year in 1994." And after each of these brief sentences, he backs up his introductory statements with proof through the numbers of why and how GE had done so well.

But, as quickly as that, Welch segues into the part of the letter that he likes the best, the part that takes up almost 95 percent of the document: a discussion on the company's values.

Here's an example, from the 1990 letter: "Those are the numbers, and we are pleased with them. For the remainder of our letter, we would like to share with you the progress we continue to make in turning our 1980s vision into reality and the promise we see in the vision we outlined last year for our Company in the 1990s." In other words, let's get on to the important stuff.

Just as significantly, when a list of GE's values is compiled, there is never a direct reference to the numbers part of the business. Rather, leaders who adhere to GE's values are expected to create a clear, simple, reality-based, customer-focused vision; they are supposed to have a passion for excellence; to stimulate and relish change; to have enormous energy. What Jack Welch doesn't say, in compiling that list of values, perhaps because it's all too obvious, is that anyone at GE who adheres to these values is going to *automatically* help in the overall effort to produce the good numbers that GE strives for.

What is crucial in understanding Jack Welch's business philosophy is to grasp one of the most fundamental truths about his management principles: it's about people, not numbers.

Welch urges GE employees to face reality; to lead, not manage; to change before it's necessary; to be boundaryless; to pursue simplicity; to be self-confident. He doesn't say, Get your numbers up. He doesn't believe in that. For one thing, he knows it's unrealistic to expect workers to attain superbowl-like financial results year after year. Even if they worked around the clock, there are simply too many external factors at work—a surprise new product introduced by a rival, a sudden surge of inflation, bad weather, whatever—that could make it impossible to "make the numbers."

Let's be clear: Jack Welch does care about the bottom line. He cares deeply about General Electric's financial performance. He'll deny it. He says he takes little comfort from what the company has done in the past under him. But, don't believe for a second that he doesn't care deeply about results.

This is just his way of emphasizing the company's culture.

Welch assumes that if he can get his people to come up with the right business values—and integrate them into their behavior—GE's financial record will be fine.

Playing Up the "Soft Stuff"

That's why he talks mostly about what he calls the "soft stuff"—the company's values and culture. That's why he'll spend lots of ink in his

Letter to Share Owners on the notion of a "boundaryless" company, or on the virtues of GE's Work-Out program or quality initiative.

Playing up the soft stuff is Welch's key to taking GE to even greater heights in the future.

For a GE business leader, coming up with a strong, market-leading product is crucial. So is knowing how to market that product. But to Jack Welch, it is absolutely essential for a leader to buy into the company's value scheme—its corporate culture, if you will—and be able to sell those values to everyone else.

Delivering the numbers is simply not enough. GE business leaders who bring home the numbers but fall short in living up to the company's values will find themselves out of a job. That may sound harsh. After all, isn't making the numbers the most important goal for any manager? Maybe for most managers, but not for Jack Welch. "Even senior people with good results, doing great jobs in terms of numbers but not walking the talk, have to be removed to support our values. We have to part company."

Welch provides one more clear example of how numbers don't really seem to matter to him. When it is suggested that people listen to his business ideas because of his strong financial performance at the company, he recoils, saying simply that it is not for him to say that GE has done well, but for others. He doesn't want to be quoted saying such things.

But wasn't it Jack Welch who said back in the 1980s that he wanted to make GE the most competitive enterprise on earth? Wasn't he saying then that he wanted GE to improve its numbers? Yes, he replies, but "I'll never get it there. Because if I ever think I've got it there I'm dead."

But there are still a lot of people who are impressed by GE's great numbers, who might look at GE's results and say, "Well, I guess that Welch has exceeded his own wildest dreams." That sort of talk irks the chairman. He doesn't want to say anything that makes it sound as if he's satisfied with where he's taken GE. So he makes a point of telling people that he takes no comfort in where GE is today.

Ironically, Welch has been accused of putting pressure on his managers to make their numbers:

- By insisting that his businesses become, and remain, number one or number two in their markets

- By making it clear that he wants only A level managers at GE
- By insisting that his business leaders stretch, and seek to reach financial results that are above and beyond their yearly budgets
- By demanding that business leaders adhere to GE values—or face dismissal

He's been called the toughest boss in America.

Welch doesn't think he should be faulted for wanting GE to do well—for insisting that his managers perform at their best. After all, isn't that their job, to make sure GE does better year in and year out?

CHAPTER

10

Plagiarize— It's Legitimate: Create a Learning Culture

"The operative assumption today is that someone, somewhere, has a better idea"

IN THE LATE 1980S AND EARLY 1990S, Jack Welch pushed for an open and informal GE.

In the mid-1990s, he began to focus on the need for GE employees to learn from one another—and from outsiders. He liked to say that GE's core competence was sharing ideas across businesses, across what he called the "boundaryless organization," and that the company viewed itself as a series of laboratories that shared ideas, financial resources, and managers.

It was critical for GE to be open so that it could learn, both from within and from without:

> We soon discovered how essential it is for a multibusiness company to become an open, learning organization. The ultimate competitive advantage lies in an organization's ability to learn

and to rapidly transform that learning into action. It may acquire that learning in a variety of ways—through great scientists, great management practices, or great marketing skills. But then it must rapidly assimilate its new learning and drive it.

An Appetite for Ideas

It was the Work-Out program of the early 1990s that gave birth to GE's voracious appetite for new ideas. This program put to rest the long-held view that only the CEO and GE's senior management knew what was best for its employees. As chief financial officer Dennis Dammerman observes: "Historically, at GE, inventors and creators, rather than doers, were made into heroes. You wanted to take personal credit for everything good that happened, because that's how you got to be a hero. Look at Thomas Edison. He wasn't a very good business-man. It was J. P. Morgan who bailed him out in 1892, but it was obviously Thomas Edison, not J. P. Morgan, who was the hero of our company in the 1890s. Well, today, you get to be a hero not just by inventing but also by recognizing a good idea and having your team implement it."

If GE had to rely on Jack Welch for all its ideas, the CEO remarks wryly, "it would take only an hour for it to sink."

By the late 1990s, the Work-Out process had permeated GE's culture. This learning culture was reflected in the openness of a company that encouraged an exchange of ideas at virtually every level of the organization. This boundaryless behavior reached beyond the halls of GE, since Welch encouraged a free flow of ideas not only among GE businesses but also between GE and other companies as well.

Welch has been talking about a learning culture for years, but called it something else in his early days as GE chairman. Back in 1990 he talked about "integrated diversity," and described it as the "elimination of boundaries between businesses and the transferring of ideas from one place in the company to another":

Integrated diversity . . . means the drawing together of our thir-teen different businesses by sharing ideas, by finding multiple applications for technological advancements, and by moving peo-ple across businesses to provide fresh perspectives and to develop

broad-based experience. Integrated diversity gives us a company
that is considerably greater than the sum of its parts.

GE's Uniqueness

He observed that integrated diversity only works when the elements of
that diversity, the thirteen businesses, were strong in their own right;
GE would not succeed by propping up small businesses with larger ones
or having weaklings rely on winners. That was why Welch had always
emphasized the importance of creating strong, stand-alone businesses
in the 1980s.

Welch liked to say that GE's uniqueness was based on its being a
multibusiness enterprise *with a learning culture;* that made its diversity a
competitive advantage rather than a handicap.

A large company like GE has access to a whole world of ideas, but
the only way to turn into a competitive advantage is to develop a pervasive and insatiable thirst for those ideas.

There has to be a compulsion to share and implement those ideas:

This boundaryless learning culture killed any view that assumed
the GE Way was the only way, or even the best way. The operative
assumption today is that someone, somewhere, has a better idea;
and the operative compulsion is to find out who has that better
idea, learn it, and put it into action—fast.

Welch goes on:

The quality of an idea does not depend on its altitude in the organization. . . . An idea can be from any source. So we will search
the globe for ideas. We will share what we know with others to
get what they know. We have a constant quest to raise the bar,
and we get there by constantly talking to others.

Welch credits GE's learning culture with improving the company's
performance in several ways:

- *Operating margins,* under 10 percent for the last 100 years, have
  risen to the 15 percent level in the last 5 years.

- *Inventory turns*, a key measure of utilizing assets, had run in the three to four range for a century, but now has doubled, and created a record $6 billion in cash in 1996; half was paid out in dividends and half was used in a stock buy-back effort.
- *Company revenues*, showing single-digit increases throughout the 1980s, have been reaching double-digit levels in the mid-1990s.

Taking a card out of his pocket with the nine GE values on it, Welch asserted, "Among the values we advocate is this one, 'Be open to all ideas . . . no matter where they come from.' Anyone who doesn't understand that, God help them, has no business with us."

How, some asked, could an employee in one business make use of an idea from another GE business if those businesses are so radically different? Wasn't GE simply an unfocused conglomerate with no real coherence? How could such a large institution exchange ideas?

Welch's reply was that the businesses were not all that different from each other—that business was really simple.

He implored GE people not to make things complicated.

GE, he liked to say, knows how to move money and people. But ideas are probably the hardest to move. "So Welch says moving ideas is really simple," notes Crotonville's Steve Kerr: "You wonder why you wouldn't learn from, say, the plastics business, because Welch has convinced you that some 'best practice' is there, and you feel bad if you don't find it."

Welch was not embarrassed to admit, as he did in his Letter to Share Owners in 1993, that GE had benefited from a flood of ideas taken from other companies.

GE has adapted new product introduction techniques from Chrysler and Canon, effective sourcing techniques from GM and Toyota, and quality initiatives from Motorola and Ford. (Speaking of the quality program, Welch crowed: "I'm very proud of the fact that we didn't invent it. Motorola invented it. Allied followed up with it. And we've taken it. That's a badge of honor. That's not something bad. That's a great thing to do.")

GE was also able to move effectively into the Chinese market by adopting advice and best practices from IBM, Johnson & Johnson, Xerox, and others.

Welch also noted with great pride that GE businesses share a great many things, including technology, design, personnel compensation and evaluation systems, manufacturing practices, and customer and country knowledge:

- Gas Turbines shares manufacturing technology with Aircraft Engines.
- Motors and Transportation Systems work together on new locomotive propulsion systems.
- Lighting and Medical Systems collaborate to improve x-ray tube processes.
- GE Capital provides innovative financing packages that help all GE businesses.

For example, GE Capital was able to obtain solid market intelligence from GE Power Systems, which, because it builds power plants, is well acquainted with the utility industry. GE Capital was able to generate new business after it learned that Power Systems was having problems with some of its backroom operations. Evidently Power was looking for a way to outsource some of its more troublesome backroom activities, such as billing and collection. When GE Capital's Retailer Financial Services group, which handles billing and collections for 75 million store-brand credit cards, learned of this, it sprang into action to secure the account—and new business opportunity for GE Capital.

Welch cites another example, from Medical Systems, to explain how GE businesses learn from one another. The service people in Medical Systems have made tremendous progress in applying state-of-the-art technology to their service business. They learned how to monitor—from a remote sight—a GE CT scanner as it is in use in a hospital setting. Even more remarkable, they have learned to detect and repair an impending malfunction on-line, often before the customer even knows there's a problem!

Medical Systems shared the technique with other GE businesses in Aircraft Engines, Locomotives, Motors and Industrial Systems, and Power Systems. Now these other GE businesses have learned how to monitor the performance of a whole slew of GE products, including jet engines in flight, locomotives and paper mills in full operation, and turbines operating in customer power plants.

That capability has given GE the opportunity to create a multibillion-dollar service business by upgrading installed GE equipment.

Another example of the GE learning culture in action is an incident that took place in Orlando in March 1997.

Welch was meeting with salespeople from Medical Systems. After he and other executives made their presentations, a young salesman stood up and complained that he and his colleagues were not getting paid; their paychecks were showing up late week in and week out. And because he wasn't getting paid on time, he was having a hard time supporting his family. Other companies might have fired the man for complaining directly to the CEO.

But four days later the vice president of sales penned Welch a note saying that the problem had been fixed, and also noted that he had called the man to thank him "and make sure he understood thoroughly how proud I was of him for raising the issue."

Welch sent a "modest CEO Award of $1,000" to the young sales representative as a reward for having the courage to speak up. Call this brashness on the part of the salesman, call it crazy, call it what you will. Welch boasts that the outspoken young man helped GE in its quest to create a learning culture.

To encourage a learning culture, Welch believes in compensating his employees generously, but he makes it clear that they are being compensated for teamwork and for sharing ideas. How generously are GE executives being paid? When he became Vice Chairman in 1979, Welch possessed fewer than 10,000 GE stock options. When he became CEO in 1981, only 200 executives had been awarded stock options. In the late 1990s, when someone became vice chairman, he probably had close to 1 million options! By the end of 1997, some 27,000 GE employees had been awarded stock options, and employee investment in GE stock through 401k plans had increased fivefold: from $2 billion in 1991 to $10 billion in late 1997. These numbers certainly bear out the fact that Welch is willing to spend lavishly on what he deems GE's most valuable resource: its people.

The Most Knowledgeable People in the World

How can Welch ensure that knowledge is shared between and among the various GE businesses? Perhaps the best way is through the Corporate Executive Council, that forum of senior GE executives that meets for three solid days every quarter, gathering for the first time in the year on March 15th. That date is not an arbitrary one; the CEC meets a few weeks before the end of each business quarter.

Next to the board, the CEC is the most senior GE forum. It includes some twenty-five to thirty people: Jack Welch, the vice chairmen (Paolo Fresco, John D. Opie, and Eugene F. Murphy), the twelve business leaders, the five senior corporate officers, and many of the seventeen corporate staff officers. From time to time junior executives will be asked to give presentations to the CEC.

Welch likes to keep the CEC sessions loose, so there is never an in-depth, formal agenda put before the group. Chief financial officer Dennis Dammerman may distribute a brief memo to participants in advance of the get-together to alert them that Welch may want to focus on a specific topic, such as the quality initiative, but other than that, there is no set program.

In the 1980s, the CEC meetings were held at Fairfield headquarters; later, they were moved to Crotonville. Welch feels that the informal, campuslike atmosphere of the Leadership Development Center encourages better exchanges among the business leaders.

The CEC begins its sessions with dinner on Monday night, followed by informal gatherings. Sessions are held in one of two seminar rooms called the Cave or the Lyceum. The Tuesday session gets under way at 8 A.M. and goes until 6 P.M., with one break for lunch. Welch always starts off the session, but he seldom opens the same way twice.

Sometimes he kicks things off by doing an encore of the slide presentation that he presented to the GE board the week before. Or he might opt to recount the details of a recent visit he has made to a particular GE business. Or he might launch into a discourse on the U.S. and world economy. And all of this just to get the ball rolling! After the introductory remarks, CFO Dennis Dammerman reports on the company's financial position; this is followed by other reports from several corporate staff officers.

And that's just the first ninety minutes.

Then the business leaders deliver in-depth quarterly and annual performance forecasts for their respective divisions. Included in this discussion are war stories on big-ticket sales and accounts, with plenty of details on why they won or lost a particular sale. They also discuss any interesting new technological developments or product breakthroughs, as well as new alliances, acquisitions, or dispositions. While all of this is serious business, the entire session is surprisingly informal. There's a great deal of give and take, with the speaker responding to questions and comments off the cuff.

The GE business leaders are also asked to comment on how several companywide initiatives are affecting their businesses. Quality is very much on the chairman's mind, so he inquires about that: How is the quality training of their people coming? What about the projects? Is there anything other GE businesses can learn from their experience?

Some ideas are picked up; others are discarded. At one CEC meeting in 1997, Gary Wendt, head of GE Capital, mentions that his employee orientation program now devotes a full day to six sigma training. Welch loved the idea. A few business leaders like that idea and plan to adapt it to their businesses; others say they see no need to change their current employee orientation programs.

There is no pressure from Welch to adopt every new "best practice" aired at these sessions. All Welch wants his top staff to do is generate ideas and adopt any that they like. That would certainly be plenty for him.

It is not all that uncommon to have other GE staffers attend a CEC meeting. For example, if a class in business management or executive development (two Crotonville training programs) has just completed research on a topic of interest to the CEC, Welch and Crotonville director Steve Kerr may arrange for members of the class to brief the CEC on that topic. They might talk about business opportunities for GE in eastern Europe or Latin America, a topic that is certainly relevant to members of the CEC.

There are three more CEC sessions later in the year: in mid-June, mid-September, and mid-December. No one sits at the meetings taking notes or recording the sessions. The last thing Welch wants is for his business leaders to be bogged down in more paper. The idea behind CEC is to provide a learning experience, a meaningful forum in which to exchange ideas, not just another deadly meeting that adds to the bureaucratic burden. "It's almost like a collegiate atmosphere," observes Robert L. Nardelli, head of Power Systems. "No one feels that they have to one-up the other person. There is a genuine sense of sharing."

Welch boasts that when CEC members leave there after forty-eight hours, they may not be the smartest people in the world, but they are the most knowledgeable:

We have been exposed to all these relevant topics. What's happening in China? What's happening in this business or that business? For forty-eight hours people share ideas, all knowing that everything counts toward the whole. . . . It's like a family clubhouse. We have a great time. I sit in the corner and facilitate ideas. It's like being back at university. No one can miss a meeting. No one has ever missed one.

Learning—it's all about learning. We live this principle. The idea of a learning organization is very real and tangible in GE. Most organizations don't go for ideas in a meeting. Why not? Because everybody present comes from the same business. They talk about the vertical business. We talk about compensation plans, about China, about generic experiences.

Building a learning culture has put pressure on GE's leaders. Steve Kerr says, "Sometimes these leaders have said to me, 'I have a best practice, and Jack Welch is coming to visit. Help me move the best practice around the company. I don't want to get caught with it alone when Jack arrives.' The point is that the manager understand there will be no reward for having a good idea, only in sharing it with others."

The CEC is designed to produce ideas, but Welch devotes much of his energies to making sure that good ideas are implemented quickly. GE Aircraft Engines CEO W. James McNerney notes that only 10 percent of the discussion at CEC meetings focuses on the intrinsic value of the idea; 90 percent has to do with the challenges surrounding its application. "In some organizations they talk about the ideas and they leave the meeting. Only then do they have to think about how to apply the idea. Jack forces the twelve of us to think quickly about any idea's application. So GE is not just a learning culture. It's the application of a learning culture. That is what we hope differentiates us. Jack applies learning more than most people. He forces us to."

At the September 1997 CEC meeting, Jeff Immelt, head of GE Medical Systems, mentioned that GE Transportation performed the "dashboard" customer service tracking process better than his business did. When Immelt returned to his headquarters he called John Rice, the CEO of GE Transportation, and said he wanted to send a team over to see how Rice's business did dashboards. And a few weeks later, Immelt's team was learning how Rice's people had done dashboards. "It starts with Jack," notes Immelt. "The philosophy is, 'We're never as good as we can be.' When you're at the CEC, you notice that everyone is stretching, everyone is trying—even though everyone has it tough. I always walk out of those meetings with four or five new ideas that I can go to work on."

Eugene Murphy, vice chairman of GE, recalled that when he ran Aircraft Engines, he had proposed an idea to the CEC that he had picked up from Ken Meyer, who ran the Aircraft Engines quality program. Meyer had produced a precise two-page report that measured the progress that a particular business made in the quality program. Again, Welch loved the idea, and Meyer's proposal was adapted at other businesses.

David Calhoun, head of GE Lighting, cheerfully suggests that the learning culture has become a natural part of the way people at GE think. He saw it when he ran GE Locomotives and wanted to improve the way the business delivered parts to customers. A team was assigned to visit various GE locales to learn about their experiences. It's now part of the GE way of doing business. "It's a more fun place to work," says Calhoun. "One of the hardest things is sitting in your own closet and dreaming up a new idea by yourself. Now we have a license to go out and learn and implement. Now you have so many ideas, you have to narrow it down to what you want."

"People today look for an idea anywhere," said Welch in the summer of 1997. "It is a badge of courage if I learn from Larry Bossidy, the CEO at AlliedSignal, or Motorola or somewhere else. It used to be a badge of weakness. Rank isn't important. Title isn't important. It's the idea that wins. And that's a big deal."

He proudly pointed to employee surveys showing that 87 percent of GE employees believe that *their* ideas count. "That's a number beyond belief. *Beyond belief.* If you did this twenty years ago, it would have been five." And he's pleased that employees appear to be taking to the learning culture without much prodding. He was especially pleased in the summer of 1997 when GE Appliances sent a two-person team to another GE business in search of "best practices":

Now that was their energizing program. And they're going to meet at the end of August with all the best ideas and see what

can be done then. It's a whole different way of thinking. "Let me learn." I don't use the word "synergy" because it's a trite little word. If everybody in our place gets up every day trying to find a better way, it'll all take care of itself. Those appliance guys going out for the rejuvenation of all the businesses to bring back the best ideas. Now I couldn't edict that if I wanted to. That has to happen because they're thinking, "How can I learn every day?"

When a reporter noted that some people feel a single-product company is stronger than a multibusiness company, Welch refuted that assertion, observing that single-product organizations like IBM, Sears Roebuck, and Kodak were getting into trouble:

That's because their organizations are closed. People only communicate within their divisions. When they're on the way up, they think they're invincible. Then they go down and they think they can't solve anything. Some business is always in trouble at GE. But we've got experience that can be used to help divisions that are down. That's our advantage, and our snowball is rolling downhill in a snowstorm picking up more and more snow. If you use the integrated-diversity idea, it'll multiply the value of a company. A decade ago, you used to keep your ideas to yourself at GE. Now, you're rewarded for how many ideas you exchange. We have changed the behavior system and the evaluation system.

Learning Culture Pressures

The learning culture produces its own built-in pressures.

The CEC, for example, creates a burden on all those at GE not attending the meetings. They wait and wonder what new ideas will emerge from the forum, what new ideas their CEO will want implemented tomorrow as a result of attending the CEC.

GE employees want to be the ones to initiate a "best practice." They don't want to be told by their CEO about some great new idea that exists at some other GE business.

Apart from such pressures, the learning culture helps those at GE who want to get ahead. Patrick Dupuis, head of GE's auditing staff, explains how GE Appliances improved its situation by trying to learn from others. "GE Appliances was doing very well on the production quality level and quite well on the commercial quality level, but it was not coming across as aggressive and involved as other businesses in the quality program. It took Dave Cote [who took over as head of Appliances in June 1997] two weeks to take his entire staff around the United States, coming back with best practices. Two months later, we think Appliances is ahead of the game on commercial quality. A business that is middle of the pack will be frustrated. It's not just stealing; it wants to stay ahead. The pressure to be ahead, to keep learning, is immense. You can never sit back and say, 'We can rest for a while.' There's a high level of pride to have implemented a best practice and bring it to the next level."

Some believe that it is mainly the corporate culture, highlighted in the late 1990s by the learning culture, that explains GE's financial success. A pair of Merrill Lynch analysts, first vice president Jeanne G. Terrile, and assistant vice president Carol Sabbagha, wrote:

> **We have often observed that GE is a big, sweet, low-tech, middle-American company that could have easily fallen into a kind of shabby gentility long ago. But it did not. Its products probably didn't make it great, since they apparently need [the quality initiative] today. NBC was once last; motors, lightbulbs, locomotives and appliances are not inherently growth businesses. Even the most exciting parts of industrial GE—power generation, medical equipment and aircraft engines—are cursed with having the most impressive competitors. There seems to us to be no real tide that carries most of GE.**

> **Intel rides a tide; so do Disney and Nike and Microsoft. Yet GE, in good times and bad, delivers earnings and delivers performance. The answer must be the management culture. . . . Like Britain in the sixteenth century, when a lot of great art and exploration and economics grew in a place where the weather is bad, at GE, an impressive management culture has developed in a place where the products are sometimes dull and the atmosphere usually intimidating. Companies that are big and old usually lumber. At the management, level, GE does not.**

What these analysts have picked up on is the Welch factor. The "impressive management culture" referred to by Terrile and Sabbagha was created by a man who has convinced most people that the best way to run a company is not to convince yourself that you have all the answers.

Most people don't. Why assume, says Jack Welch, that he has all the right answers?

And yet the right answers are out there—somewhere. The trick is to find them and, once they're found, get them implemented as quickly as possible.

It may seem like plagiarism, but it's legitimate. And it can be profitable. History has shown that it has helped one particular company become one of the most competitive enterprises in the world.

PART III

Forging the Boundaryless Organization

"We had to get rid of anything that was getting in the way of being informal, of being fast, of being boundaryless."

Get Rid of the Managers, Get Rid of the Bureaucracy

"Every layer is a bad layer. The world is moving at such a pace that control has become a limitation. It slows you down."

W HEN JACK WELCH took over in the early 1980s, General Electric appeared to be one of the strongest companies in the United States. It was not in the throes of a crisis, nor was it suffering from any of a dozen maladies that plague large companies from time to time.

Still, Welch decided to act, and act decisively.

Concerned over what he perceived to be an uncertain future, Welch feared that GE's rivals would get stronger at General Electric's expense.

He wanted to make the company more competitive.

To achieve that goal, Welch felt he needed a sleek and aggressive General Electric, and this meant a smaller GE—a *much* smaller GE.

At the time the company had 412,000 employees. Welch believed that GE's bloated ranks had become a failed strategy, costing GE inordinate amounts of money.

At that time, no other American business leader was prepared to do what Jack Welch did. He became the pioneer of—

Downsizing.

"Tampering" with General Electric

Until the early 1980s, the American worker had asserted a right to a job for life and pretty much could depend upon lifelong job security.

Yet Jack Welch countered that nothing—including one's job—could be considered sacred, and he had a forceful argument for this reasoning. Ultimately, all that mattered was the survival of the company. That was what counted most, not any particular job. He knew that his downsizing program would cause pain, a great deal of pain, yet it could not be helped. Not if General Electric was to survive and flourish in a more competitive global arena. Welch was prepared to be stoic, though he admitted in later years that downsizing was the worst part of his job.

Restructuring in the early 1980s left no facet of General Electric untouched. Every one of GE's 350 business units was a candidate for the CEO's restructuring.

He did not simply strip away a little bureaucracy or divest a few businesses. He reshaped the face of the company.

The effect of Welch's massive restructuring was to put thousands of GE employees out of work. In time, he reduced his workforce by almost 35 percent, to 270,000.

The "Welch Revolution" of the early 1980s was one of the great shifts in American corporate life. Welch found himself in uncharted waters. Because it was both bold and painful, the GE Chairman needed both vision and guts to stand up to the accusations that he was heartless, insensitive, and brutal.

No one dared to tamper with the powerful General Electric mystique. That mystique was based on 103 years of history and tradition, from its beginnings with Thomas Edison to its emergence as one of corporate America's great success stories. Why would Jack Welch or anyone else tamper with such success?

But tamper he did, earning himself the hated nickname "Neutron Jack." The phrase clung for years, like a bad odor that simply would not go away even though Welch argued constantly that GE's workers were given plenty of warning, treated generously, and provided with retraining. In the late 1990s Welch looked back at the period and noted how times had changed. "Today, people sort of get a badge of honor for ten thousand [layoffs]. It's terrible to take out people. It's the worst part of the job. But we had to get rid of anything that was getting in the way of being informal, of being fast, of being boundaryless."

A Blow to Bureaucracy

Welch believed that a vast, bloated bureaucracy had grown up at GE and it was choking initiative and enthusiasm. Some saw virtue in the decentralized, bureaucratic system. It created order, provided control.

Nonsense, cried the CEO of General Electric. All it did was promote excessive sluggishness.

Soon after taking over, he began to tear the bureaucracy apart, attacking layer upon layer of management that he felt obstructed swift, simple communication. Those extra bureaucratic layers simply wasted time and left managers to spin their wheels. "The world is moving at such a pace that control has become a limitation. It slows you down," says Welch. "You've got to balance freedom with some control, but you've got to have more freedom than you ever dreamed of."

Bureaucracy had always seemed like the enemy to Jack Welch, even before he became chairman and CEO of General Electric. In 1960, when he was hired to develop new businesses in GE's Chemical Development Operation, he and his superiors were appalled at the vast bureaucracy they encountered around the company, especially at headquarters in Fairfield, Connecticut. "We had a Green Beret, almost SWAT team, mentality," recalled Reuben Gutoff, Welch's boss for twelve years. "The enemies were not just outside competitors but the GE bureaucracy as well. We talked a lot about that—the bureaucracy-speak, the bureaucracy-babble. We had met the enemy, and it was us."

Before Welch started his revolution, the basic task of GE managers was to monitor their subordinates' performance. But that sort of command-and-control management style did not permit managers to spot trouble soon enough. Senior managers all around GE were merely firing memos at one another. They prevented the CEO from talking directly with junior managers and rank-and-file workers.

Too Many Titles

To the chairman, all of the strategic planning and control and formality inherent in these management layers did little more than sap the entrepreneurial spirit that GE so desperately needed.

GE had grown so huge and diverse that it seemed as if one out of every two employees was a manager of one kind or another.

That wasn't quite true, but when Welch became CEO in 1981, an astounding 25,000 employees bore the title of manager. There were some 500 senior managers and 130 at vice president level or higher:

- Too much bureaucracy
- Too many managers
- Too many titles

GE's businesses had been organized in sectors and each sector leader was a senior vice president. Welch understood that the sector heads possessed no real power; all they did was transmit information, acting as filters. Sector heads would spend three days preparing for a meeting with Welch. But when they did meet, it soon became apparent that they were not well informed. Then they had to spend more time digging up the answers to the pointed questions that he asked.

Welch abolished this system, removing layers between himself and the divisional CEOs. The number of management levels between the chairman and those in the field dropped from nine to between four and six a decade later. When Welch was through discarding much of his senior management, each business was left with only ten vice presidents, rather than the usual fifty found at other companies the size of GE. Now he could talk directly to his business leaders.

Welch had a name for his attack upon GE's bureaucracy. He called it—

Delayering.

Without all those layers, the company could become lean and agile, a major Welch goal. Critics argued that delayering reduced necessary command and control. Not so, countered Welch:

Big corporations are filled with people in bureaucracy who want to cover things—cover the bases, say they did everything a little

bit. Well, now we have people out there all by themselves, there they are, accountable for their successes *and* their failures. . . . Some who looked good in the big bureaucracy looked silly when you left them alone.

Years after he had successfully cut down GE's vaunted bureaucracy, Welch remained adamant that it had been the right thing to do. On a visit to Crotonville in the fall of 1997, he took another whack at de-layering. "By the time you get through the levels, the barn has burned down, and you've got to get closer to the game," says Welch. "Every layer is a bad layer. Now we don't have all that nonsense. If Delhi wants something, they fax me. It's much easier."

Delayering is one of the hardest parts of being a manager. Getting rid of the folks who work on the factory floor, far removed from the corporate office, is one thing. But it's quite another to tell a fellow manager that he's not cutting it and has to go.

Delayering probably takes more courage than any other management task. If you are content to remain just an ordinary manager, you'll find Jack Welch's tactics too painful. Who wants to fire a buddy, an associate?

But, if you want to become a high-performance business leader, you really ought to take a hard look at all those layers of management—and then decide where to cut, how to improve communications with the people below on the factory floor.

Try it, even though it will hurt, at least for a while.

CHAPTER

Be Lean and Agile Like a Small Company

"Small companies move faster. They know the penalties for hesitation in the marketplace."

JACK WELCH BELIEVES that to survive in an increasingly competitive world, large companies like General Electric must stop behaving and thinking like . . . large companies. They should:

- Get lean
- Get agile
- Start thinking like a small company

"We [have] to find a way to combine the power, resources, and reach of a big company with the hunger, the agility, the spirit, and the fire of a small one," says Jack Welch.

Welch's goal has been to make GE as lean as possible, as fleet as a small company. First, he dealt with those layers of management that, he believed, were clogging the GE machine. Then he removed the entire second and third echelons of management—the sectors and groups. In the 1980s business leaders had reported to senior vice presidents who reported to executive vice presidents, all of whom had staffs of their own. Welch changed that so that the fourteen business leaders reported directly to the three people who occupied the CEO's office—Welch and his two vice chairmen:

> **The new arrangement has proved breathtakingly clean, simple, and effective. Ideas, initiatives, and decisions move, often at the speed of sound—voices—where once they were muffled and garbled by a gauntlet of approvals and the oppressive ministrations of staff reviews . . . .**

> **We found ourselves in the early 1980s with corporate and business staffs that were viewed—and viewed themselves—as monitors, checkers, kibitzers, and approvers. We changed that view and that mission to the point where staff now sees itself as facilitator, adviser, and partner of operations, with a growing sense of satisfaction and cooperation on both sides. Territoriality has given way to a growing sense of unity and common purpose.**

After slicing away bureaucratic layers and removing the monitoring role of senior managers, Welch made another important stride in instilling the small-company soul into the body of GE, when he formulated the Work-Out program in 1988. Although the chairman did not know it at the time, Work-Out would prove to be one of his most important initiatives, one that would leave its mark on the company for decades to come.

The Virtues of Being Small

For GE to behave like a small company might seem paradoxical.

Ambitious businesspeople, after all, want to develop their companies, make them bigger. Jack Welch is not against bigness per se. He loves the idea that GE is one of the world's largest corporations and getting larger every day.

But he wants GE to avoid the inherent pitfalls of being big. Big companies have a tendency to become bureaucratic wastelands. They move too slowly, think to slowly, and, more important, *act* too slowly. Trying to build a sleek, competitive enterprise while saddled by those red-tape accoutrements is like trying to win a race wearing cement shoes.

Welch feels that small, sleek companies have huge competitive advantages:

> **For one, they communicate better. Without the din and prattle of bureaucracy, people listen as well as talk; and since there are fewer of them they generally know and understand each other.**
>
> **Second, small companies move faster. They know the penalties for hesitation in the marketplace.**
>
> **Third, in small companies, with fewer layers and less camouflage, the leaders show up very clearly on the screen. Their performance and its impact are clear to everyone.**
>
> **And, finally, small companies waste less. They spend less time in endless reviews and approvals and politics and paper drills. They have fewer people; therefore they only do the important things. Their people are free to direct their energy and attention toward the marketplace rather than fighting bureaucracy.**

Robert L. Nardelli, head of Power Systems, has organized his business into a number of profit and loss centers, "to get people focused on managing markets and customer relationships. We try not to burden people with the bureaucracy commonly associated with a $7.5 billion behemoth. Rather, we develop centers of excellence focused on meeting customer needs within specific markets. In that way, we have clear ownership and quick, innovative responses to marketplace needs." But that doesn't mean that each business has its own sales force. Nardelli has also restructured his sales force internationally, setting up 25 regional customer teams around the world. "These teams are a vital link back to the business, providing a single port of entry that helps ensure customers are fully aware of the company's entire portfolio of services and products."

Speed Is the Key Ingredient

Welch understands that small companies fear bureaucracy, and all that usually accompanies it. Employees of small companies must be fast on their feet all the time, or risk falling into the same traps as larger companies. Speed "is the indispensable ingredient in competitiveness," says Welch. "Speed keeps businesses—and people—young. It's addictive, and it's a profoundly American taste we need to cultivate."

Welch's love of speed in business began early in his career when he was working at GE Plastics. He had one employee. He took him home to meet his wife and have dinner. They talked about everything and had genuine rapport. That was in the 1960s, but Welch feels that the philosophy is as relevant today. Companies need to be informal.

All through the 1980s Welch preached the virtue of small-company speed. "There is something about speed that transcends its obvious business benefits of greater cash flows, greater profitability, higher share due to greater customer responsiveness and more capacity from cycle time reductions." Speed exhilarates and energizes: "This is particularly true in business, where speed tends to propel ideas and drive processes right through functional barriers, sweeping bureaucrats and their impediments aside in the rush to get to the marketplace."

Welch notes that companies appear to follow predictable life cycles. At the beginning, new businesses are gripped with an urgency to get to the marketplace. In such an environment, bureaucracy has a hard time getting a foothold—just as ice cannot form in a fast-moving stream. But, as institutions grow and become more comfortable, their priorities shift:

- From speed to control
- From leading to managing
- From winning to conserving what they had won
- From serving the customer to serving the bureaucracy

"We begin to erect layers of management to smooth decision making and control that growth," says Welch, "and all it does is slow us down. We put barriers between the functions of our businesses, which create turf and fiefdom." And that is where the emphasis on speed makes the difference. "If you're not fast, you can't win. You must get products to market faster and response from customers quicker. You've got to make decisions fast. If you're not boundaryless, and you've got a bunch of layers, that's like going out in the cold with six sweaters on. Your body doesn't know what the temperature is."

With speed a cardinal virtue at GE, Welch and his team make closing a deal in record time a badge of honor. They take great pride in talking about how in 1989 they took only three days to seal an alliance with the British firm GEC—a deal that increased their share of the European market for four of its businesses: Medical Systems, Appliances, Industrial and Power Systems, and Electrical Distribution and Control.

And they love to point to 1995 when it took NBC only a weekend to sew up the exclusive rights to televise five of the next six Olympic Games for $4 billion. GE is proud of the fact that NBC was able to move so quickly, despite the size of the deal. After all, how many other companies can decide to spend $4 *billion* in a single weekend?

In his 1992 Letter to Share Owners, Welch noted what it is about small companies that he admires:

Most small companies are uncluttered, simple, informal. They thrive on passion and ridicule bureaucracy. Small companies grow on good ideas—regardless of their source. They need everyone, involve everyone, and reward or remove people based on their contribution to winning. Small companies dream big dreams and set the bar high—increments and fractions don't interest them.

We love the way small companies communicate: with simple, straightforward, passionate argument rather than jargon-filled memos, "putting it in channels," "running it up the flagpole," and worst of all, the polite deference to the small ideas that too often come from big offices in big companies.

Everyone in a small company knows the customers—their likes, dislikes, and needs—because the customer's thumbs up or down means the difference between a small company becoming a bigger company tomorrow—or no company at all. It comes down to something very simple: Small companies have to face into the reality of the market every day, and when they move, they have to move with speed. Their survival in on the line.

Steve Kerr comes to GE from the academic world. He was dean of faculty at the University of Southern California (USC) School of Business and then visiting professor of management at the University of Michigan before becoming director of GE's Crotonville Leadership Development Center.

He admits that he is not used to the quick pace at GE. "At USC you couldn't prepare a course in less than a year. But at GE the attitude is, 'Do something. Get the ball in play.' In the Work-Out program, the decision maker has to make a decision on the spot. We find that mistaken decisions are made only 10 percent of the time in Work-Out sessions. That's not bad. So the feeling is, 'Do something. It probably will be the right decision.' "

In small decisions such as starting a management course—and bigger ones, like gaining the television rights to the Olympics—Jack Welch prides himself on running a company that moves fast:

> **Speed is the product of an open organization. Enormous energy and the ability to energize others is one of our critical values. Involve everyone and move quickly. If you can't come to a fast decision, and you can't get everybody in the game quickly, then you don't have the right values. Being a brilliant administrator is not enough. You've got to excite people. Get them going.**

GE Capital is the classic example of a business thinking and behaving like a small company. Capital's CEO, Gary Wendt, runs his $33 billion enterprise as if it were a string of niche businesses. His headquarters staff in Stamford, Connecticut, is small and lean. Wendt says he wants the leaders with GE customers, not with him. So the leaders remain close to their markets and focus on the part of the business they know the best.

With this narrow focus, GE Capital's businesses can function with a clear understanding of where profit and loss stand all the time, a distinct advantage over businesses that have trouble creating accurate income statements.

Just what is Jack Welch saying here? Isn't the goal of a business leader to make the business grow and grow and grow—to have it become as large an enterprise as possible so that profits will grow?

Of course it is. There's no question that companies should try to become more and more profitable.

All Jack Welch is saying is this: As you grow, don't lose sight of the virtues of what small businesses offer, and what they do better than their larger counterparts. While you're growing, don't permit the attributes of bigness to stand in your way, to overwhelm you, to weigh you down like that cement-shoed runner.

Make your business grow, but do everything possible to get that small-company soul into the body of your big business—and you'll have the best of both worlds.

Tear Down the Boundaries

"Our people must be as comfortable in Delhi and Seoul as they are in Louisville or Schenectady."

JACK WELCH FELT that there were far too many boundaries within General Electric. Everywhere he turned, he found boundaries:

- Between management layers
- Between engineers and marketing people
- Between GE and its customers
- Between GE employees who worked full-time and those who worked part-time
- Between GE and the whole outside community

Boundaries, barriers—same thing. Welch hated boundaries and wanted to get rid of them. They slowed down the company. They complicated matters. They got in the way.

Welch felt that the boundaries between GE and the outside world were due to a long-standing GE belief that he labeled the "not invented here" (NIH) syndrome: if an idea is not invented at General Electric, it's worthless.

Welch hated NIH thinking. In his 1996 Letter to Share Owners, he wrote that NIH "limited our ability to learn from suppliers, our customers and other global companies that had 'best practices' that could be of enormous use to us."

Of all of Welch's business strategies, none is more important to him than boundarylessness. He knows it's an awkward term. But it best sums up the ideal he is seeking for General Electric, and it is probably the term most closely associated with GE's CEO.

Boundarylessness, for Welch, defines GE: an open, informal company where employees can move swiftly and effortlessly and where they can connect to the outside world just as quickly and effectively.

The strategy is intimately caught up in the struggle for higher productivity rates:

Productivity is not the squeezing out of a rag. Productivity is the belief that there's an infinite capacity to improve anything. We live here knowing we don't have the answers. We know somebody has the answers. We're out there chasing every day to find them, because it's intellectual capital that creates the productivity. And that's why in GE today the value of boundarylessness is without question the most important value that's occurred in our company.

Going to Market Separately

Jim Baughman cites an example of how boundaries hurt GE. At one stage GE sold billions of pounds of plastic, billions of lightbulbs, and millions of electric motors to the automobile industry. And yet the sales staffs of each of these GE businesses called on the automobile industry as if they didn't work for the same company. The left hand didn't know what the right was doing. The problems were due to decentralization, which had created profit and loss units that were too small to compete. Decentralization had also created too many layers of approval and other functional boundaries. Engineering would design something only to find that GE's manufacturing people were having difficulties making it, the sales force couldn't sell it. Once the product did get sold, the service people found it hard to fix.

"There was no horizontal flow," says Baughman, "so we had hierarchic boundaries that slowed down the decision process. Things took too long. We had boundaries between the businesses. Where we should have been going to market as a team, we were going separately."

In a speech he gave in March 1990, Welch articulated what was behind the notion of boundarylessness:

> **The pace of change will be fleet in several areas. Globalization is now no longer an objective but an imperative, as markets open and geographic barriers become increasingly blurred and even irrelevant. . . .**

> **Simply doing more of what worked in the 1980s—the restructuring, the delayering, the mechanical, top-down measures that we took—will be too incremental. More than that, it will be too slow. The winners of the 1990s will be those who can develop a culture that allows them to move faster, communicate more clearly, and involve everyone in a focused effort to serve ever more demanding customers.**

> **To move toward that winning culture we've got to create what we call a boundaryless company. We no longer have the time to climb over barriers between functions like engineering and marketing, or between people—hourly, salaried, management, and the like. Geographic barriers must evaporate. Our people must be as comfortable in Delhi and Seoul as they are in Louisville or Schenectady.**

Boundarylessness has been a key strategy in Welch's effort to achieve General Electric's productivity goals. But the strategy calls for much more than simply getting rid of bureaucratic waste and boosting productivity.

Welch's view of the 1990s is based on the premise that the workplace needs to be liberated. That workers should no longer be told what to do, but should be empowered and given responsibility. To reap the full benefit of every employee requires a new way of thinking, a new world where employees run free. In this brave new world all employees are permitted to participate in decision making and have full access to vital information needed to make those decisions. This may not be a radical thought in 1998, but it did represent a fairly radical departure from the traditional command-and-control model that ruled corporate America when Welch first introduced these thoughts in the 1980s. Welch would move toward boundarylessness by liberating the workers, letting them speak for themselves.

Working with Everyone

What does boundarylessness mean for the GE of the late 1990s? Gary Wendt, head of GE Capital Services, observes that "boundarylessness was necessary to have us act like a small company. Boundarylessness meant to Jack Welch that we are all in this business together and we need to be sharing things with each other and working to cooperate with each other; not simply to do what we're supposed to do, go home, and don't talk about it. In a large corporation, you can see how people could get the feeling that they don't make a difference. But boundarylessness encourages people to behave in a way that they have to work with everyone."

Every once in a while, the General Electric chairman himself would confront examples of boundaries—and he would act immediately to tear them down. He once discovered that whenever he called a meeting, certain GE staffers spent countless hours preparing page after page of possible answers to questions he might throw at them. This canned material represented a "boundary" that the staffers were imposing between themselves and Welch. He told the staff that he didn't want them going through those preparations. It wasted too much time.

But even after Welch put an end to that practice, the staff was still concerned that Welch might ask them something they couldn't answer. So they stationed an employee outside the meeting, ready to research an answer as quickly as possible. That employee became another boundary, preventing the staff from dealing with Welch directly. Once he caught on to that boundary, Welch halted that practice as well.

The next time there was a meeting, the CEO put a question to one staff member, a question he couldn't answer.

"I don't know the answer," the person confessed, bewildered, but unable to think of what else to say.

Welch applauded. Then he said, "That's OK, but make sure you find out and let me know."

The chairman was thrilled. He had created a sense of boundarylessness among the staff that would pay off in less time wasted, less unnecessary effort expended.

How Many GE People Does it Take?

Crotonville's Steve Kerr and his colleagues teach boundarylessness in the classroom by example. "We teach that when someone comes to you for a decision or approval, you must look at the number of people who have already signed off on the decision. If it's two or more people, you have to ask what value you are adding. If everyone's accountable, no one's accountable. Also, you should ask, 'What is keeping me from letting my subordinate make that decision?' You have to ask, 'How often have I reversed a decision or approval?' If the answer is seldom or never, why feel the need to sign off on it?"

Kerr developed boundaryless forms of behavior outside the classroom as well. When he began directing Crotonville in March 1994, he learned that his division was responsible for hosting GE's Corporate Executive Council meetings. As one of those CEC meetings was about to start, Kerr noticed a man sitting outside the meeting hall and asked him what he was doing.

"I go into action if there's some technical problem," the man explained proudly.

Kerr was taken aback. What kind of technical problem was he talking about?

"Well," said the man calmly, "let's say a bulb in the overhead projector has to be changed."

Kerr couldn't believe his ears. He thought to himself: We have Ph.D.s and engineers inside the room. And we need someone *outside* the meeting?

Kerr spoke quietly but forcefully to the man. "There are five engineers in that meeting, including the chairman. I'll bet one of them could change a lightbulb!"

Knocking down one more boundary at GE, Kerr told the man to go back to his regular duties.

It's How We Act

With the creation of the Corporate Executive Council in 1986 GE's senior executives began engaging in boundaryless behavior—talking to one another directly and informally, learning from one another, adapting "best practices" for their own use.

But Welch's most aggressive attempt to rid GE of its boundaries was the launching of the massive companywide initiative called Work-Out in 1990. Welch noted in 1996 that Work-Out had eliminated insularity at GE by going after NIH and eradicating it. Through Work-Out, GE began to systematically explore the world's best companies for better ways of doing things. That created the basis for GE's learning culture—another critical Welch business strategy of the late 1990s.

While the town meeting approach was originally designed to dismantle GE's internal ceilings and walls, Welch began to sense that the Work-Out process would also help to get rid of external walls by strengthening ties with customers and suppliers.

Welch says that the development of a boundaryless learning culture is the most important product of Work-Out and that culture defines how GE employees should behave. "Today, we would never knowingly hire someone who would not or could not adopt that behavior."

Speaking to a group of junior executives at Crotonville in the fall of 1997, he explained that "boundaryless behavior is how we act. People help each other as natural acts. There's an open dialogue. You now debate things. You never told us ten years ago what you thought. Before if you had an idea you held on to it."

Welch's vision of the boundaryless company has long appealed to Paolo Fresco, GE's vice chairman of the board and executive officer.

Back in the early 1980s, even when Welch was using the word *openness* to describe the concept of boundarylessness, Fresco felt the chairman was on the right track. He wanted to get everyone highly involved. "And," said Fresco, "he believed in calling things what they are—facing reality. Not the way you'd like them to be. Learning from best practices. Hating bureaucracy. Getting rid of sacred cows. Just bringing a fresh look. If you are a young man and you join a traditional company, you are overwhelmed by the bureaucratic arrogance you find and this is true in any organization. We were suffering from that as much as everyone else was. This fresh wind [in the form of Jack Welch] came in and said, 'You can challenge everything.' That is the one thing I found the most exciting."

David Calhoun notes that when Welch first instituted boundarylessness, most senior GE executives thought about it in the context of their own organizations. Function to function. Department to department. How could they get people to work together? How could they go after common measures? The challenge for GE people now, he says, is to break down the boundaries that exist between companies, between countries, between suppliers and customers. When he ran GE Transportation, Calhoun noted, he had to buy 70 percent of what was in the locomotive, so he was extremely dependent on suppliers. Those suppliers not only provided GE with the components, but helped design the locomotive itself. Calhoun had to find out not only how to design the part but how the part would affect the overall performance of the locomotive. "It is an enormous opportunity and it is very complicated. Not only do you need to convince your own organization to be boundaryless but the suppliers as well. That's not easy. Why? Because we expect a new level of resource commitment from the supplier. We're saying, 'If you want to do business with me, I want you in the middle of the design process. We do not want just an engineer, we want your *best* engineer. Once we get their best engineer, our responsibility is to listen and implement. That is where the real leverage is.'"

The removal of walls, Welch said in his 1993 Letter to Share Owners, meant that

> **. . . we involve suppliers as participants in our design and manufacturing processes rather than treat them as vendors, left to cool their heels in waiting rooms. It means having major launch customers like British Airways, Tokyo Electric Power, or CSX in the room and involved in the design of a new jet engine, a revolutionary gas turbine, or a new AC locomotive, or a panel of doctors helping us develop a new ultrasound system.**

The message that the CEO of General Electric is trying to convey is this: If you're a business leader, at whatever level, you've got to ask yourself, What parts of my business are slowing us down? What parts are bottling us up? It should be clear by now that Jack Welch's business philosophy aims in large measure at systematically dismantling all the obstacles inside one's own business that hamper the successful production and marketing of products.

Becoming boundaryless is one important step in helping you, the business leader, to remove every possible roadblock that impedes speeding a product to the marketplace.

Yes, boundarylessness is an awkward word. But as Welch hammers home, it's a concept that can truly pay handsome dividends.

PART IV

Harnessing Your People for Competitive Advantage

"My whole job is people. I can't design an engine. I have to bet on people."

Three Secrets: Speed, Simplicity, and Self-Confidence

"Bureaucracy is terrified by speed and hates simplicity."

Getting rid of the bureaucracy.

Delayering.

Downsizing.

All of that had to do with restructuring the mighty business engine known as General Electric.

The restructuring effort proved to be a crucial element in creating the streamlined GE that Welch knew was needed.

But Jack Welch sensed that it was not enough, and that to create a truly agile, competitive enterprise required more—much more.

To transform GE into a world-class company, he would have to devise a new strategy. A strategy capable of supercharging an arguably weakened workforce. The downsizing of the 1980s had reduced the number of GE employees by almost a third, and those still standing were reeling, consumed by worry for their own jobs. After all, they wondered, if GE could simply snap their fingers and eliminate all those jobs, what's to stop them from cutting mine next?

Welch recognized the problem, and he knew that he needed to give GE employees—the survivors—a sense of how to behave in the new, lean environment. He would have to do something that would help diminish the uneasiness and rebuild confidence and self-worth.

So as the 1980s waned and the 1990s dawned, Welch started to give some serious thought to these matters, and to exactly what type of company GE should become. He noted how the 1980s had forced business to change. "The complacent and timid had a date with hostile-takeover people. Ten million manufacturing jobs were eliminated and shifted to the service sector. Seventeen million new jobs were created, and unemployment dropped to its lowest point in fifteen years. American firms began to globalize."

As corporate Darwinism weeded out the weak companies, the 1980s created a more productive business environment. Millions of manufacturing jobs were lost, but many more were created in the service sector. While this constituted a natural and healthy business evolution, the worst thing a leader could do was to assume that what worked in the 1980s would work in the 1990s. "Fighting the last war" would bring disastrous results, said Welch, because American productivity still lagged behind Japanese.

And Welch's other predictions were also being put to the test. In the early 1980s he had said that the world would soon become far more complex, and history was proving him right: the field of competition had turned into a crowded battleground, as Europe, Korea, and Taiwan joined Japan in the global fray. Simply pursuing more of the hardware solutions of the 1980s—downsizing, plant closings, and so forth—would not be nearly enough to triumph in the cutthroat 1990s:

> **The competitive world of the nineties will make the eighties look like a walk in the park. How does America win in the nineties? To win we have to find the key to dramatic, sustained productivity growth. . . . We have to turn in the nineties to the software of our companies, to the culture that drives them. . . . We have to move from the incremental to the radical, toward a fundamental revolution in our approach to productivity and to work itself—a revo-**

lution that must touch every single person in the organization every business day.

Speed, Simplicity, Self-Confidence

He summed up his prescription for winning in three words:

- Speed
- Simplicity
- Self-confidence

If he could get GE employees to work with speed, simplicity, and self-confidence, Welch was confident that the dividends would begin to show up on the bottom line.

GE would become more productive—and more profitable.

Speed Decreases Control

Welch knew that in order to get speed, *real* speed, decisions at virtually every level would have to be made in minutes, not days or weeks. He also knew that decisions had to be made face-to-face, not memo-to-memo. This meant that people had to think on their feet, and that the forests of meaningless paper trails and approvals—so common in large organizations—would have to be eliminated.

Welch looked to the lessons of the 1980s to help create a speedier, more streamlined GE. The 1980s had shown that there was an inverse relationship between speed and control: as speed increased in an organization, control decreased. The management apparatus that had worked in the 1970s had become a handicap in the early 1980s, so Welch and GE changed with the times.

Welch was primarily thinking about speed when, in December 1985, he eliminated the sectors, those excess layers of executive vice presidents who stood between the CEO and the heads of the company's thirteen major businesses.

This delayering sped communications and helped to get products to markets more quickly.

In his 1993 Letter to Share Owners, the chairman harped on speed. In fact, in that memorable letter, he talked more about speed and boundarylessness than any other topic. He gave some examples of GE's speed:

- There was a new product announcement at GE Appliances every ninety days—unthinkable years ago.
- The GE90, the world's most powerful commercial jet engine, was designed and built in half the normal time.
- Another team developed a breakthrough ultrasound innovation in less than a year and a half. Others designed and built a new AC locomotive in eighteen months.

In his 1994 Letter to Share Owners, Welch talked about new product introduction as one of the best ways to measure GE's speed. He gave these examples:

- The Lighting company introduced hundreds of new products, ranging from the expansion of its Halogen IR line, to a whole new range of compact fluorescents, to the introduction of GE/ Motorola-brand electronic fluorescent ballasts.
- GE Power Systems, which once took years to develop new products, had designed and brought to market three new gas turbine generators in 1994.
- NBC launched America's Talking, a new cable network that featured a diverse roster of talk shows.
- Product development in Medical Systems had gone from a two-year cycle to less than one, and 70 percent of GE's computed tomography products were less than one year old.

Simple Enough for Cocktail Party Chatter

As for simplicity, Jack Welch likes to proclaim that business is simple. He implores people to have the courage to be simple. Don't make business harder than it is, Welch pleads.

No matter how different GE businesses seem one from the other, he urges everyone in the company to think simply, to see themselves as performing essentially the same two processes—inputs and outputs— and not to make anything more complicated out of business than that.

The inputs are the same, he says. They are people, energy, and physical space.

Some people perform mechanical feats, some do financial things, but when you think about what you do conceptually, you're really not doing different things, says Welch. Simplicity is practically an art form, with many definitions:

To an engineer, it's clean, functional designs with fewer parts. For manufacturing it means judging a process not by how sophisticated it is, but how understandable it is to those who must make it work. In marketing it means clear messages and clean proposals to consumers and industrial customers. And, most importantly, on an individual, interpersonal level it takes the form of plain-speaking, directness—honesty.

Simplicity is also indispensable to a business leader's most important function: creating and projecting a clear vision. Says Welch, "The leader's unending responsibility must be to remove every detour, every barrier, to ensure that vision is first clear, and then real. The leader must create an atmosphere in the organization where people feel not only free to, but obliged to demand clarity and purpose from their leaders."

A business leader needs what Welch calls an "overarching message—something big but simple and understandable. Whatever it is—we're going to be number one or number two, or fix/close/sell, or boundaryless. Every idea you present must be something you could get across easily at a cocktail party with strangers. If only aficionados of your industry can understand what you're saying, you've blown it."

One of the most difficult things for a manager to do, says the head of GE, is to reach that all-important threshold of self-confidence in which being simple is comfortable. "Simple messages travel faster, simpler designs reach the market faster, and the elimination of clutter allows faster decision making. All this happened in the upper echelons of GE," wrote Welch in his 1995 Letter to Share Owners. "We saw the leadership come alive with energy, excitement, and the crackle of small-company urgency."

Self-Confidence: The Antidote to Insecurity

Welch knew that the survivors were shaken by the massive changes, and above all else were in dire need of a healthy dose of self-confidence:

"Some people get it at their mother's knee, others through scholastic, athletic, or other achievement. Some tiptoe through life without it. If we are to create this boundaryless company, we have to create an atmosphere where self-confidence can grow in each . . . of us."

The root cause of many of bureaucracy's ills—the bitterness, the turf battles, the in-fighting and pettiness so rife in many organizations—is insecurity, says Welch. Insecurity makes people resist change because they see change only as a threat, never as an opportunity. And the way to build self-confidence is to give people a voice, to get them talking and listening to and trusting one another:

> **Self-confidence does not grow in someone who is just another appendage on the bureaucracy, whose authority rests on little more than a title. Bureaucracy is terrified by speed and hates simplicity. It fosters defensiveness, intrigue, sometimes meanness. Those who are trapped in it are afraid to share, can't be passionate, and—in the nineties—won't win. . . .**

> **Self-confident people are open to good ideas regardless of their source and are willing to share them. Their egos don't require that they originate every idea they use, or "get credit" for every idea they originate. We began to cultivate self-confidence among our leaders by turning them loose, giving them independence and resources, and encouraging them to take big swings. The inevitable surge of self-confidence that grows in people who win leads to another natural outgrowth: simplicity.**

Welch made a heartfelt plea for self-confidence in the organization and extolled the virtues of a self-confident leader: "Self-confident people don't need to wrap themselves in complexity, 'businessese' speech, and all the clutter that passes for sophistication in business—especially big business. Self-confident leaders produce simple plans, speak simply, and propose big, clear targets."

A company cannot simply manufacture or distribute self-confidence. But it can provide an atmosphere that affords employees that opportunity to dream, risk, and win—and ultimately earn self-confidence. What it takes is speed, simplicity, and self-confidence, re-iterates Chairman Welch. That way it is possible to develop

> **. . . a work ethic that plays to our strengths, one that unleashes and liberates the awesome productive energy that we know resides in our workforce. If we can let people see that what they do counts, means something; if you and I and the business leadership of the country can have the self-confidence to let people go— to create an environment where each man and woman who works in our companies can see a clear connection between what he or she does every day, all day, and winning and losing in the real world—we can become productive beyond our wildest dreams, certainly beyond the abilities of our international competitors, most of whom are hobbled by cultures that make it virtually impossible for them to liberate and empower their people.**

"If you don't have self-confidence," says Welch, "you can't be simple. You just can't. You're scared to death that you'll look simple. The way to sabotage your chances of producing great bottom-line results is to bog the organization down in complicated, distracting clutter. The surest path to failure is to create the kinds of bureaucratic sloth and sluggishness that slow your business down."

But, a business leader asks, justifiably, How can I avoid all these things—the monitoring, the checking, the approvals? We've been doing these things for years. And they seem to work.

Welch's answer is, not surprisingly, a simple one: Have the self-confidence to make meaningful changes in your business. Have the self-confidence to simplify and speed up your business procedures. Speed, simplicity, and self-confidence may sound like dozens of other business aphorisms. But when they are truly encouraged and developed, they are powerful management tools that can help streamline your organization and boost the productivity of your entire workforce. It's really as simple as that.

Use the Brains of Every Worker— Involve Everyone

"Get the management layers off their backs, the bureaucratic shackles off their feet, and the functional barriers out of their way."

JACK WELCH'S FIRST REVOLUTION at General Electric brought massive change: 350 businesses transformed into 13.

- The core electrical manufacturing businesses were no longer the focus of the company; high-tech and service segments now were.
- Plants were shut, buildings were leveled, existing factories were made state-of-the-art.
- New plants were built and layers of management were cast aside.
- The number of employees dropped by a third, from 412,000 to 279,000.
- Revenues and earnings were on the rise.

Welch called these years the "hardware phase."

The hardware phase had made General Electric more competitive, but it also had a totally disorienting effect on the employees.

The good news was that they had survived the cut. But they weren't out of the woods yet; most of the survivors still faced a difficult and uncertain future, and they were feeling those difficulties every day. They worked in new plants, with new bosses and new jobs. More workers competed harder for the fewer promotions that remained. To make matters worse, they all lived in fear for their job. They needed to feel more sure about themselves and their futures. At the very least, *they needed to feel wanted.*

A Plan to Capture Good Ideas

The CEO of General Electric was certainly cognizant of the negative side effects of his downsizing. He could no longer promise GE employees a job for life, and yet he had to find a way to motivate them to work harder than ever.

He needed to make his employees feel less like overworked cogs in a machine and more like "owners" of the business—like direct participants in the way the business was run. How could he get them to feel highly involved and empowered? How could he show them that they truly did make a difference?

His solution was Work-Out, a program designed to foster, capture, and implement good ideas, regardless of their origin. By getting more involved, Welch argued, employees would be helping to strengthen GE's businesses—and healthy, growing businesses were the best guarantee for job security:

> **The way to get faster, more productive, and more competitive is to unleash the energy and intelligence and raw, ornery, self-confidence of the American worker, who is still by far the most productive and innovative in the world.**

> **The way to harness the power of these people is to protect them, not to sit on them, but to turn them loose, let them go—get the management layers off their backs, the bureaucratic shackles off their feet, and the functional barriers out of their way.**

In the past GE managers had been responsible for improving productivity. "We generally used to tell people what to do," says Welch. "And they did exactly what they were told to do, and not one other thing." Now this task is be shared with the men and women on the factory floor, and "we are constantly amazed by how much people will do when they are *not* told what to do by management."

Even as Welch was deciding to empower his employees, he understood that there was a certain contradiction between what he was advocating and the hierarchical leadership he still believed in. "Can you put in an empowering methodology in a nonempowering way?" asks Crotonville's Steve Kerr. "Jack caught the wonderful contradiction when he realized that what he was decreeing here would be no more autocratic leadership. Welch said one of the ways we'll know if Work-Out will be successful is if my style of leadership won't be tolerated."

Though he was empowering his employees through Work-Out, Welch didn't want to label the new process *empowerment*. He preferred the phrase *high involvement:*

> **That doesn't mean abdication of decision-making authority by leadership. And that gets confused sometimes. We want everyone to have a say. We want ideas from everyone. But somebody's got to run the ship. Now, that doesn't mean somebody runs the ship by directing it. Somebody runs the ship with a total input from everyone. Empowerment is OK as long as it's understood. Empowerment doesn't mean anarchy. Involvement is less misleading—high involvement, a say in the decision-making, a stake in the institution, a voice. And I'll tell you one thing: With voice comes responsibility.**

By making his employees feel that they had a stake in the company's future, Welch was hoping to inject a spirit of common purpose among GE's employees and businesses.

Too Bad We Waited So Long

Welch regretted waiting seven years to empower his workforce, but he felt that starting any earlier did not make sense. There had been too much ferment at GE as workers wondered whether they would still have jobs in the near future. GE was undergoing quite a transformation: thousands of employees were leaving, while thousands of others were joining the company's ranks. It was simply not possible to make employees feel better and at the same time boost productivity amid such uncertainty and sweeping change. Empowering employees any earlier, acknowledged Welch, "would have produced a mixed message because we were shocking them. I'm not sure you could have sold that and been credible."

GE's CEO got the idea for Work-Out one day in September 1988 when he visited Crotonville, GE's Leadership Development Center.

On that particular day, Welch was speaking to both upper and lower levels of GE management. Some complained that the real problem lay with their bosses, who they felt did not share GE values and therefore had little interest in improving the day-to-day operations of the company.

Several staffers spelled out the problem for Welch: after all the downsizing and delayering, there were fewer employees left to perform the work. Rather than empathize with their situation, the bosses simply dumped the extra workload on the remaining workers, with little or no concern for how that might affect them.

After his appearance at Crotonville, Welch was annoyed. He was not happy with what he had heard, and complained that he had heard the same questions asked over and over, questions that should have been addressed by the bosses back home in the businesses.

Why, he asked himself, was there no dialogue within those units?

Sadly, he knew the answer all too well:

Despite all the changes Welch had put into effect, GE was still a giant hierarchy. Senior management only spoke to intermediate management, who only talked to junior management, who were the only ones who seemed to talk to the workers on the factory floor.

The floor workers were not expected or encouraged to engage in dialogue with superiors. They were expected to work.

Shouldn't this rigid, dinosaur-like chain of command be put to an end? Wasn't it time to harness the talent and energy of the employees and force the bosses to answer the questions raised at Crotonville that day?

It seemed crucial to Welch to get lower-level management on board the GE revolution. The top managers were already there. But down below, managers remained resistant to change.

Welch sensed that the solution lay in getting GE personnel to raise work-related issues with managers back home—instead of with the General Electric chairman: "We have to create an atmosphere where people can speak up to somebody who can do something about their problems." Welch alone couldn't solve those issues.

Engaging the Workers' Minds

Welch began to dwell on this challenge: how to engage the minds of his workers. The time had come for managers and workers to talk with one another, to explore ways to improve the day-to-day functioning of the business.

Welch wanted GE's business leaders to stand eyeball-to-eyeball with the employees and do something they evidently had not done for quite some time: actually *listen* to them. It was quite likely that managers would resist such dialogue at first. Why would they find it easy to turn over the "managing" of the company to unqualified "soldiers"?

Welch was ready to take the risk and put his plan into action. He had a strong conviction that much of the creativity and innovation that drove productivity lay with the men and women closest to the actual work. Managers, after all, did not have a monopoly on ideas or solutions to day-to-day problems.

Welch's ardent desire to liberate the GE worker was very much in keeping with the American dream. He liked to say that the United States had the most truly free enterprise system in the world; that the American system was based on the individual's freedom; that the system had enabled him to become GE's chairman in one generation and permitted talented young engineers in the company to move up fast. If the United States injected bureaucracy and rigidity into its economic system, it would play directly into the hands of its global competitors. But if it permits its employees to flourish and grow, if it nurtures and implements the best ideas its people have to offer, then it has a real chance to succeed.

Welch called GE's urge to liberate and empower its workforce a competitive necessity. After all, the United States doesn't receive the benefits that other countries do from protected markets, government support, and relationships with senior officials.

Notes Welch:

We complain, on occasion, about all of this, but it is we who have the ultimate advantage, one that few of us, if pressed, would ever wish to trade. It is the fact that we are, despite our mix of global cultures and enterprises, an *American* company; and, as such, our system, while providing no guarantees, also has the fewest barriers to innovation, boldness, and risk taking—the stuff that will propel the real winners in the 1990s.

Welch became most concerned that his managers might stifle the process of empowerment. So, he argued, "If you are controlling two people and just getting them to do what you say, I'd get rid of you and keep those two. If there are three people, I want three ideas. If you're only giving orders, I will get only your ideas. I'd rather select from the ideas of three people. That's GE's basic thinking."

In seeking to empower his workers, Jack Welch appeared to be imposing one more difficult demand on his business leaders. As hard as it was for his managers to fire an employee, it would be almost as difficult to turn over decision making to the workers who remained behind.

But that's what Welch wanted. He wasn't advocating empowerment out of some altruistic impulse simply to be nice to his staff; or out of some sense that the business leaders aren't as smart as the employees on the factory floor.

No, Jack Welch is saying something else: You simply have to treat your employees as an integral part of your business. Do that, and you will find employees responding by becoming more engaged and conscientious. And an engaged, conscientious worker is a more motivated, productive worker. It's really no more complicated than that.

Every employee wants to feel important to the company. And getting workers involved and empowered will make them feel important. Workers want to feel needed and important, a simple fact that business leaders can exploit, but it will require some sacrifice. Managing less is managing more, is how Welch would put it. And although managing less is not always easy to swallow, it has some tremendous advantages.

Take the "Boss Element" out of Your Company

"You've got to balance freedom with some control, but you've got to have more freedom than you've ever dreamed of."

WORK-OUT WAS Jack Welch's bold, ambitious ten-year program to push cultural change throughout General Electric.

Starting in 1989, its primary goal was to broaden the scope of debate throughout the entire company. It also had the ambitious goal of removing the "boss element" from General Electric. Through Work-Out Welch strived to redefine the traditional concept of management, making listening to employees an integral part of every manager's job. At the same time the program gave employees the right—and the responsibility—to come up with their own ideas for solving those nagging problems. The goal was to give everyone a say in the way the organization was managed—and to keep bosses from dictating every step in the decision-making process.

While other companies experimented with similar empowerment efforts, GE was the first enterprise to undertake such a program on a companywide scale. Ultimately, of course, the goal of the Work-Out program was to "clean up" GE, to make workers more productive and processes simpler and more clear-cut. Work-Out was also designed to reduce, and ultimately eliminate, all of the wasted hours and energy that organizations like GE typically expend in performing day-to-day operations.

In Welch's words, Work-Out is meant to help people stop "wrestling with the boundaries, the absurdities that grow in large organizations. We're all familiar with those absurdities: too many approvals, duplication, pomposity, waste."

The Work-Out effort is in itself somewhat of a GE paradox. Here was one of the nation's toughest, most aggressive bosses saying to his employees: You've been bossed around too much, and now we realize that we've been hurting the company by not letting you become your own bosses.

The program lacked a name at the start. Because Welch had talked about "working out" the nonsense of GE, and of dealing with problems that had to be "worked out," not unexpectedly the name Work-Out was chosen. (Some incorrectly viewed the name as yet another way to justify downsizing, that Work-Out was simply another fancy name for "taking out" people, but Welch insisted such was not the case.)

Confronting the Boss Face-to-Face

Work-Out was initially supposed to help define and foster the new business culture that Welch hoped to create: a boundaryless culture that encouraged workers to act with speed, simplicity, and self-confidence, a culture that was informal and open: a place where everyone was expected to share ideas and learn from one another.

Work-Out had two defining aspects:

1. Employees had to be able to make suggestions to their bosses face-to-face.
2. Employees had to be able to get a response—on the spot, if possible.

The most appropriate model for Work-Out, one that would help break down the walls of hostility between managers and employees, was the New England town meeting, which had once provided a forum for dialogue between local citizens and town fathers.

The GE "town meetings" (Work-Out sessions) began in March 1989. Welch wanted everyone at GE to have at least a taste of Work-Out by the end of its first year. The program was *not* optional, but the chairman did not live in a fantasy world: he understood that many employees were suspicious of Work-Out, fearing that the program was just another brand of GE downsizing. So in order to soften the blow, he began the program as a volunteer effort.

At first, the emphasis was on getting as many employees through the program as possible, not on developing and refining the Work-Out technique. In early phases of Work-Out, workshops were not limited to workplace topics; rather, invitees were encouraged to raise any issue at all. In later phases, however, as participants became more comfortable and less suspicious of the program, the workshops had more specific agendas and goals, such as cost reduction or new product introductions.

Before a Work-Out session was to begin, business leaders urged potential participants to brainstorm with colleagues in order to generate additional ideas for the session. Work-Out organizers always urged those attending to feel free to raise any topic they wished.

Once the organizers had decided who they wanted in a given Work-Out session, they sent out letters of invitation, explaining what Work-Out was all about, but always making it clear that attendance was not compulsory. Then they sent out a second letter to those who had expressed interest in the program with details about when and where the session would be held.

Chinos and T-Shirts

Employees and managers alike were asked to dress casually at the workshops, in chinos and T-shirts, in order to blur distinctions between managers and workers.

The workshops, which usually lasted three days (although some were only two and a half days), were always held off-site, usually at a hotel. Organizers felt this was very important; otherwise, attendees would sneak away at coffee breaks to listen to voice mail and collect faxes. Also, the off-site locale helped people to break out of their everyday office thought patterns.

Since some employees could not afford to be completely out of touch with their offices, someone was always assigned to sit outside a Work-Out session in order to pass on emergency work messages and collect the nonemergency messages for session breaks. The Work-Out site had to be close enough to allow a participant to dash to the office if necessary. For example, a participant might need to consult a colleague in order to come up with an answer to a Work-Out question, such as why a certain policy had been instituted or whether a policy regarding some work practice had already been approved. A phone call might suffice, but at times, someone back at the home office might be asked to attend the Work-Out session for, say, half a day. Some work manuals were brought to the meeting and placed at the back of the workshop room, but not all documents and manuals were so readily available. Being close to the office meant that a participant could quickly retrieve any papers or manuals that were needed. Such departures from the workshops, however, were generally frowned upon, and messengers were used whenever possible in order to save the GE staffer the trip.

Often needing to get their hands on a fact, figure, or policy quickly, Work-Out organizers came up with one more solution for obtaining information: the hot line. Prior to the workshops, organizers had arranged for "experts" from the business's various departments (legal, finance, etc.) to make themselves available by phone from 9 A.M. to 11 A.M. on the second day of the Work-Out gathering. Often, the expert rendered an opinion on an important Work-Out topic on the spot, such as how easy it would be to change a work policy or practice.

All Work-Out sessions followed a certain pattern. On the first day there would be forty or fifty invitees (some sessions had only twenty participants). The participants would represent a diverse cross-section of GE personnel, from senior and junior managers to salaried and hourly workers. A facilitator was also on hand, to help break the ice, move the Work-Out process along, and encourage the audience to speak out frankly. The facilitators, who were most often academic types with hands-on corporate experience, played an important role in keeping the session on track.

The business leader (or some other senior representative of the business) kicked off the first-day session by discussing the strengths and weaknesses of that particular business and explaining how that business fit into General Electric's overall strategy.

The facilitator then arranged for the group to break into four small groups, eight to twelve in each room, to brainstorm about some of the weaknesses that the keynote speaker had highlighted. These "break-out rooms," as facilitators called them, were close together, allowing the facilitator to move quickly from one room to another. One of the facilitator's tasks was to check on whether participants at two or more of the minisessions were discussing the same topic.

Why Is That Approval Needed?

It was not a sin for two groups to discuss the same topic, but the facilitator would inform the two groups that they were tackling the same issue so that they could decide whether one group should move on to another subject. The facilitator had no veto power over what topics were discussed; however, like a baseball umpire, he or she sought to keep the playing field level: high-ranking employees were constrained from dominating the conversation or bullying others in the room. And, like the umpire, the facilitator stayed aloof, letting the attendees do most of the talking.

From time to time, the facilitator would ask the minigroups to join forces. During this plenary session, the groups would report back and everyone could learn what the others were discussing.

Throughout the session, discussants were expected to evaluate four aspects of the business:

- Reports
- Meetings
- Measurements
- Approvals

Which of these made sense, and which did not? What could be eliminated and which had to be kept? The idea was to get people talking.

After making an initial appearance, the "boss"—the leader or senior representative—stayed away. Not only did bosses have to leave; they were even told that interfering with the session could jeopardize their careers.

No one was supposed to take notes during the first two days of the Work-Out session. Jack Welch feared that note taking would add wasteful bureaucracy to the exercise. It may have seemed an odd decision, with all those valuable ideas being aired, but the chairman of General Electric was adamant: note taking was just one more brand of bureaucracy.

During the last few hours of the third day, the boss was finally permitted back into the meeting to confront the employees, listen to their ideas, and respond positively to as many of their proposals as possible—on the spot!

Only Three Ways of Answering

It is this final-day encounter between the boss and the employees that gives Work-Out its special power, its real significance. Take a moment to imagine what the boss was going through at this juncture. For two full days, employees have spent hour upon hour discussing the boss, dissecting his strengths and weaknesses, reviewing him as one might a movie or a play. What's more, this broad-based critique had been initiated and sanctioned by none other than Jack Welch himself.

None of this is lost on the participants in Work-Out, and the boss's return to the session is usually a dramatic one. The boss takes a position at the front of the room. Up to this point, that mere act of moving to the front of the room had given the boss an aura of authority, of respect and power. Now the boss stands in front of the employees, to listen to *them*. In this new world of role reversal, who is the boss, and who is the underling?

As the boss approaches the front of the room on that final day, he or she has no idea what has transpired in the past few days. But that soon changes. In this final stage of Work-Out, participants put forward their proposals, and the boss is permitted to make only one of three responses:

1. Agree on the spot to implement a proposal.
2. Say no to the proposal
3. Ask for more information, in effect postponing a decision. If that occurs, the boss must authorize a team to get that information by a certain set date.

Routinely, 80 percent of the proposals receive immediate answers. If additional study is required the manager has to come up with an answer within one month.

One of the Work-Out participants is selected to put together a memo on all the proposals discussed (which may be as many as twenty-five), along with the steps to be taken by management as part of determining the feasibility of a particular proposal. The memo is then quickly distributed to all Work-Out participants, who certify that it accurately reflects what went on at the final session with the boss. Lastly, the memo is circulated to everyone else in that particular GE business. Next to each recommendation is the name of the Work-Out participant who raised the issue—the issue's "champion"—who must then follow up on his or her recommendation and inform the attendees, through the Work-Out leader, of progress.

Steve Kerr, one of the Work-Out facilitators, notes that the goal of Work-Out is to come up with specific, actionable items that leave little room for ambiguity: in fact, he bars recommendations that contain vague language, such as "We want to have this new policy," and encourages participants to be as exact as possible. Each recommendation may contain as many as three action items, and each action item has to be accompanied by a deadline. Finally the Work-Out leader assigns a "roadblock buster," who has the task of following up to make sure that each deadline is met.

A Work-Out Primer

Here are the seven steps required to implement Work-Out:

1. Choose the issues to be discussed.
2. Select the appropriate cross-functional team to tackle the problem.
3. Choose a "champion," who will see any Work-Out recommendations through to implementation.
4. Let the team meet for three (or two and a half) days, drawing up recommendations to improve your company's processes.
5. Meet with managers, who make decisions on the spot about each recommendation.
6. Hold more meetings as required to pursue the implementation of the recommendations.

7. Keep the process going, with these and other issues and recommendations.

Initially, the whole notion of Work-Out seemed so counterintuitive. Employees comfortably speaking out and confronting a boss? Bosses required to take a back seat to employees, who systematically critique the business with no fear of repercussions? Yet Welch wanted to give the idea a chance. If it didn't work, little would have been lost. But if it succeeded, a whole new method for improving the company would have been created—and GE would benefit from all the candor and ingenuity that had remained bottled up for so long.

The premise of Work-Out was devastatingly simple: those closest to the work know it best—even better than the bosses. The single best way of getting workers to pass on that vital knowledge was to give them more power. And in exchange for that power, an employee would be allowed—nay, *would be expected*—to assume more responsibility for his or her job.

When Jack Welch initiated Work-Out, he knew that GE would reap huge benefits if it worked:

- Productivity would be higher.
- Needless tasks would be jettisoned.
- Workers would feel liberated and satisfied at having those tasks done away with.

All he had to do was hope and pray that it worked.

Create an Atmosphere Where Workers Feel Free to Speak Out

"Those who actually did the work . . .
had some striking ideas on how things
could be done better."

AT FIRST, as the Work-Out program got under way, the invisible walls between managers and employees remained firmly in place, inhibiting a free-flowing dialogue. The chains of history and tradition were too strong to be sundered so quickly. Employees had no experience in advising bosses on how to improve the business—and no previous incentive to do so. It just hadn't been done before. So, at the start, there were many awkward silences.

But here and there, the concept of Work-Out began to catch on.

It began with someone having the courage to ask a question—and with a manager being willing to answer the question and change policy on the spot. Once the ice was broken, others in the audience overcame their timidity and raised their hands as well.

Work-Out was catching on at some of the GE businesses, but in the beginning there was no shortage of problems.

Union members, who naturally harbored suspicions whenever company executives came forward with an idea, any idea, viewed Work-Out with their usual skepticism. Some called the program "Jobs-Out" or "Heads-Out," convinced that Welch and his senior colleagues had a far more sinister goal for Work-Out. They were convinced that Welch sought to cut payrolls, not learn from workers on how to improve the company.

But it didn't take long for even these union members—as well as the other participants—to understand that Work-Out was no ordinary flavor-of-the-month management fad. They soon realized that Welch actually meant it when he declared that he wanted to turn over decision-making power to the workers.

Of course, not every Work-Out session ran like clockwork: in some sessions, the program was little more than a glorified opportunity for workers to squeal on one another for such infractions as reading a newspaper or "hiding behind" a machine all day instead of working. But in other sessions, the boss was quickly put on the spot.

That's what happened to Armand Lauzon, the head of plant services at the GE Aircraft Engines factory in Lynn, Massachusetts.

We Have 108 Proposals for You

When Armand Lauzon was invited into the room to face Work-Out attendees on the third and final day of the session, he was forced to stand with his back to *his* boss. One by one, the recommendations of the group were placed before him for one of those three answers (yes, no, or I need more information), and it was clear to him that he was not supposed to make eye contact with his boss.

The group put 108 proposals in front of Lauzon that day, ranging from designing a plant-services insignia as a morale booster to constructing a new tinsmith shop. He said yes on the spot to 100 of the 108 proposals! One proposal was to let Lynn's employees bid against an outside vendor on new protective shields for grinding machines; evidently, an hourly worker had sketched the design for the shields on a brown paper bag. Lynn won the bid for $16,000, far lower than the vendor's quoted $96,000. The shields proposal was considered an ideal Work-

Out result: It saved GE money and brought work to the Lynn plant. This was no small feat for Lynn, since their employee rolls had been downsized by over 40 percent—from 14,000 in 1986 to 8,000 five years later.

One electrician felt no qualms about confronting his boss: "When you've been told to shut up for twenty years and someone tells you to speak up, you're going to let them have it." Not only did employee Work-Out proposals save GE $200,000 that year; they saved jobs as well.

Rattlers and Pythons

At some Work-Out sessions the facilitator broke work issues into two categories.

Rattlers and Pythons.

Rattlers were the simple problems, the ones that could be "shot" like a dangerous rattlesnake, and solved on the spot.

Pythons were issues too complicated to unravel right away, just as no one could easily unravel a python entwined on itself.

One "rattler" involved a young woman who had been publishing a popular plant newspaper, but in doing so had encountered a wall of bureaucracy. GE policy required her to obtain an astounding seven signatures every month in order to get her newspaper published. She pled her case emotionally: "You all like the plant newspaper. It's never been criticized. It's won awards. Why does it take seven signatures?"

Her boss stared at her in amazement. "This is crazy. I didn't know that was the case."

"Well, that's the way it is," she replied.

"OK," the general manager said, "from now on, no more signatures."

The newspaper editor beamed.

Another factory worker tossed out another rattler. "I've worked for GE for over twenty years, I have a perfect attendance record. I've won management awards. I love this company. It's put my kids through college. It's given me a good standard of living. But there's something stupid that I'd like to bring up."

The man operated a valuable piece of equipment that required him to wear gloves.

The gloves wore out several times a month. To acquire another pair he had to call in a relief operator or, if none was available, shut his machine down. He then had to walk a fair distance to another building, go to the supply room, and fill out a form. He then had to walk around the plant to track down a supervisor of sufficient authority to countersign his request. Only after he had returned the signed form to the supply room was he given a new pair of gloves! Frequently he lost as much as an hour of work.

"I think it's stupid."

"I think it's stupid too," said the general manager in front of the room. "Why do we do that?" At that point everyone in the room was dying to hear the answer. Finally, from way back in the room came the answer: "In 1973, we lost a box of gloves."

"Put the box of gloves on the floor, close to the people," the manager ordered. Another rattler shot.

At the Research and Development Center in Schenectady, New York, an employee attending a Work-Out session asked why managers were given special parking places. No one could think of a good reason. The managerial privilege was rescinded on the spot.

At a Work-Out session for the company's communications personnel, a secretary asked why she had to interrupt her own work to empty the "out tray" on her boss's desk.

Why couldn't he drop the material off on her desk the next time he left his office?

No one had a good answer and a few steps of unproductive effort were scratched from the secretary's routine—again, on the spot.

At a Work-Out session involving GE Power Generation personnel, someone noted that the Purchasing Department chose welding equipment without conferring with welders, the employees who actually used the equipment. That led to inappropriate equipment being selected for certain tasks. Why not have the welders join the purchasing team when visiting vendors to order equipment?

Without hesitation the manager said fine.

Changing such procedures—eliminating the seven signatures needed for the newspaper, revoking parking privileges for managers, or even asking bosses to empty their own out trays—required little time or study to implement.

But pythons proved far more stubborn than rattlers. At one session, a python appeared at a Power Generation Work-Out.

Attending the session were personnel in turbine manufacturing, sales, and field service. One gripe came from field service engineers, who complained about having to write these mammoth, 500-page reports. The reports were supposedly needed because they forecasted which turbines might need to be replaced the next time an outage occurred.

Despite the massive effort necessary to prepare such unwieldy documents, no one paid much attention to the reports. Knowing that, the field service engineers often turned them in as much as six months late, if at all. Eventually, thanks to some intense Work-Out sessions, the gargantuan reports were scrapped and in their place briefer, more up-to-date reports were turned in immediately—and were actually read!

Even as employees were dealing with the trivial, easy issues, Work-Out was giving them an increased sense of participation in their jobs and a good feeling about themselves.

These Are Not "Rat Sessions"

It became a major test of the program to make sure that town meetings did not degenerate into "rat sessions," meetings to find out who was lazy or who hated the boss.

In time, GE's union members began to sense that management's motives were indeed sincere: that their true purpose in Work-Out was to get rid of bad work habits, not simply to uncover laggards. Welch urged GE managers to resist adding up the number of Work-Out sessions they had arranged, convinced that all that extra time and energy could be put to better use elsewhere. "Don't ever tell me you had forty-one Work-Outs," he told them. "I don't want to know."

If the program was working, he noted, it would show up in the only measurement that counted: increased productivity. Still, businesspeople rate success and failure in quantitative terms. Some managers could not help but brag about how many Work-Outs they had under their belts.

By the spring of 1998, nearly every GE employee had taken part in Work-Out sessions.

Work-Out sessions found ways to improve the company, no matter how insignificant the issue. If it was important enough for an employee to mention it, it was fair game for Work-Out. In Louisville, Kentucky, where GE makes appliances, employees at a Work-Out session sought to find ways to improve the environment in Building One, where clothes washers and dryers are made. The place turned into a virtual steam bath in the summer, even before the machines on the assembly lines were turned on! The recommendations were incredibly simple: Open some vents that had been closed for years (no one could remember why they had been closed in the first place). Buy a few fans and blowers. As a way of emphasizing their point, Work-Out participants asked their boss to walk out with them to the parking lot where they took their time setting up easels and flip charts while the boss melted in the noonday sun. The overheated boss got the point and gave a quick OK to cooling off Building One.

Elsewhere in the company, Work-Out sessions attacked the GE bureaucracy. At NBC, the operations and technical services department were streamlined by ridding the department of forms that added up to more than 2 million pieces of paper per year. At GE Plastics in Burkville, Alabama, where Lexan, a polycarbonate used in auto bumpers and milk bottles, is made, a Work-Out team wanted to increase the "first-pass yield"—the percentage of resin that wound up as salable pellets without having to be melted and rerun through the factory's extruders. A solution was found: install a computer terminal on the extrusion floor that provided employees with an early warning of problems.

In Erie, Pennsylvania, where GE manufactures locomotives, a Work-Out team discovered that delays and rework were being caused by the inconsistency in the paint. It turned out that GE was purchasing it from two different suppliers. Team members convinced their boss to buy the paint from just one supplier. As a result, a paint job took only ten shifts instead of twelve. At GE Capital, it was proposed that GE's Retailer Credit Services, which manages Montgomery Ward's charge card business, link its cash registers directly to GE's mainframes, thus cutting the time for opening a new customer account from thirty minutes to just ninety seconds.

Quite a number of the recommendations at Work-Out sessions proved incredibly simple to implement. One computer lab technician, for example, noted that every report printout from his department contained about ten unnecessary pages on it because it first ran out an initial computer code. The Work-Out participants asked him how he might cut this, and he said, "Just hit the suppress button." When one of his managers approached the man and asked him in a friendly manner why he had not told the managers about this before, the man replied, "No one ever asked me."

Here is what Work-Out has accomplished, in Jack Welch's view:

> As we took down much of the clutter and scaffolding of layers and organizational structure and got rid of the useless noise bureaucracy always generates . . . we started to see deeper into the organization and hear the voices of those who actually did the work, ran the processes, . . . and dealt with the customers. They had some striking ideas on how things could be done better.

> Our desire to tap into this creativity, to listen more clearly to these ideas . . . and draw more of them out all over the company led us to a process we call Work-Out.

> Work-Out is many things . . . meetings . . . teams . . . training . . . but its central objective is "growing" a culture where everyone's ideas have value . . . everyone plays a part . . . where leaders lead rather than control . . . coach rather than kibitz. Work-Out is the process of mining the creativity and productivity that we know resides in the American workforce . . . the most creative . . . but irreverent . . . the most energetic, but independent . . . workforce in the world.

In the summer of 1997, Welch was as great an advocate of high involvement as he had been nearly a decade earlier:

> The most important thing a leader has to do is to absolutely search and treasure and nourish the voice and dignity of every person. It is in the end the key element. Because if you give people voice and dignity and incentives and other things to participate, to enrich themselves, to pour out ideas, and if you have an atmosphere where you're open to accepting, [then all will be fine].

There is much for any business leader to learn from GE's Work-Out. At first business leaders may be incredulous about the true value of Work-Out, and employees are likely to be equally suspicious. Certainly, it was difficult for GE leaders to figure out why it was so important to nourish the voice and dignity of every person. And it was equally hard for employees to buy into a program that seemed to be aimed at getting rid of more bodies.

But in time, a dialogue ensued at GE, in fact, thousands of dialogues, and the concept and practice of Work-Out spread through the entire company like wildfire. That can happen in any company. It takes some courage. No business leader is going to find it comfortable—at least at first—to stand in front of employees, be critiqued, and listen to a whole set of recommendations for change. And few employees are going to feel totally relaxed, at least at first, about taking on the boss.

But it can be done. GE has done it—with much to show for opening up its decision-making to the rest of the company. Consider this: Welch took GE from $25 billion to over $90 billion (and counting) in sales and has made GE the most valuable company in the world. While it's not possible to quantify the financial impact of Work-Out, most would argue that it has played a leading role in helping to ignite a revolution at GE, helping thousands of employees feel like they have a stake in the business, like the company really does want to hear what they have to say. Imagine unleashing that spirit of involvement and belonging in your organization—and then imagine the potential results.

S–t–r–e–t–c–h!
Reach for the Stars!

"In a boundaryless organization with a bias for speed, decimal points are a bore."

J ACK WELCH BELIEVES in doing the best possible—and then reaching beyond. He calls this business strategy *stretching*. To Welch, stretching means exceeding goals. Often business leaders exceed goals even as they fall short of the stretch. That's fine with Welch.

Reward a business leader even for falling short of a stretched goal, says Welch. Don't mete out punishment. What's critical to the GE chairman is setting the performance bar high enough; otherwise, it's impossible to find out what people can do.

What Welch calls "stretch" simply means figuring out performance targets—on everything from profitability to new product introductions—that are achievable, reasonable, and within GE's capabilities. And then raising sights higher—much higher—toward goals that seem almost beyond reach, goals requiring superhuman effort to achieve. As Welch notes, "We have found that by reaching for what appears to be the impossible, we often actually do the impossible; and even when we don't quite make it, we inevitably wind up doing much better than we would have done."

Stretch Targets Energize

Reaching and stretching, argues Welch, is a major breakthrough. It ends all those petty, internal negotiations about budget targets that accomplished little in forging a manager's vision.

Budgets enervate.

Stretch targets energize.

Welch insists on asking managers and employees to reach for their dreams—and skip the niggling negotiations that are so typical of large companies.

Haggling over budget plans is simply an exercise in compromise: "People work for a month on charts and presentations and books to come in and tell the CEO that, given the economic environment, given the competitive scenario, the best they can do is Two. Then the CEO says 'I have to give the shareholders Four.' They eventually settle on Three and everyone goes home happy."

Does that signal the end of conventional rigorous budgeting, a reporter asks him?

Yes, Welch replies, because when it comes to budgets, everyone fights for the lowest common denominator when they should be thinking about stretching:

> **Rigorous budgeting alone is nonsense. I think in terms of . . . the best you can do. You soon begin to see what comes out of a trusting, open environment. But the most important thing you have to put in place is a human resource system and a compensation system that works. . . . When things break down it is because the measure system and the compensation system do not coincide with the objectives of the organization. The danger is that you could drive behavior with suboptimal measurements.**

Bullet Train Mentality

In order to illuminate the importance of stretch, Welch points admiringly to the Japanese executive who was thinking stretch when he talked about the "bullet-train mentality."

The executive noted that to double the Japanese bullet train's speed, it would be necessary to do far more than merely refine the engine.

Every aspect of the infrastructure surrounding the bullet train, including the rails and the overhead cable, would have to be looked at and possibly altered.

In order to double the speed of the bullet train, far more would be required than some incremental improvement in one aspect of the train. What was needed was a new paradigm, some monumental improvement to each and every aspect of the infrastructure. "You've got to think out of the box," says Welch. "It's not the same train with a little more tweak. It's a whole new thought. So all the talks are about big things! Double the speed of the bullet train—don't go ten miles an hour faster. That's what stretch is."

Dreams Are Exciting; Decimal Points Aren't

Stretching, Welch asserts,

> . . . allows people to constantly reach for the goal. And people are getting more and more comfortable with the idea that you get the best out of people not by fighting budgets, which are all about minimal numbers, but by getting people to do the best they can, and measuring their progress toward it—against last year, against what competitors are doing.

> We're in the process of enriching our organization through the stretch concept. Operating margins are 50 percent higher than they were for the first one hundred and eight years of our company, and in a tougher global environment.

In one of his Letters to Share Owners, Welch said this about "stretch":

> Stretch is a concept that would have produced smirks, if not laughter, in the GE of three or four years ago, because it essentially means using dreams to set business targets—with no real idea of how to get there. If you do know how to get there—it's not a stretch target. We certainly didn't have a clue how we were going to get to ten inventory turns when we set that target. But we're getting there, and as soon as we become sure we can do it, it's time for another stretch.

That is classic Jack Welch thinking. Never be content with the present. Never let the present dictate your future. Don't be comfortable with the present.

Make the Pizza Delivery Man Rich

Welch began talking about stretch only in 1993. He recalled how it was in earlier years:

> We used to timidly nudge the peanut along, setting goals of moving from, say, 4.73 inventory turns to 4.91, or from 8.53 percent operating margin to 8.92 percent; and then indulge in time-consuming, high-level, bureaucratic negotiations to move the number a few hundredths one way or the other. The point is, it didn't matter. Arguing over these petty numbers in conference rooms certainly didn't inspire the people on the shop or office floors who had to deliver them. In most cases, they never even heard of them. We don't do that anymore. In a boundaryless organization, with a bias for speed, decimal points are a bore. They inspire or challenge no one, capture no imaginations. We're aiming at ten inventory turns, at 15 percent operating margins, and at the introduction of more new products in the next two years than we've developed in the last ten. In a company that now rewards progress toward stretch goals, rather than punishing shortfalls, the setting of these goals, and quantum leaps toward them, are daily events.
>
> Across this company, stretch targets are making seemingly impossible goals exciting, bringing out the best from our teams; and the pizza delivery people are getting rich as our people celebrate each milestone along the way to those targets. Boundaryless people, excited by speed and inspired by stretch dreams, have an absolutely infinite capacity to improve everything.

"Decimal points are nonsense," said Welch in a 1994 interview. "Dreams are exciting, not decimal points. Unless you get a bureaucracy that rewards on the route to progress and it doesn't punish for the shortfall against this year's micro plan, it doesn't work."

Keep Stretching

Welch is right that the stretch concept has had a positive effect on GE's inventory turns. Vice Chairman Paolo Fresco notes that in 1992, the ratio stood at four. GE looked at some of its best competitors and decided it should strive for ten inventory turns in five years. The goal seemed crazy to some since it had taken GE twenty years to get from three to four. In mid-1997 Fresco predicted that GE would reach eight and a half or nine turnovers by the end of the year. "I don't think we could have done it if we'd said, let's go for 10 percent improvement a year. Now I think it's time we went for twenty turns—we need to keep this objective moving in front of us. I don't think we or anybody else knows the limits to our ability to improve."

In one of his Letters to Share Owners, Welch notes that a stretch atmosphere

> . . . replaces a grim, heads-down determination to be as good as you have to be and asks, instead, how good can you be? "How good can we be?" was the question in 1991 when the company set two big stretch targets: ten inventory turns and 15 percent operating margins by the end of 1995. At that time, those two numbers represented big stretches. After all, it had taken over a century—since Edison's time—and we still hadn't reached five turns and had barely achieved an 11 percent operating margin.

With the arrival of 1995, Welch predicted, ten inventory turns may be just beyond GE's reach, but by the year's end GE would be over nine "In GE today, this is not a 'miss,' a 'broken commitment,' or a 'black eye'—but a triumph to be celebrated."

The CEO of General Electric noted in early 1995 that far more was required before GE executives were entirely comfortable with the stretch concept.

More trust had to be developed. People still felt comfortable with the old way of doing budgets. Jack Welch insists that budgets suppress, budgets depress.

As for 15 percent operating-margin stretch targets by 1995, in the period leading up to that year, Welch said it was possible.

What mattered, he said, is that GE had broken out of its 110-year pattern. He now cringes at numbers he crowed about some years back.

In the 1995 Annual Report, Welch acknowledged that GE did not achieve two of its stretch targets: operating margins and inventory turns. Over the previous three decades, GE's highest corporate operating margin had hovered around 10 percent; and inventory turns were around five. In 1991, GE set two stretch targets for 1995: 15 percent operating margins and ten inventory turns.

At the end of 1995, GE fell short of both goals, Welch admitted. It achieved a 14.4 percent operating margin and almost seven inventory turns. "But in stretching for these 'impossible' targets, we learned to do things faster than we would have going after 'doable' goals, and we have enough confidence now to set new stretch targets of at least 16 percent operating margin and more than ten turns by 1998."

For 1997, the operating margin was 15.7 percent and inventory turns were at 7.8 times.

According to Crotonville's Steve Kerr, Welch seems to be defying the conventional wisdom when it comes to the stretch concept. The commonly held view is that if someone sets a goal too high, the outcome will be more disappointing than if the goal had been set lower. Yet Welch has been able to achieve superior results through stretch.

What happens if employees fail to reach goals?

Welch calls this a "crucial issue."

If they don't have the team operating effectively, you give them another chance. If they fail again, you hand the reins to another person. But you don't punish for not meeting big targets. If ten is the target and you're only at two, we'll have a party when you go to four. We'll give out bonuses and go out on the town and drink or whatever. When you reach six, we'll celebrate again. We don't waste time and money budgeting 4.12 to 5.13 to 6.17.

Eugene Murphy, GE vice chairman, recalls his experience as head of Aircraft Engines: "If we look at a product and say it will take four years to do that product, we then look at how to improve the schedule. We say we can improve it by a year. When all is said and done, we have a ways to get to the year; but we may add two months."

Murphy used the concept of stretch to attain $50 million in benefits from GE's six sigma quality program when he was running Aircraft Engines earlier in 1997. "We took a stretch to try to get to $70 million.

It's going to be very difficult to accomplish. I don't know at this point if we'll achieve it or not. We may end up getting to only $60 million. But if we had set the goal at $50 million, the likelihood is that we'd have worked like hell and we'd have gone to $50 million. If we set it at $70 million, there's a better chance of going beyond $50 million." (*P.S.:* Engines did achieve the $70 million.)

To Robert L. Nardelli, head of GE's Power Systems, stretch is a concept not to be taken too literally. "Stretch," he suggests, "means really challenging yourself and believing there is an infinite capacity to improve upon everything you do. Once you get through the denial period, then you really embrace stretch as something you want to do, not as something management tells you to do. It is far better to challenge yourself and then experience the satisfaction of winning, than to be driven to the same point anyway. With this mindset, the term stretch becomes secondary to the way you run the business. You expect to get top-line growth regardless of the industry environment because it's ingrained in your attitude."

The Dangers of Stretching

David Calhoun, head of GE Lighting, is all too aware of certain dangers and risks associated with the stretch concept.

Stretch, he notes, can on occasion conflict with the original commitment that a business leader promises to deliver in the annual business plan. A problem arises when Jack Welch asks the leader to go beyond the original commitment of, say, $100 million in sales a year and stretch his sales to, say, $200 million in that same year. Calhoun observes, "You can abuse stretch. Stretch is designed to make us think out of our box. It makes us reach for things that our operating plan doesn't. We may think about acquiring a new company or doubling sales efforts, or cutting our costs over 50 percent. And there are risks associated with that. Dropping prices out of the bottom to get to a stretch goal would be crazy. In other words, stretching forces us to do stuff we wouldn't otherwise do. You want to make sure we do the right stuff. You want the business leaders to think out of the box but to stick to our commitments as well. That's a big challenge for the leadership."

Agreeing that there are risks associated with the stretch concept, Patrick Dupuis, head of GE's auditing staff, suggests that GE minds are so prone to try stretching that they quickly merge commitment with stretch: "We don't know how to live with commitments and stretch. If you give us three numbers, we're going to concentrate on the stretch. We will forget about commitments. So you could lose control if you aim for stretch. But if you don't reach for stretch, you can lose your commitments by not paying too much attention to costs. GE people love stretch, but they might love it so much they might get ahead of themselves. Leadership in GE today is all about walking this fine line."

Even Welch seems aware of the pitfalls of stretch. For example, someone at a lower level works hard to improve upon the previous year's performance, and at the end of that year succeeds. But that person's boss, striving for a much higher stretch performance target is disappointed and berates the worker for "only" delivering what he or she deems to be mediocre results. Now we have an unhappy manager and an unmotivated employee. So, acknowledges Welch, stretch is not an easy concept. It takes time to implement successfully, and depends a great deal on senior managers and junior managers building trust in one another. Welch observes:

> **If you have a lousy relationship where a boss takes a stretch goal and stamps it as a plan and then nails you because you didn't reach it, the stretch program is dead. I have no issue with people who work for me who come in with big plans, big dreams, big stuff. They know we're not going to nail them because they didn't make their plan. We're going to nail them because they didn't execute in the context of the environment they're in. Or we're going to reward them for getting close to the plan they wanted in the context of the environment they're in.**

Jeff Immelt, head of GE Medical Systems, observes that when the CEO of General Electric began the stretch concept in the early 1990s he focused on financial goals; but by the late 1990s he was concentrating on getting GE business leaders to stretch goals dealing with process (the new introduction of products, cycle time, etc.): "You'll never succeed if you don't do process and output. Now the emphasis is more on both. We want to become a six sigma company and use that to get results. We know that if we do that, we'll hit every financial goal that Jack has set for us, and that Wall Street has for us."

Notice that Jack Welch only began his stretch program in the early 1990s—knowing that it would have been too much to ask for in the painful years of restructuring. Just as he could not expect to empower employees through Work-Out until the major downsizing efforts were concluded, he could not introduce stretch until those leaders had the self-confidence that their businesses were performing optimally.

Stretch may seem a luxury to most business leaders. And it was a luxury at GE during Welch's early years. But the chairman's advice to all business leaders is this: Don't automatically settle for second-best when you can achieve more. Reach for the stars. You may fail. In fact, you probably will fail. But stretching yourself, stretching your business, is going to bring better performance results to your business.

He's saying more than that, though. Welch's message is also this: Be more creative, be more imaginative, be more thoughtful about your business. The more you think about how to get more out of your business, the higher your stretch targets, the better off you're going to be.

PART V

Push Service and Globalization for Double-Digit Growth

"The opportunity for growth in product services is unlimited."

Grow Your Service Business—It's the Wave of the Future

"The [service] market is bigger than we ever dreamt. However, we will continue to expand and to manufacture. . . . Without products, you're dead."

IN THE PAST, GE's manufacturing businesses—lightbulbs, aircraft engines, appliances, etc.—were the company's primary growth engine. But that has been changing. The explosive growth of GE Capital Services and the acquisition of the NBC television network has gradually transformed GE from a purely manufacturing company into a more diversified company with an increasingly important service component.

GE Capital Services earned $4 billion in 1996 and NBC earned $953 million; together, they account for nearly half of GE's $10.8 billion in operating profits. It's the same on the revenue side: GE Capital had revenues of $32.7 billion in 1996 and NBC had revenues of $5.2 billion—nearly half of GE's overall $79.1 billion in revenues.

Perhaps more significant, Welch appears to see services as the key to the company's future earnings growth. This includes not only products such as insurance and annuities, but services for users of manufactured goods, GE and non-GE products alike.

The word *service* has taken on new meaning at GE. It's part of the new reality around the company.

In 1997 GE embarked on a companywide effort to provide more sophisticated value-added services. When asked why he had waited so long to embark on this program, Jack Welch replied: "All these things you learn. If Jack Welch knew seventeen years ago what he knew today, it would be a better company. This is a learning organization. I learn every day. Keep searching. I don't know diddley. I got guys here trying to learn more."

GE's increasing emphasis on its service dimension was inevitable. GE Capital Systems, its greatest growth engine, experienced a 17 percent increase in 1996, compared to only about a 5 percent increase for Aircraft Engines and 7 percent in Appliances. GE Plastic's revenues actually declined—albeit slightly—from 1995 to 1996. Of the $707 million in increased net profit at GE from 1995 to 1996, GE Capital Systems represented an astounding $402 million, or almost 57 percent of the total increase. Its profits have averaged a remarkable annual 18 percent increase since 1992.

A Surge in Services

In 1990, manufacturing represented 56 percent of GE's portfolio of businesses, financial services constituted only 25.6 percent, and the after-market service side contributed 12.4 percent (broadcasting represented another 6 percent).

But by 1995 the manufacturing portion had dropped to 43.5 percent, while the financial service side had grown to 38.2 percent. After-market services and broadcasting remained steady, at 12.3 percent and 6 percent, respectively.

But estimates for the year 2000 suggest that manufacturing will constitute a smaller portion of the GE business mix. Manufacturing will drop to only 33.2 percent of all GE business, while the financial service side is expected to rise to 45.8 percent; the after-market service component will also rise, to 16 percent, and broadcasting will remain steady, at 5 percent.

The decision to convert GE into a service-oriented company made perfect sense. As manufacturing receded, the company's revenues grew on average only 5.4 percent a year between 1990 and 1995. In 1995, however, its revenues were up an impressive 17 percent, to $70 billion, as earnings rose 11 percent, to $6.6 billion; then in 1996, its revenues rose 13 percent, to a record $79.2 billion, while earnings increased 11 percent, to a record $7.28 billion.

What made the transition from a manufacturing-oriented to a service-oriented enterprise was GE's hidden asset: its installed base of industrial equipment, which included 9,000 GE commercial jet engines, 10,000 turbines, 13,000 locomotives, and 84,000 major pieces of medical diagnostic equipment. As Jim McNerney notes: "That asset had been underwhelmed. We were more enamored with product technology than service technology."

But all that changed in the late 1990s. In October 1996, GE hauled in $7.8 billion—some 11 percent of its total revenues—servicing its huge installed base of industrial equipment. Those service revenues could more than double by the year 2000, to a whopping $18 billion. This certainly bodes well for GE's future, since margins routinely are 50 percent higher on services than on the product sales.

A Strategic Commitment Begins

The strategic commitment to build up GE's service component was made in 1994, and by 1995, GE's first piece of purely service business was in place.

GE Medical Systems supplied CAT scanners, magnetic resonance imagers, and other medical imaging equipment to the 300 or so hospitals run by the health-care giant Columbia/HCA.

In the spring of 1995, GE convinced Columbia to let it service *all* of Columbia's imaging equipment, even those made by GE's competitors. In 1996, GE agreed to provide another service for Columbia: managing nearly all medical supplies, most of which were product lines GE didn't even sell. The deal proved to be profitable for both partners: GE got the business, and Columbia saved millions of dollars.

In October 1996, GE Medical Systems was heavily into service, with fully 40 percent of its $3.5 billion in revenues coming from that side of the business. The company was so successful that it was held up as a model for other GE businesses to emulate. To build up the service end, Medical Systems began buying independent medical service shops. For instance, in February 1996, it purchased National Medical Diagnostics, a leading independent servicer of imaging equipment. Later that year, it added a private equipment-maintenance insurance company.

GE Medical also spent $80 million developing a modern training center, including a TV studio, in order to develop educational programming. Charging fees from $3,000 to $20,000, it offered hospitals the chance to tune in to live broadcasts on topics such as proper mammography techniques. One day in 1996, senior executives at Medical Systems offered the executive team of a regional hospital chain a half-day management seminar, discussing strategic planning, employee evaluations, and time management.

Medical Systems' increased service profile resulted in growth despite a flat global market for medical equipment.

In January 1997, Jeff Immelt took over Medical Systems from John Trani, who left to run Stanley Works. Immelt stepped into a $4.5 billion division with 15,000 employees worldwide, a business with the number one market share in diagnostic imaging techniques such as CAT scanning and ultrasound.

Immelt asked himself: How can I look for opportunities to grow?

The service segment seemed his best bet. It accounted for roughly 40 percent of revenue and was growing at 10 to 15 percent annually. Immelt's five-year goal is to develop the business by expanding market opportunities.

One service, Integrated Imaging Solutions, could grow by 20 to 30 percent a year. It provides customers with remote diagnostic capabilities, for example, transmitting scans from a mobile base to a hospital miles away. Medical Systems also made this technology available to other GE units, including Aircraft Engines, Transportation, and Power Systems, allowing them to monitor the performance of jet engines in flight, locomotives pulling freight, and turbines in power plants.

In 1997, in San Francisco, a crucial scanner broke down in the middle of an operation. Warned via a satellite link, GE's maintenance crew, located in Buc, near Versailles, France, was able to reinitialize the optical disk on the faulty machine by remote control, and the surgery in San Francisco resumed. GE Medical maintenance teams have mastered this procedure so well that they now carry out work on competitors' equipment in the United States, forcing their manufacturers to offer the same services.

David Calhoun, head of GE Lighting, recalls the impact of adding a service component to Transportation, which he headed before running Lighting: "The service business is an eye-opening venture. In the locomotive business, we sold locomotives forever, bigger, strong. Yet if you were a railroad, your productivity wouldn't be in the locomotive, but in getting your utilization from 50 to 80 percent. Pursuing that avenue, we've come up with a whole variety of products and options that we now go to the railroad with—all in the service field."

This included selling computer-aided dispatching systems to help the railroad manage its fleets more efficiently; equipment is placed on the locomotives that informs the railroads of the locomotives' locations at any given time. As Calhoun comments: "We know the technology. We can discern more quickly what broke. Before we got into the service business, the railroads did it all themselves. But we'd have to give them big, long maintenance instructions. Then they would come back to us with all sorts of questions. But now, since the new products have so much electronics, the mechanical people in the railroads have difficulty coping. We can eliminate the middleman."

Calling Card for the Late 1990s

Welch has seized upon services as one of GE's major calling cards for the late 1990s, and has established the service side of the business as an independent entity. GE's Jim McNerney observes: "Where the temptation is to manage the service side functionally, Jack has pushed us hard to manage the service business independently, to break it down by product, to keep it apart from the equipment side of the business. Everyone else's instincts were to try to control the service business within the equipment business. It's easy to blend the two together and come up with the wrong answers for both. But when they're separate profit and loss centers, you are more likely to come up with the best results. The management challenge, however, is to bring the two sides of the business back together as your customer sees you."

The large equipment businesses—Aircraft Engines, Power Generation, Medical Systems—have been given mandates to bolster the service of their businesses. Some of those businesses are learning the value of acquisition as a way of bolstering the service side. For instance, in May 1995, GE signed a joint venture with the power company Societa Nordelettrica of Milan, Italy; the two began offering utility maintenance and operation services throughout Europe. GE Power Systems was also trying to grab a share of the $1 billion market managing power plants for independent power producers and coordinating fuel purchasing for deregulated utilities. GE, accordingly, was running a 500-megawatt gas-fired power plant for Ocean States Power in Rhode Island.

Vice Chairman Paolo Fresco notes that GE had always been involved with service, but that service was called "after-market," which carried the connotation of "after-thought." "Now, we think servicing the customer is our primary market," says Fresco. "We happen to give the customer a piece of equipment in the process of serving this customer." Fresco feels that GE is ahead of the curve, compared to other businesses in providing service for its product lines, particularly in power generation, aircraft engines, industrial products, and medical systems.

According to GE officials, it is not so much that the manufacturing side of GE has been atrophying. Rather, the rate of growth in the service sector is potentially higher than the rate of growth for manufacturing. The reason for this is readily apparent: only so many pieces of industrial equipment can be sold in the world.

Welch has concluded that it would be a mistake to switch entirely from product to service because GE's reputation is still based on its product lines:

> We offer companies complete solutions not so much in order to increase our equipment sales, but because they have a need for them. That said, we will always be a company that sells high-tech products. Without products, you're dead. You go out of business and become obsolete. If I fail to introduce a new medical scanner, how many hospitals are likely to come and see me for new services?
>
> Take aeronautics. I don't know how far my guys would go, but one day they could end up maintaining a whole plane. But if that's

what the customer wants, they'll find a way to do it. The market is bigger than we ever dreamt. However, one thing remains absolutely certain: we will continue to expand and to manufacture aircraft engines.

No Fun in Service

Fresco isn't worried that GE will lose the attractiveness as a manufacturing company by stressing services: "I would be concerned if we had taken it to the extreme of abandoning the products. Then we would have lost some of our roots. The roots are still in strong technological competence. It goes back to the broader issue: If you are going to be faithful to your origins, you are destined to be a dinosaur. You have to evolve. We're trying to maintain the best of what we had, but to remain anchored to something that was good twenty years ago and not change would mean failure; that's what happened to so many companies. We have changed a lot. That is why we are the only member of the original Dow Jones Industrial Average still in the listing a century later."

Welch knows that a major obstacle to expanding the service dimension still exists: product innovation is fun while service efforts are not. Still, he feels that there are marvelous untapped opportunities for service.

Paolo Fresco agrees. "The problem," he says, "is to convince the engineers that [servicing the equipment] is as rewarding as inventing the turbine for the year 2010. Obviously there is a certain macho feeling on the part of the technicians that they always have to go for the most advanced product."

To deal with this challenge, GE established a Services Council headed by Fresco. It brings together the leaders of various businesses dedicated to service, and together they form a sort of executive corporate council devoted to thinking about GE's services.

Paolo Fresco observes that the new focus on the service component somewhat contradicts Welch's number one, number two business strategy. "Once you strive to be number one and number two, you may be tempted to try to define the market in such a way that you have a high chance to achieve number one or two status. But once you want to not just sell the engine but provide an amount of services around that engine, the market becomes ten times bigger and your market share becomes ten times smaller because you are competing with other service companies. The universe of competitors and potential customers gets much larger."

For example, GE once competed *only* with Pratt & Whitney and Rolls-Royce, but now it must compete with a number of service providers, among them some airlines that have their own internal service components.

Eugene Murphy, who headed Aircraft Engines from 1993 to August 1997, explains how and why that business expanded its service aspect. During the early 1990s, with drastically reduced defense spending and a recession, Aircraft Engines faced mounting pressures. A number of commercial airlines went bankrupt. The surviving airlines began demanding more and more value.

Accordingly, Aircraft Engines has developed an engine services business that is growing at a double-digit rate, with annual revenues in excess of $2 billion in 1996. It has landed ten-year maintenance and overhaul contracts from British Airways, US Air, and Atlas Air. It also acquired a majority interest in Celma, a rapidly growing overhaul operation in Brazil, and set up joint-venture accords with airlines and other leading engine maintenance providers. In 1995, Aircraft Engines integrated the overhaul and component repair services and spare parts businesses into GE Engine Services as part of Welch's plan to give the service effort independent status within General Electric.

Under the ten-year, $2.3 billion contract GE signed with British Airways PLC in March 1996, GE was to perform 85 percent of the engine maintenance work on BA's fleet—including engines made by competitors Rolls-Royce PLC and Pratt & Witney.

Indeed, the service business is the wave of the future for GE. It's hard to ignore that fact. How easy it would have been for Jack Welch to play down the service side of the business. After all, General Electric has been associated with manufacturing high-quality products for generations dating back to the age of Edison. For more than a century it was content to leave the service business to others. But, as we have seen time and time again, the chairman of GE is not enamored of the past just because it's the past. He's only interested in the future. And that is why he has had the vision and the courage to push GE, one of the great product companies of the modern age, so far into the service side of the business.

CHAPTER

20

Look to Financial Services to Bring in Earnings

"Our vision for the next century is a . . . global service company that also sells high-quality products."

SERVICE IS ONE of the key words in the GE lexicon. And what drives service at GE is Capital Services. No other business has done as much to contribute to GE's growth and profits in the 1980s and 1990s.

In 1995 and 1996, GE Capital Services had an operating profit of $3.5 billion and $4 billion, respectively, a substantial portion of GE's total (pretax) operating profits of $9.8 billion in 1995 and $11 billion in 1996.

Remarkable Growth

The growth of GECS is an amazing story. It began in the Depression days of 1932 as GE Credit, lending money to financially strapped GE customers who wanted to purchase major appliances such as refrigerators. GE Credit continued to finance installment buying for such products until the mid-1960s, by which time banks and independent financing companies were performing this function, making it unnecessary for GE Credit to remain in the business.

But GE Credit employees balked at the idea of shutting down the business; they were proud of the experience they had acquired in financing a whole variety of products. The business remained intact, changing its name to GE Capital. Today it is one of the great success stories, going from a paltry $77 million in earnings in 1978 to $205 million in 1982; since 1985, it has grown sevenfold, from revenues of $3.8 billion in that year to $32.7 billion in 1996 (along with $4 billion in operating profits).

GE Capital has twenty-seven businesses, including Americom (a provider of satellite communications services); Auto Financial Services; Aviation Services; Commercial Equipment Financing; Commercial Finance; Commercial Real Estate Financing & Services; Consolidated Financial Insurance; Consumer Financial Services; and Employers Reinsurance Corporation.

The impact of GE Capital on the whole corporation cannot be overemphasized: GE's overall revenue growth of 9.1 percent from 1991 to 1996 would have shriveled to only 4 percent without GE Capital. Its businesses, which range from credit cards to satellite leasing to computer programming, are generating 39 percent of GE's earnings, up from 29 percent in 1990. The driving force in GE's stellar stock performance—rising at 123 percent in 1996 and 1997 (compared to 63 percent for the S&P 500)—has been GE Capital.

GE Capital Services had record net earnings in 1996: $2.8 billion, up 17 percent, or $400 million, from 1995. Compare this with the 5 percent growth of Aircraft Engines and Appliances. GE Capital had $39.9 billion in revenues in 1997 and $3.3 billion in net earnings.

Nineteen of its twenty-seven businesses had double-digit growth. It increased its assets outside the United States by nearly 30 percent.

If GE Capital stood on its own, and not as one of GE's twelve major businesses, it would rank in twentieth place on the *Fortune* 500 list.

If it had been a stand-alone business in 1997, GECS would rank in the top 10 U.S. commercial banks, with $227 billion in assets.

In 1997, GECS was providing other companies with capital, financial services, transaction-processing capacity, and heavy equipment. Some services, such as aircraft and railcar leasing, were related to GE's manufacturing lines, such as making jet engines and locomotives. GE Capital:

- Finances everything from airplanes to cars
- Owns and leases fleets of trucks, cars, railcars, planes, and business equipment
- Leverages technology to deliver consumer services over the Internet
- Sells insurance and mutual fund products
- Is the nation's largest issuer of commercial paper

In late 1997 it was the world's largest equipment lessor, with over 900 airplanes (bigger than any other airline); 188,000 railcars (larger than any railroad); 750,000 cars; 120,000 trucks; and 11,000 satellites.

It owned the third-biggest reinsurance company in the United States, Employers Re (also the fourth-largest business at GE for 1997, trailing only Aircraft Engines, Plastics, and NBC, but slightly ahead of Power Systems).

In the late 1990s, GE Capital moved into computer services and life insurance and invested billions of dollars overseas. It has made seventy-six acquisitions in Europe since the mid-1990s, hoping to earn $1 billion by the year 2000 (double what it was earning in late 1997).

GE Capital had some major setbacks in the 1990s: the controversial, embarrassing fall of Kidder Peabody and the bankruptcy of Montgomery Ward. But offsetting those difficulties, notes Gary Wendt, the fifty-five-year-old CEO of GE Capital, is a sterling 18 percent average annual profit growth rate (from 1991 to 1996).

Stretching GE Capital

Wendt has had to stretch his business in accordance with the GE chairman's targets, and he has not done badly: half of GE Capital businesses missed their three-year growth targets in 1996; yet GE Capital beat its overall three-year $750 million target by a stunning $1.1 billion as total 1996 profits soared to $2.8 billion. In 1997, Wendt raised his profit target to $3.3 billion. He sounded as if he were on some roller-coaster that he couldn't jump off: "You know how it goes. Jack gives me targets. I raise them 15 percent and the people I talk to raise them to 25 percent."

What's GE Capital's secret?

In part, it benefits enormously from the parent company's triple-A credit rating. It also benefits from Jack Welch's low-cost learning culture that gives the business easy, continuous access to some of the best-run businesses in the United States.

A good part of GE Capital's success lies with Gary Wendt as well. One of the smartest people at GE, he has spent all of his twenty-two years with the company at Capital, taking over the business in 1990. He's known to have a great eye for spotting trends and an ability to move fast when necessary. After he graduated from the Harvard Business School in 1967, he began selling undeveloped land parcels for a Texas auto dealer who promised him a new Cadillac if he took the job. He also promised to make Wendt a millionaire. Wendt got the car, but not the million bucks. (The auto dealer's business collapsed before that could happen.)*

It has taken outsiders some time to appreciate GE Capital's strengths, as Nicholas Heymann, an analyst for Prudential Securities, notes: "The old idea was that you shouldn't pay a premium multiple for GE stock because nearly 40 percent of earnings comes from financial services, a low P/E (price/earnings) business. But the market is learning that Capital is different from cyclical financial service firms, that its better-than-15 percent growth rate is practically guaranteed."

Another reason for success is GE Capital's ability to manage a business that gets into trouble, saving it from having to write off a bad loan or swallowing a leasing loss. This occurred when loans to Tiger Inter-

---

*Always a behind-the-scenes figure, Wendt was suddenly catapulted into the public eye when his estranged wife, Lorna, filed for divorce. Gary and Lorna had been college sweethearts. When they married in 1965, they had only $2,500 in the bank. To put Gary through Harvard Business School, Lorna worked as a music teacher and then turned to homemaking, raising the couple's two daughters. According to one magazine report, when Gary Wendt told his wife he wanted out of the marriage in 1995, she filed for divorce, demanding half of his net worth. Gary offered her $11 million, far below the $50 million she was seeking, and so *Wendt vs. Wendt* went to trial. Through a spokesperson Gary defended his $11 million offer. "He is not saying, 'You weren't a good wife to me,' " noted Gary's publicist, Cathy Callegari. "He is saying, 'You are not responsible for my business success.' " On December 3, 1997, Connecticut Superior Court Judge Kevin Tierney ordered Gary Wendt to turn over assets worth $21 million, including a $3 million home in Stamford, Connecticut, and one in Key Largo, Florida. He also has to pay $21,000 a month in alimony for life. "The judge," said Lorna, "has found that this [was] a partnership between equals." Gary got to keep most of his future earnings. Lorna felt she had earned every penny of the judge's settlement: "He brought home the bacon, but I shopped for it, cooked it, and cleaned up after it."

national, the parent of North American Railcar, went belly-up in 1983. GE Capital entered the picture and became a railcar leasing business, which has since become profitable. And when a number of its passenger planes ended their leases and entered a soft market, GE Capital turned the planes into cargo carriers and provided some seed capital before launching Polar Air, an independent cargo line. When the Houston Astrodome consortium went bad in the 1980s and the banks involved took large writeoffs, GE Capital helped to run the Houston Astros baseball team for some two years instead of writing down its loans. Even though the Astros kept up their losing ways, GE Capital saw a good return.

Growing by Acquisition

Acquisitions has been an integral part of Capital's growth.

Its strategic acquisitions in the 1990s turned GECS into a global player in information technology, in providing customers with business solutions, and in systems management.

Since 1994 it has spent $11.8 billion on dozens of acquisitions. Hundreds more were examined and eventually scuttled as unworthy. But with the rising price of assets, GE Capital is not expected to make as many acquisitions as in the past. Taking that into account, Wendt is shifting priorities at GE Capital toward internal growth driven especially by value-added services.

Such service growth has two giant advantages: it doesn't require a good deal of investment, and it offers higher returns. Take the leasing business. The trains, planes, and cars under GE Capital's sway require much repair work. By taking on such work, GE Capital can save clients time and money and charge a handsome fee for performing the service. By keeping the equipment in good shape, it can lease it out for longer and thus increase profits.

Service in GE Capital's lending businesses has been given fresh priority as well. One example: Not only will GE Capital finance state-of-the-art semiconductor equipment for a high-tech firm, it will also repurchase the equipment after a number of years, fix it up, and find a lower-tech user for it.

GE Capital has moved into insurance in a big way since the mid-1990s. Hence, GE has become a savings business, concentrating on what Welch calls "consumer wealth accumulation," with $46 billion in assets. This is an activity that GE did not even participate in until 1992. The activity has been created by the acquisition of insurance and annuity companies like First Colony Life of Lynchburg, Virginia; GNA; Harcourt General; AMEX-LT Care; Union Fidelity Life; and Union Pacific Life.

Starting in 1996, GE Capital has spent billions of dollars taking advantage of the rapid consolidation that has swept the insurance field. It purchased three life insurance companies in 1996, at a cost of $3.2 billion, including $1.8 billion for First Colony of Lynchburg, Virginia, a leader in term life insurance.

A Change of Strategy

GECS is changing its own internal strategy. With Gary Wendt proclaiming that "you can't make money selling money anymore," GECS has decided to compete head-on with IBM and EDS for multimillion-dollar deals running computer networks for other companies. By October 1996 it had built up a $5 billion global computer outsourcing business.

In May 1996 it bought Ameridata Technologies, a $2 billion Stamford, Connecticut, company that sells personal computers to corporate buyers. In July 1996, it added CompuNet, a rapidly growing German outsourcer. These two purchases doubled the size and strength of its Technology Management Services business. It created Information Technology Solutions, a $5 billion global information technology company, with more than 9,000 employees and operations in thirteen countries throughout North America, Latin America, Europe, and the Asian-Pacific rim region, providing integrated products, services, and financial solutions to local, national, and international commercial and government customers on a global basis.

It has also become truly international. In 1990, it had virtually no income outside of the United States and Canada. By the late 1990s, GE Capital had a net income of $800 million internationally. Among its international projects in 1996 were co-managing the debt and participating in equity financing for Samalayuca II, the first large, privately funded power project in Mexico; and forming a precedent-setting joint venture with the Shanghai power system to fund and operate the Shanghai Zhabei Power Project, China's first long-term, nonguaranteed, commercially financed power project. GE Capital also took part in some telecommunications and airport privatization projects in Hungary.

Jewel in the Crown

Nearly 60 percent of GE's profits now comes from services, up from 16.4 percent in 1980. Jack Welch says he wishes it were 80 percent. And there is no doubt that he will do whatever he can to push the service end of the business—especially GE Capital—as far and as fast as he can. Welch knows that GE Capital is the jewel in GE's crown, and he has every reason to believe that the jewel will sparkle for many years to come.

Have Global Brains— and Build Diverse and Global Teams

"Businesses are global, not companies."

F ROM THE TIME he took over GE, Jack Welch understood that the business environment was changing:

- That GE's competitors were increasingly non-American
- That there were important opportunities for GE in overseas markets

In the early 1980s globalization was an alien concept to most businesspeople. In fact, most American business leaders were mystified by the global marketplace. For years their businesses had concentrated on the American market—and these leaders saw no reason to change.

Welch, on the other hand, saw every reason to change, and felt that GE didn't have a moment to lose.

The New Reality

He saw globalization as a new reality, as a great opportunity for GE. And he was not afraid to move quickly in order to capitalize on his ever-increasing vision of a global economy.

In 1980, the year before Jack Welch became CEO of General Electric, only two of GE's strategic businesses, Plastics and Aircraft Engines, were truly global.

GE Vice Chairman Paolo Fresco felt that he had been pushing for globalization for some time, but he understood that GE had to conclude the "fix, close, or sell" period before it could focus on its international operations: "It's very difficult to jump in the world arena if you don't have a solid base at home. But once the solid base was created we really took the jump."

Between 1985 and 1995 revenues from overseas operations increased from 20 percent to 38 percent of GE's total revenues.

By 1996, General Electric had a $33 billion "global business" that had grown 18 percent over the previous year.

By the spring of 1997, more than 40 percent of GE's revenues were derived from non-U.S. markets—markets where GE has grown at three times the U.S. rate. By the end of 1997, the figure had grown to 42 percent.

A Timely Swap

Welch's globalization revolution began in the summer of 1987 when in the space of half an hour he clinched a deal with Alain Gomez, the chairman of Thomson S.A., the largest French electronics company. GE exchanged its television set business for CGR, a Thomson company specializing in medical imaging. Thomson had a virtual monopoly in France, and the deal marked both GE's move into Europe and the start of its globalization program.

After Thomson, GE moved quickly to expand its reach in overseas markets. First there were joint ventures with the German company Robert Bosch, an industrial engines firm, and Toshiba, the Japanese electrical equipment company. GE then made an outright acquisition, buying Sovac, the French company specializing in consumer credit.

Until 1990, GE Lighting was almost totally an American business, with less than a 2 percent market share in Europe. Once the Iron Curtain lifted and the European Community created pan-European markets, GE moved quickly, acquiring a majority interest in the Hungarian lighting company Tungsram and then, in early 1991, a majority of the THORN Light Source business in the United Kingdom. With those acquisitions, GE had the number one lamp business in the world, with a nearly 20 percent market share in Western Europe.

By the early 1990s, GE's global presence had increased dramatically. Its operating profits from overseas markets had grown by 30 percent a year since 1987, and the $2.8 billion in non-U.S. earnings represented 40 percent of the company's total.

It is interesting to note that Welch did not simply wake up one day with the idea of taking GE global. Welch's global roots can actually be traced back to the 1960s, when he worked in GE's Plastics business: "Plastics eventually emerged as a truly global business. When I was twenty-nine years old I bought land in Holland and built the plants there. That was 'my land' for 'my business.' I was never interested in the global GE, just the global Plastics business . . . the idea of a company being global is nonsense. Businesses are global, not companies."

Gary Wendt notes that "Jack's perception of the world changed in the late 1980s from trying to sell things *to* the world, to understanding that GE has to be *all over* the world. . . . That's when globalization started to be understood."

With globalization under way, Europe was high on GE's list. Since the end of the 1980s, GE has invested nearly $10 billion in Europe; half has gone to finance fifty or so acquisitions. Behind the scenes, Paolo Fresco, a native Italian who speaks five languages, has been directing GE's global expansion. Fresco was the first foreigner to join GE's executive committee.

The acquisition of those fifty businesses in Europe resulted in almost $20 billion in revenue—Welch's original target for the year 2000. Welch has revised his goal and is now hoping for an astounding $30 billion by 2000! Typically, Welch says these figures "don't mean a thing. They're there to encourage people and you can set any target you like. It's only the product of your work that counts."

To give some perspective on how remarkable that $30 billion figure is, consider this. When Welch took the reigns in 1981, GE's *total* worldwide sales were at $25 billion. Looking ahead, when Welch retires, it is likely that GE's revenues will top the $100 billion mark, with more than half of that astronomical sum coming from its overseas operations.

Ten Years Ago We Were Nothing in Europe

Even if GE's European arm does not yet enjoy the international standing of other blue-chip companies, like IBM or Ford, overseas sales are soon likely to account for half of GE's revenues for the first time in their history.

A French reporter once interviewed Welch in a hotel in Paris and asked the CEO why GE was still not well known in Europe? Welch hated the question. Wanting to prove to the reporter just how ubiquitous the GE franchise is, Welch grabbed the remote control, switched on the TV, and flicked between NBC and CNBC while making the following proclamation:

> There's one **GE** company and there's another. Okay? There are already 50 million subscribers in Europe. . . . Apart from that, we're not big on the consumer goods market. The general public hasn't heard of us because we're not yet flooding Europe with our fridges. So what's the point in investing in advertising? Our industrial customers know us, and for the time being, that's the most important consideration.

> In lighting we have a market share of around 15 percent in Europe, but we face two serious competitors, Philips and Siemens. We are growing extremely rapidly in Asia, and in the United States we have a dominant position. Globally, we're strong. Extremely strong. Europe is only a part of the picture. What counts is the fact that we're powerful overall. Ten years ago, we were nothing in Europe. Nothing!

GE began its full-scale charge on Europe in 1989; since then, it has invested $17.5 billion there, half on new plants and facilities and half on its acquisitions. The strategy has paid off handsomely: GE's European forces raked in their largest net profit in 1995, an estimated $1 billion on revenues of $14.1 billion, roughly 15 percent of GE's overall net profits.

Operating profit for GE in Europe jumped 59 percent to $1.4 billion. Unfortunately, GE's Asian operations didn't fare as well; operating profit in Asia declined 10 percent in 1995, to $585 million.

Not all of the news coming out of Europe was glowing, however. The consumer appliance business has been a disappointment. In 1995 they turned a meager profit on revenues that did not top the $1 billion mark; five years earlier GE predicted that European consumer appliance sales would reach $5 billion by the mid-1990s. As recently as 1992, the Tungsram faculty had a negative cash flow of as much as $1 million day, and it took many millions of dollars—and another two years—to get it into the black.

Global Brains

As part of its global strategy, GE has promoted a number of non-U.S. nationals to senior management. Most of these appointees are men in their forties and fifties. Today, half of GE's dozen divisions on the Continent are led by locals.

In September 1997 Welch named Swedish-born Goran S. Malm president of GE Asia Pacific and senior vice president of GE. And he appointed Japanese-born Yoshiaki Fujimori as president and CEO of GE Medical Systems Asia and a vice president of GE Asia Pacific, succeeding Malm. That same week Welch named Cuban-born Ricardo Artigas vice president of Global Parts and Services for GE Power Systems; and Spanish-born Joaquim Agut president and CEO of GE Power Controls, succeeding Artigas.

Welch's foreign operations are a top priority for him, and he makes sure to visit his overseas personnel regularly. He spends a few weeks in Europe every January and three weeks in Asia each October. Along with visits to GE businesses, he also meets with partners and potential partners. When in Europe, he routinely visits six or seven countries, most often England, France, Germany, the Netherlands, Italy, and Spain. He sometimes goes to Hungary to visit GE's Tungsram lighting unit. Paolo Fresco always accompanies Welch. Fresco is GE's "Mr. International," a man whom Welch describes as "the classic global leader."

Though Welch is pushing hard toward his global goals, GE still lags far behind some of the other blue-chip corporate juggernauts.

In 1995 it ranked fifth on the UN list of the world's 100 largest companies, with the most overseas assets. But it ranked only ninety-fifth among those with the highest percentages of total assets, sales, and employment overseas. Exxon (21), IBM (35), Du Pont (55), and Ford (66) all rank higher.

The centerpiece of the company's European strategy—and the most dramatic example of how GE is shaking up the commercial status quo in Europe—is GE Capital Services Europe, which has consumed over $5 billion of capital. In 1995, it looked at roughly 100 deals, bid on about 40, and closed on 21. In 1996, GE Capital Services Europe generated 20 percent of the $2.8 billion net income of GE Capital Services worldwide.

Being global, to Welch, gives GE a strong growth platform by expanding its presence all over the world. In addition, its growing strength in the global arena helps GE to become a stronger competitor on all fronts, since it prevents rivals from gaining a foothold in any of the key foreign markets.

Going global has always been a difficult challenge for GE. "There's almost no expansion globally that isn't fraught with risk, different cultures, says Welch. "The Germans can pay a bribe. The French can pay a bribe and take it off their taxes. So you have to be diligent. You have to have training. But you can't stay home. Clearly, the risk side is long, but the opportunity side's longer. That, I think, is the difference."

In Europe, GE revenues grew by 42 percent per year from 1994 to 1996—and almost tripled profits. As of 1996, there was an $18 billion "European GE." In Asia, where there was double-digit growth, there was an $18 billion "Asian GE," making it a sizable player in the fastest-growing market in the world. As Welch noted in his 1996 Letter to Share Owners, "The constant sharing of business experiences and cultural insights, from around the world, is creating a Company whose brains, as well as its businesses, are truly global."

Welch has set stretch goals for his foreign operations, and has targeted Europe and Asia as GE's greatest growth markets. He hopes to reach $20 to $25 billion in sales in Europe by the year 2000, producing between $2 to $2.5 billion in net profits, clearly a "stretch" goal.

In his 1992 Letter to Share Owners, Welch noted that the reality of the global marketplace as GE's true arena was reinforced by a major shift of senior management and resources toward India, Southeast Asia, China, and Mexico—the megamarkets of the twenty-first century. GE continued to move its center of gravity in the direction of these high-growth markets.

A year later, Welch noted that speed had permitted GE to quickly shift the company's center of gravity toward the high-growth areas of the world, especially Asia. Forty percent of GE sales were coming from outside the United States, up from 30 percent just five years earlier. GE's foreign sales had grown at a compounded rate of almost 10 percent over the previous five years. Lighting, for example, one of GE's oldest businesses, which less than five years earlier had only 21 percent of its sales come from outside the United States, had pushed foreign sales to 38 percent by 1993.

In the 1994 Letter, Welch commented that GE revenues from outside the United States continued to outpace its domestic growth. In Europe, they totaled more than $9 billion in 1994. Globalization continued with double-digit top-line growth in the key emerging markets of Mexico, India, China, and Southeast Asia.

In 1996, GE did $1.3 billion worth of business in China. Welch knows that Asia is a big challenge for GE, but he refuses to be swayed by warnings that China may be the one market that GE cannot crack:

> **You know, people say, "You're taking too big a risk in China." What are my alternatives? Stay out? China may not make it, and we may not make it in China. But there's no alternative to being in there with both feet, participating in this huge market, with this highly intelligent crowd of people. We don't know China. Every time I leave China, I know how much I don't know.**

Paolo Fresco feels that Europe and Japan offer the biggest opportunities for GE because their economies are largest in absolute terms. While GE has a strong interest in breaking into Southeast Asia, China, India, and elsewhere in Asia, the markets there are smaller, so the challenge is that much greater. Take India and China:

> **Today we like India very much, but we have to recognize that in the last couple of years India has slowed down substantially. The bureaucracy is making life more difficult in India, so we have to be**

realistic and take the long view for India and accept that the movement is going to be a bit slower.

China has to learn how to live with the market economies. It's still a country where they say they want to play market economics, but they still have a centralized concept and they still believe that profit is good only if it is made by the Chinese government. But it's not very good if it's made by foreigners. So you have to be careful in China, and you have to use certain cautions because it's going to be a tough, long way. Tactically I'm not particularly in favor of making large investments in China at present, but I'm very much in favor of taking a very determined entry strategy, being patient, and being there when the time is right.

We have this kind of discussion all the time. Recently, we have decided to intensify our effort in South America, for instance. One of these days we should put more intensity into Russia when it finally emerges from its internal mismanagement and becomes again an attractive market. There's a lot of talent there, so I think there should be an opportunity.

A 1997 Lehman Brothers report written by Robert T. Cornell suggests that GE was doing very well globally:

Overall, we were impressed by the scale GE has achieved in Europe and the degree its acquired businesses have been integrated. This is not a loosely coupled organization but the same aggressive business machine as is operating in the United States. We were also impressed with the growth flavor in all the presentations. One tends to think of Europe as mature, but GE is moving with a high level of entrepreneurship and is making headway despite the fact that traditional European business "cooperation" still can make life difficult for newcomers and outsiders. Bottom line, GE is already huge and very profitable in Europe with most of its businesses talking about a further doubling in size with existing or higher levels of profitability in a reasonably short period of time.

GE competes in many major world markets:

- *Aircraft Engines:* GE is the world's largest producer of large and small jet engines for commercial and military aircraft, including the GE90, the largest jet engine ever built, which powers the new Boeing 777 twin jet. In 1995, more than half of the world's large commercial jet engine orders were awarded to GE and its joint venture, CFM International.
- *Appliances:* GE serves some of the world's fastest-growing markets, including India, China, Asia, Mexico, and South America.
- *Capital Services:* Financial services is expanding its operations globally, and placing special emphasis on Asia and Europe.
- *Lighting:* GE is a world leader in lighting products for consumer, commercial, and industrial markets, with a complete line of incandescent, fluorescent, quartz, high-intensity, tungsten-halogen, and holiday lighting. Its global operations include joint ventures in China, Indonesia, India, and Japan and acquisitions in the United Kingdom, Germany, Italy, and Hungary.
- *Medical Systems:* Its global operations include sale, service, engineering, and manufacturing organizations in the Americas, Europe, and Asia.
- *NBC:* International ventures include entertainment and news channels in Europe and Asia. It also includes NBC's highly rated coverage of the Atlanta Olympics.
- *Power Systems:* GE Power Systems serves customers in 119 countries.

While Welch and GE have made tremendous progress in making the company a global powerhouse, there is still much more to be done. By the year 2000, Welch expects the majority of GE's revenue to come from overseas, and he is fiercely determined to meet that goal. In fact, he places great importance on this particular objective, and feels that securing this goal is one of the best ways to ensure GE's survival in the new millennium.

Drive Quality throughout the Organization

"You've got to be passionate lunatics about the quality issue."

Live Quality—and Drive Cost and Speed for Competitive Advantage

*"As boundaryless learning has defined
how we behave, six sigma quality will . . .
define how we work."*

I N T H E L A T E 1 9 9 0 S , one concept is driving General Electric with unwavering intensity, an intensity that is evident at every GE business throughout the world. And this concept can be summed up in one word.

Quality.

Of course, by the late 1990s quality was hardly a new concept. Companies like Motorola had been living quality for years. But when Jack Welch embraces an idea, he does so with his own brand of fiery commitment, and his customary all-consuming passion. And as history has shown throughout the years, it's this firebrand enthusiasm that helps turn ordinary company programs into GE strategic initiatives powerful enough to transform the company.

As he did with restructuring in the early 1980s. With speed, simplicity, and self-confidence in the mid-1980s. And with boundarylessness in the early 1990s.

He exhibited that same excitement as he embraced the notion of quality in the late 1990s. He is so taken with quality that he is almost smothering it with his attention, mobilizing the entire company in the effort. For he is convinced that quality improvement will be the breakthrough business strategy that will make General Electric the most competitive company on earth.

Once again, Welch is trying to stay one step ahead of the pace, changing before it is absolutely necessary to do so.

Why now? And why the focus on quality? It's not as if GE has overlooked quality in the past. On the contrary. Quality for General Electric has always been important. And GE's durable products have always been widely regarded as high-quality products.

Yet, GE's products and processes have not yet attained *world-class* quality. Other companies have taken on the role of quality leaders. Companies like Motorola, Toyota, Hewlett-Packard, and Texas Instruments have long since been associated with world-class quality. However, Welch couldn't care less that other companies have beat him to the punch on quality. In fact, he will use the knowledge and experience gleaned from other companies to create an even better, more powerful program. And, he has determined to put GE's stamp on the quality effort from start to finish.

Fighting an Asian Hurricane

During the 1980s and early 1990s, GE penetrated markets only where it held powerful competitive positions and technological edges. The company abandoned businesses like consumer electronics, where it simply did not have that edge.

The strategy worked exceedingly well as GE's revenues tripled, earnings quadrupled, and the average annual return to shareholders leaped to 23 percent.

But while GE has had the luxury of choosing its market battlegrounds, some companies like Motorola, Texas Instruments, Hewlett-Packard, and Xerox did not. As Welch describes it, those companies were caught "in the eye of the Asian competitive hurricane" and had to deal head-on with the Japanese invasion that struck many American industries. Because their Asian competitors achieved new levels of quality in their products, Motorola and the other American firms had to improve quality levels or close their doors to business. As a result, after years of exceptional effort, they have a quality level that matches or exceeds all of their global competitors.

When GE benchmarked itself with those companies, it became abundantly clear that there was much room for improving the quality of GE's products and processes. "It's gotten better with each succeeding generation of product and service," says Welch. "But it has not improved enough to get us to the quality levels of that small circle of excellent global companies that had survived the intense competitive assault by themselves, achieving new levels of quality."

Learning from the experience of those American enterprises, Welch decided to make quality a crucial management focus at GE. Quality, to be blunt, has become a Welch obsession.

It wasn't as if Welch had rejected quality improvement all these years. He had simply assumed—incorrectly, in his judgment—that he could attack the issue of quality by concentrating on other aspects of business: by improving speed, increasing productivity, and getting employees and suppliers more involved in the company. It had always made sense to Welch that if an organization was fast and agile, it automatically had to have quality: "But we proved you could get fast and agile, and not have perfect quality," confessed Welch.

Speed Will Give Us Quality

Welch had never assigned quality a high priority at GE, and for one good reason: GE products always *seemed* to have better quality than the next guy's. No one really argued the point.

Sure, Welch and his associates knew that there was room for improvement. But the GE chairman simply assumed that the best—or perhaps only—way to improve quality was by pushing speed, simplicity, and self-confidence. Only when Jack Welch discovered that the three S's weren't doing the trick did he become convinced that something else was needed.

GE had launched quality programs in the past, but they weren't taken seriously. "So many of us grew up in the company with quality programs," says GE's CFO Dennis Dammerman. "We had a little gopher with the hat on, running around with the GE logo on it. We had posters on the wall on which was written 'Zero defects today.' Those were the signs that I used to walk under when I first started at GE Louisville in the 1960s. The goals and objectives were nice, but there wasn't a lot of substance to them. They didn't have measurements and approaches that involved everybody. They were slogans."

For a number of years, Jack Welch had been urging greater levels of productivity from GE personnel. Yet, by the mid-1990s, employees argued that greater productivity was not possible without improving the quality of GE's products and processes. Too much time was spent on fixing and reworking a product before it left the factory. That cut down on GE's speed, one of Welch's supreme corporate tenets, and also reduced productivity. "One of the things that became pretty obvious to us," notes Paolo Fresco, "is that our customers were pretty happy with our quality because compared with the competition our quality was as good as or better than our competitors. But as we started looking at the way we were spending our money, we saw there was a lot of waste because of mending bad quality before it hit the customer."

No one really looked at how much time was being wasted by the failure to produce a high-quality product on the first round, by having to rework it a good deal before it was ready to be shipped. "When we say a lack of quality," says Fresco, "we're talking about all the retesting and the reworking until the product is ready to be delivered to the customer. We thought of the waste and reworking as the cost of doing business. It was always called the cost of doing business. People currently identify high quality with high cost. We've now found that to achieve good quality is cheaper than to have bad quality. Now we've found that doing the right thing at the high-quality level the *first* time saves a lot of useless work."

Welch remained dissatisfied with GE's quality. As Bob Wright, head of NBC, observes, "Jack always thought of quality programs as basically an excuse to spend money to fix an engineer's problems which shouldn't exist in the first place. The programs were an excuse to have more inspectors and more overhead to cover up problems in the system."

Still, the inertia at GE over quality had a long-standing basis. First of all, Welch had made the Work-Out program the focus of General

Electric's key strategic initiatives in the late 1980s and early 1990s. Work-Out appeared to embrace all of Welch's most important goals: openness, informality, boundarylessness, high involvement, self-confidence, productivity, learning from one another. It was taken for granted that Work-Out would keep General Electric's quality high. Then, too, the Crotonville experience, where GE's managers learned how to manage large-scale change, would, it was assumed, lead to high quality levels. Finally, GE's bottom line was always improving, mitigating the incentive for Welch to promote a companywide quality program.

The Only Real Value Choice

The CEO of General Electric applauded people who worked hard to improve quality—those who traveled all night in a snowstorm to fix a locomotive part; or worked for days without sleep, troubleshooting some obscure part on a turbine or CAT scanner so that equipment would perform perfectly by its shipping date. But he wanted to avoid such needless work. He wanted to improve the processes so that the first effort was as close to perfect as possible.

He felt that it wasn't enough to have products and services that were merely equal to and better than those of GE's competitors. "We want to be more than that," said Welch. "We want to change the competitive landscape by being not just better than our competitors, but by taking quality to a whole new level. We want to make our quality so special, so valuable to our customers, so important to their success that our products become their only real value choice."

The question was how to come up with a companywide quality campaign that didn't repeat the mistakes of the prior programs. Welch and his colleagues found the answer in "six sigma," the concept that had been pioneered by Motorola, the Illinois-based maker of communications equipment and semiconductors.

Six Sigma

Six sigma is a measurement of mistakes per one million discreet operations—and applies to all transactions, not just manufacturing. The lower the number of errors, the higher the quality. One sigma means that 68 percent of the products are acceptable; three sigma means 99.7 percent are acceptable; six sigma, the ultimate goal, means that 99.999997 percent are acceptable. Six sigma denotes more quality than three sigma: at six sigma, only 3.4 defects per million operations occur; At three and a half sigma, which is an average quality measure for most companies, there are 35,000 defects per million.

Quality has long since been associated with the Japanese. Companies like Motorola knew that to be truly competitive meant taking on the Japanese in their own quality ballpark. Japanese goods like watches and televisions have for some time met six sigma standards. The quality of American goods, in contrast, was hovering around four sigma. But Japan's high standards of quality applied only to products such as electric equipment, cars, and precision instruments—and only to the area of production. Japan continued to lag behind in the effort to improve quality and productivity by improving business *processes* (as GE would attempt to do through its six sigma quality initiative).

Should We Follow Motorola?

In the late 1980s and early 1990s, Motorola pioneered the six sigma initiative and in the process reduced the number of defects in its products from four to five and a half sigma, yielding $2.2 billion in savings. Other firms, such as AlliedSignal and Texas Instruments, began to adopt their own six sigma quality programs. Six sigma was becoming so popular that it spawned an offshoot industry of consultants and missionaries. One such missionary was Mikel Harry, who had been at the center of the quality effort at Motorola, and later became a GE consultant during the early stages of its six sigma quality initiative. Another was Richard Schroeder, who had supervised quality improvement efforts at Motorola affiliates. Together Harry and Schroeder founded a consulting firm called the Six Sigma Academy in Scottsdale, Arizona.

Throughout 1994 and early 1995, Welch and other GE executives began mulling over what to do to improve GE's quality. The chairman was in a quandary. He agreed with others that GE was ripe for a massive effort at quality improvement. But what he first saw of the six sigma approach turned him off. He worried that it was inconsistent with his other business values and strategies:

- It was centrally managed.
- It seemed too bureaucratic—with its reports and standard nomenclature.
- It called for specifically agreed-upon measures.

In short, the initiative simply didn't feel like a GE program.

Work-Out, on the other hand, felt very much like a GE program: breaking down bureaucratic boundaries, encouraging openness, and urging people to learn from one another.

But ultimately Welch was swayed by his own employees, especially the manufacturing people and the engineers. They were the first to recognize that the company needed a solid quality initiative. These "hands on" people understood that after several years of great progress in productivity and inventory turns, progress had faltered because of the high number of defects in its business processes.

In April 1995, a month before Welch was hospitalized for ten days for triple-bypass heart surgery, the company did a survey that showed that GE employees were dissatisfied with the quality of its products and processes. (It should be noted that the results of the survey had nothing to do with the chairman's heart ailments.)

It was increasingly apparent that a number of other companies, including Motorola and Texas Instruments, had achieved dramatic results through six sigma programs.

A Crucial Meeting

Then in June, the CEO at AlliedSignal, Larry Bossidy, spoke to Welch's Corporate Executive Council. Bossidy was highly regarded at GE. He was a former GE vice chairman and one of Jack Welch's closest friends. In 1994, Bossidy had launched a six sigma program at AlliedSignal. Now, a year later, he told the CEC how impressed he was with it and how he thought GE could benefit enormously from undertaking a similar effort. "GE is a great company," he told the CEC. "I know. I worked there for thirty-four years. But there is a lot you can do to become greater. If GE decides to engage in six sigma, you'll write the book on quality." Dennis Dammerman recalled that Bossidy's presentation "had a real ring of substance to it, not just posters, but real substance." Welch, who had an enormous respect for

Bossidy, obviously felt the same way. He concluded that if six sigma was good enough for Larry Bossidy, it might be good enough for Jack Welch.

What particularly attracted Welch to six sigma was its heavy reliance on statistics. This quality program would not be "fluffy," a word he had used to describe previous, discredited GE qualify efforts. "Six sigma had a systems approach to manufacturing with cost and quality emerging as major by-products," noted Bob Wright. "Quality would no longer be a hanger-on." Indeed, what truly impressed Welch was the hope that *this* quality program would not sink in a tide of indifference as previous ones had. He had now come to believe that this is not a slogan. "This is not the program of the month," he said. "This is a discipline. This will be forever."

Soon after that CEC meeting, Welch asked Gary M. Reiner, then the vice president for Business Development (currently senior vice president and chief information officer) to undertake a study of how other companies were progressing with their quality initiatives. Among the companies Reiner studied were Motorola and AlliedSignal.

Welch was also beginning to hear about the need for a fresh quality initiative from GE people attending courses at Crotonville. In August 1995 The Executive Development Course focused entirely on quality. The class took a close look at winners of the Malcolm Baldridge National Quality Award, a government award given for quality excellence in business. "We felt like we were the pawns in this game," said Gary Powell, one of the course participants. "We were reporting out some incredible stories from our customer interviews. I never had such an ugly discussion with a customer as when we went out to one of the GE Motors customers. These people absolutely worked us over on quality. They said, 'You people are terrible.' They felt like hostages. As bad as we were, competitors are worse. We simply weren't meeting their needs."

In September 1995, the EDC class addressed Welch and other members of the CEC at Crotonville, passing on examples from the field that argued for a fresh quality drive. "You could see the sparkle in Welch's eyes," said Gary Powell. "This was exactly the way he wanted it to play out. We were telling his team we really needed to improve quality. It became very real. We talked about some of the best things we had seen that we could leverage. GE Medical Systems had started to work on quality; but it was really the series of team presentations of that class that helped to cement the need for improving GE quality."

Having decided to launch a quality improvement program, it seemed natural for GE to invite expert Mikel Harry to address the Corporate Officers meeting the first week of October. Harry talked about the virtues of the six sigma approach in making quality improvements in business processes.

But, once it decided to embark on a serious quality program, GE wanted to launch it the GE Way, a way that had never been done before. As Paolo Fresco comments: "When GE decides to do something, it goes after its own objectives with a vengeance, with an intensity that is unique."

Reiner was put in charge of GE's new quality program. From his travels to other enterprises, he learned that only a quality initiative that involved all GE employees had a chance to succeed. "What we learned is that unless you have a singular focus on quality, you don't get it. We focused quite a bit on speed. We measured it and we made real progress in achieving the speed with which we developed new products and the way material flowed through a factory. But the work required to get to a six sigma level of quality is a lot and you need trained resources to really think through why you're not getting the quality you want."

If GE could pull off a successful quality program, the potential rewards were enormous. The cost of remaining at three sigma or four sigma amounted to as much as 10 to 15 percent of a company's revenues. For General Electric, that would translate into a cost of $8 billion to $12 billion. According to Gary Reiner, GE hopes to recoup that money through its quality initiative "probably within five to seven years."

Fresco notes that improved quality means not only cost reductions but increased sales. "By increasing your quality level you make much more money for the shareholder; but you also acquire market share because your customer is going to be much more satisfied with you than with your competitors."

Reiner's point was taken seriously at GE. Two years into the program, six sigma has spread through the ranks. Banners on the walls of GE businesses proclaim its importance. Conversations are peppered with references to quality efforts. Traveling around GE plants and factories and the offices of senior managers, a single phrase rings in one's ears: "Six sigma. Six sigma. Six sigma." It is GE's new mantra, its new war cry in the late 1990s.

Make Quality the Job of Every Employee

"By 2000, we want to be not just better in quality, but a company 10,000 times better than its competitors."

JACK WELCH MADE an official announcement launching the quality initiative at GE's annual gathering of 500 top managers in January 1996. He called the program "the biggest opportunity for growth, increased profitability, and individual employee satisfaction in the history of our company." GE has set itself a goal of becoming a six sigma quality company by the year 2000. Such a company produces nearly defect-free products, services, and transactions.

Our Toughest Stretch Goal

Welch calls six sigma the most difficult stretch goal GE has ever undertaken. Prior to the quality initiative, GE's typical processes generated about 35,000 defects per million operations, or three and a half sigma. While that number of defects may sound like an astronomical figure, it was actually consistent with the defect levels of most successful U.S. enterprises.

By way of comparison, airlines have a safety record that is less than one-half failure per million operations, while their baggage operations are in the 35,000 to 50,000 defect range. This is typical of manufacturing and service operations as well as the writing up of restaurant bills, payroll processing, and doctors' prescriptions.

To reach six sigma, GE would need to reduce its defect rates by 10,000. To achieve this level of performance by 2000, it would have to reduce defect levels an average of 84 percent a year! Says Welch:

> **Very little of this requires invention. We have taken a proven methodology, adapted it to a boundaryless culture, and are providing our teams every resource they will need to win.**
>
> **Six sigma—GE Quality 2000—will be the biggest, the most personally rewarding, and, in the end, the most profitable undertaking in our history.**
>
> **GE today is the world's most valuable company. The numbers tell us that. We are the most exciting global company to work for. Our associates tell us that. By 2000, we want to be an even better company, a company not just better in quality than its competitors—we are that today—but a company ten thousand times better than its competitors. That recognition will come not from us but from our customers.**

Motorola took ten years to reach six sigma. Welch hopes to do it in five years. Is that possible?

To the GE chairman, his goal is realistic. Motorola, after all, had to pioneer the program. It had to develop the tools. GE has the advantage of coming along later. And it benefits from having the Work-Out culture that enables its employees to be more responsive to a quality initiative. Welch is confident that GE will do what other companies took much longer to accomplish: "There is no company in the world that has ever been better positioned to undertake an initiative as massive and transforming as this one. Every cultural change we've made over the

past couple of decades positions us to take on this exciting and rewarding challenge."

The New Warrior Class

The six sigma program relies upon an entire new "warrior class" within
the company to carry out its aims and procedures. This warrior class
consists of:

- Green belts
- Black belts
- Master black belts

The various "belts" represent managers who have undergone the complex statistical training of six sigma.

On July 19, 1997, Welch sent a letter, written in longhand, to all
Corporate Executive Council attendees, describing what he felt should
be the five characteristics of the people who steer the quality program
through its rigors:

1. Enormous energy and passion for the job—a real leader—sees it
   operationally, not as a "staffer."
2. Ability to excite, energize, and mobilize organization around six
   sigma benefits—not a bureaucrat.
3. Understands six sigma is all about customers winning in their
   marketplace and GE bottom line.
4. Has technical grasp of six sigma, which is equal to or bettered by
   strong financial background and capability.
5. Has a real edge to deliver bottom-line results and not just technical solutions.

From Billing a Customer to Making a Lightbulb

Initially GE is concentrating on cutting out wasteful expenditures of
time and effort. The focus is on such disparate elements as:

- Billing a customer
- Making the base of an incandescent lightbulb

- Approving a credit card application
- Installing a turbine
- Lending money
- Servicing an aircraft engine
- Answering a service call for an appliance
- Underwriting an insurance policy
- Developing software for a new CAT product
- Overhauling a locomotive
- Invoicing an industrial distributor

In its first year or so, employees considered six sigma just another new management fad, and word of the program filtered throughout the company slowly. This was not what GE's organizers had in mind. So Welch applied his fiery zeal to promoting the program personally. He talked it up in speeches every chance he got and even distributed a pamphlet about it (*The Goal and the Journey*) in the spring of 1996.

At the GE operating managers meeting in January 1997 the chairman made a startling declaration: he proclaimed that GE's managers would have to get "on board" the quality initiative—or face dismissal!

> **Simply put, quality must be the central activity of every person in this room. You can't be balanced about this subject. You've got to be lunatics about this subject. You've got to be passionate lunatics about the quality issue. You've got to be out on the fringe of demand and pressure and push to make this happen. This has to be central to everything you do every day. Your meetings. Your speeches. Your reviews. Your promotions. Your hiring. Everyone of you here is a quality champion or you shouldn't be here.**

Welch likened the program to the concept of boundarylessness and insisted that employees at every level of the company live six sigma:

> **It's no different than boundaryless behavior. People who weren't boundaryless shouldn't have been here in the eighties. Shouldn't be here in the nineties. If you're not driving quality you should take your skills elsewhere. Because quality is what this company is all about. Six sigma must become the common language of this company. Only your best can be black belts. Black belts must be**

in the middle of things—they can't be an upgraded quality organization. They've got to be central to the heart of the business. Measure the hell out of it. . . . This is all about better business and better operating results. In 1997, I want you to promote your best people. Show the world that people that make the big quality leadership contribution are the leaders we want across the business.

In the next century we expect the leadership of this company to have been black belt–trained people. They will just naturally only hire black belt–trained people. They will be the leaders who will insist only on seeing people like that in the company. . . . So in quality the warmup is over. The intensity level has to come up tenfold from where it is today. It's your central activity. It's the company's future. So 2000 will be tough as hell. But we're all going at it with an intensity never seen in business history.

No Belt, No Promotion

In his Letter to Share Owners in 1996 Welch reminded his staff of the penalty some will pay for not heeding his decree to take six sigma seriously: "The methodologies of Six Sigma we learned from other companies, but the cultural obsessiveness and all-encompassing passion for it is pure GE. For leaders who do not see how critical quality is to our future—like leaders who could not become boundaryless during the 1980s—GE is simply not the place to be."

If these messages weren't enough, Welch dropped one more none-too-subtle hint in March 1997, when he sent a fax to managers around the world, clarifying promotion requirements associated with six sigma quality. In that fax he wrote that effective January 1, 1998, one must have started green belt or black belt training in order to be promoted to a senior middle management or senior management position. And, effective January 1, 1999, all of GE's "professional" employees, numbering between 80,000 and 90,000 and including officers, must have begun green belt or black belt training.

Welch's message was a clear threat: If you don't have a belt, you won't get promoted. "We've got to say only people that have black belt training will lead businesses in this company in the next century." To drive the point home, he tied an astounding 40 percent of his 120 vice presidents' bonuses to progress toward quality results.

As boundaryless learning defined how GE employees behave, six sigma quality will, Welch contends, define how GE's employee teams work. In a speech given at an annual meeting in April 1997, he again took a tough stance: "In the next century we will neither accept nor keep anyone without a quality mind set, a quality focus. It has been remarked that we are just a bit 'unbalanced' on the subject. That's a fair comment. We are."

After Welch's repeated warnings that GE staffers had to "volunteer" for six sigma, it was hardly surprising that the number of applicants for training programs rose dramatically. And one could feel the excitement the program was generating during a visit to various GE installations in the summer of 1997. It all seemed like a boot camp whose one purpose was rallying the "troops" behind the quality program. To say the least, GE's employees have become obsessive about the program. When asked what else was new at GE besides the quality drive, Gary Reiner, who directs the program, answered half-jokingly, "Quality is the *only* thing that we do around here."

Going to War?

Welch knows he's set some pretty tough stretch targets in the quality initiative, but he has no qualms at all about setting ambitious goals. In the summer of 1997 a journalist told Welch that a former GE manager had equated working for Welch with going to war: many people die and the survivors are left to face the next battle. The GE CEO responded somewhat angrily:

> **Does this look like a war? I really don't think that's appropriate. On the other hand, I cannot achieve my objectives if I say to my people, 'I think the quality's great and I'd like you to think so too.' I have to say to my managers, 'forty percent of your bonus depends on how few faults your groups are responsible for.' I have to tell them that anyone who wants to be working here in two years' time must undergo the training.**

The company has added 3,000 employees to deal with the six sigma effort, including 400 at GE Plastics. With the addition of those 3,000 employees, some at GE have worried that the effort may create an unwanted bureaucracy. Dennis Dammerman admits it's a possibility. "There are people who would ask, 'Is all of this [quality initiative] discipline, or is it bureaucracy? My contention would be it's clearly discipline. What I like about six sigma is that we have to be very careful that it doesn't evolve into a lot of meaningless bureaucracy. That it's real, that the things that are fixed stay fixed. That it's not a new [wasted] layer."

It's the Customer, Stupid!

By the summer of 1997, Welch felt that six sigma was already paying handsome dividends:

> **Quality is the next act of productivity . . . Out of quality you eliminate reworking. You get salesman time improved dramatically. They're not spending 30 percent of their time on invoice errors. All these things create dramatic productivity. Quality is the next evolution. Everything about this enterprise is doing more with less. OK? It needs rejuvenation all the time. Quality is the next step in the learning process. Getting rid of layers. Getting rid of fat. Involving everyone. All that did was to get more ideas. The whole thing here is to create the learning organization.**

The quality initiative, contends Welch, "is both a top-line and bottom-line program. It creates customer satisfaction, enhancement, success. . . . It creates volume for everyone. Winning customers. The drive for quality is not some GE drive. The only reason for the quality is to make your customers more competitive. The focus on quality is aimed at making your customer aware. It's the customer's quality. Making him win."

Until he visited Great Britain in the late spring of 1997, the quality program had been little more than some abstract program to Jack Welch. On paper, he was quite familiar with how impressive the rewards of six sigma could be, but he still had no hands-on experience or feeling for how those rewards could be installed into the GE fabric.

Then he met David Curren, the European director of GE Capital's mortgage business. A number of things about Curren and the meeting he arranged for the CEO moved him. First of all, Curren had become a trained black belt in quality. This was a definite sign that upper management was serious about heeding Welch's call to get on board the program. Second, Curren had made a point of inviting some of his customers to participate in the meeting. This was evidence that GE's managers understood the driving theme of the quality program: it was aimed at enhancing the satisfaction of the company's *customers*. The chairman thought Curren's presentation was the wave of the future. Here was a black belt, the head of a business, helping customers to participate in GE's business reviews:

> **It was a totally different meeting. It was a meeting of GE in 2001, 2002. He brought customers with him. And the customers were talking about how six sigma had made them get more mortgage applications because they were able to respond faster because GE had responded faster. How they were "growing" their earnings. I got a customer's pitch about their success. Then our guy talked about his profitability increase in front of his customers.**

A reporter asked Welch what he would say to a GE factory employee who asked, What's in the quality program for me? "Job security. Enhanced satisfaction. Not wasteful rework. Growth."

But isn't the GE employee going to work eight hours on the factory floor whether there's a quality program or not?

Sure, was the thrust of Welch's answer, but without six sigma the employee might not have a job forever. With six sigma, with a quality program that focuses on finding out what customers want, the employee has a better chance that his job will be needed in the future. "We only have meetings about data, not anecdotes anymore," adds Welch. "It used to be you would make a promise to a customer, but it wasn't necessarily what he wanted; now it's 'Do you deliver to that customer's specified spot in time?' It has nothing to do with what you want. All these things are done in a way that the customer drives them. The customer manages your factory."

Had Welch gotten his way, six sigma would have spread throughout GE like lightning, improving products and processes overnight. But

GE was far too big for that to happen, filled with too many people who had been doing their jobs for too many years to adopt major changes that quickly. Welch is not a patient man, however. He still believes in speed and self-confidence as effective business strategies, and he wants self-confident GE personnel to inculcate six sigma into their lives quickly. By April 1997, Welch remarked in a speech, less than two years into the program, "six sigma has gone from being an alien concept, full of complex calculations and unfamiliar jargon, to a consuming passion sweeping across the company." Consuming, indeed, but the jury was still out on whether it would deliver the bottom-line results that GE was striving for by the year 2000.

To Achieve Quality: Measure, Analyze, Improve, and Control

"Quality is the next act of productivity."

Тhe six sigma approach to quality improvement in business processes entails the formation of project teams, each aimed at achieving the six sigma level of precision through a four-step process known as MAIC:

- Measurement
- Analysis
- Improvement
- Control

Essentially, these steps call for probing, measuring, and analyzing in order to discover the root causes of the problem—and then controlling the problem to keep it from recurring. The control phase is crucial. In the past at GE things got fixed, but they didn't *stay* fixed because there were few real controls. For the first time, the six sigma approach addresses this issue. GE makes a point of auditing its quality initiative projects for six to twelve months to assure that the high level of quality remains; the project is then audited every six months thereafter.

How Six Sigma Works

Here, is how the six sigma process works at General Electric: First, a project is identified. Then, critical-to-quality (CTQs) characteristics are defined. And finally, the six sigma process begins. Master black belts mentor black belts through the four MAIC steps:

1. *Measure:* Identify the key internal process that influences CTQs and measure the defects generated relative to identified CTQs. Defects are defined as out-of-tolerance CTQs. The end of this phase occurs when the black belt can successfully measure the defects generated for a key process affecting the CTQ.
2. *Analyze:* The objective of this phase is to start to understand why defects are generated. Brainstorming, statistical tools, and so forth are used to identify key variables that cause the defects. The output of this phase is the explanation of the variables that are likely to drive process variation the most.
3. *Improve:* Here the objective is to confirm the key variables and then quantify the effect of these variables on the CTQs, identify the maximum acceptable ranges of the key variables, make certain the measurement systems are capable of measuring the variation in the key variables, and modify the process to stay within the acceptable ranges.
4. *Control:* The objective of this final phase is to ensure that the modified process now enables the key variables to stay within the maximum acceptable ranges using tools such as statistical process control (SPC) or simple checklists.

Each of these phases takes one month. Each phase begins with three days of training, followed by three weeks of "doing" and a day of formal review by the master black belts and champions. After a black belt finishes the first project under the aegis of a master black belt, he takes on added projects, which are only reviewed by a master black belt. Both master black belts and black belts are expected to work full-time in their roles for at least two years.

Black Belts and Green Belts

GE has given names to the various players in the six sigma effort:

1. *Champions:* These are senior managers who define the projects. These senior management leaders are responsible for the success of the six sigma efforts. They approve projects, fund them, and troubleshoot. Some business leaders are champions. Most champions report directly to the business leader. A GE business typically will have seven to ten champions. Champions do not have to work full-time in the quality program, but they are expected to give as much time as needed to assure the program's success. Champions are trained for one week. By the end of 1997 there were 200 champions at GE.

2. *Master black belts:* These are full-time teachers with heavy quantitative skills and teaching and leadership ability. They are certified upon fulfilling two requirements: they must oversee at least ten black belts who become certified; and they must be approved by the business champion team. They review and mentor black belts. Selection criteria for master black belts are quantitative skills and the ability to teach and mentor. Master black belts are trained for at least two weeks to teach and mentor. By the end of 1997 they numbered 700.

3. *Black belts:* These are full-time quality executives who lead teams and focus on key processes, reporting the results back to the champions. These team leaders are responsible for measuring, analyzing, improving, and controlling key processes that influence customer satisfaction or productivity growth. They are certified upon successfully completing two projects, the first under the aegis of a master black belt; the second one, more autonomously. A successful project is one in which defects are reduced ten times if the process began at less than three sigma (66,000 defects per million operations), or by 50 percent, if the process started at greater than three sigma. To become certified, black belts also have to be approved by the business champion team. Black belts are full-time. By the end of 1997 there were 2,600 black belts.

4. *Green belts:* They work on black belt projects but do not work on the projects full-time; they work on six sigma projects while holding down other jobs in the company. Once the black belt

project has ended, team members are expected to continue to use six sigma tools as part of their regular job. By the end of 1997 there were 15,000 green belts.

GE also planned to train each of its 20,000 engineers so that all of its new products would be designed for six sigma production. And it planned to train all 270,000 GE employees in six sigma methodology.

The goal, by the end of 1998, is for every one of GE's 80,000 to 90,000 professional employees to be green belts. The number of champions and master black belts won't grow very much, but their role is crucial, as they will form the core level of expertise.

In mid-1997 there were still an insufficient number of master black belts to mentor the green belts during their projects. To cope with the lack of master black belts, Gary Reiner organized a computer system that provides interactive multimedia mentoring. When a green belt has a question about the measure and analyze phase, he or she is now able to engage in an interactive dialogue with an expert system to answer the questions.

Measuring Progress

GE has designed five corporate measures to help a business track progress in the six sigma program:

1. *Customer satisfaction:* Each business performs customer surveys, asking customers to grade GE and the best-in-category on critical-to-quality issues. The grade is a five-point scale, where 5 is the best and 1 is the worst. A defect is defined as either less than best in a category or a score of 3 or less. GE measures defects per million survey responses. As with all measures in the project, the results are reported on a quarterly basis.
2. *Cost of poor quality:* There are three components: appraisal, which is mostly inspection; internal costs, largely scrap and rework; and external costs, largely warranties and concessions. GE tracks the total as a percent of revenues on a quarterly basis.
3. *Supplier quality:* GE tracks defects per million units purchases, where the defective part has either one or more CTQs out of tolerance and therefore must be returned or reworked, or the part is received outside the schedule.

4. *Internal performance:* GE measures the defects generated by its processes. The measure is the sum of all defects in relation to the sum of all opportunities for defects (CTQs).

5. *Design for manufacturability:* GE measures the percent of drawings reviewed for CTQs and the percent of CTQs designed to six sigma. Most new products are now designed with CTQs identified. GE hopes to begin designing products and services to six sigma capability. This measure is very important, since the design approach often drives the defect levels.

The Snowball Is Growing

Since the six sigma initiative began in October 1995, the results have been nothing less than stunning—exceeding even Welch's lofty expectations.

GE launched the quality initiative in late 1995 with 200 projects and massive training. In 1996, it completed 3,000 projects, each averaging seven months, and trained 30,000 employees. It invested $200 million in the initiative and got a return of nearly that much ($170 million) in quality-related savings.

Welch's current six sigma effort is backed by far more resources than any past quality initiative. GE spent $300 million in 1997 and enjoyed a $600 million benefit—so its net benefit was $300 million for the year. At first, it planned to undertake 6,000 projects, but that number grew to 11,000. The average project is five months in length and yields an 80 percent reduction in defects, generating $70,000 to $100,000 in savings. Some 100,000 GE personnel were trained in 1997.

In 1998, sigma six will include 37,000 projects at a cost of $450 million, with anticipated benefits of over $1 billion. Some $400 to $450 million will be spent in 1999 in 47,000 projects, with an expected $1.3 billion in benefits. Welch crows that "the snowball is growing, and by 2000 the cumulative bottom-line impact of six sigma quality will be measured not in hundreds of thousands or millions but in billions."

Here's how six sigma is progressing in one of GE's businesses, GE Capital. During 1996, GE Capital completed more than 300,000 hours of six sigma training, in twenty-one countries and fifteen languages. By the end of the year it had 75 quality leaders on board, 135 master black belts, and 550 black belts; 560 projects were underway, 57 of which were completed during the year. It invested $88 million that year in six sigma quality and projected an investment of $153 million for 1997. The investment was beginning to pay off in improved customer retention, error reduction, and net income. In 1997 GE Capital projected a net savings from quality of $150 million.

Meanwhile, Around the Company

And elsewhere at GE the results were no less impressive. GE Lighting had a billing system that worked fine but contained one problem: it didn't mesh very well electronically with the purchasing system of Wal-Mart, one of GE's best customers. This caused disputes, delayed payments, and was a waste of time for Wal-Mart.

Then a GE black belt team used six sigma methodology, information technology, and a $30,000 investment to solve the problem from Wal-Mart's perspective. In four months, defects were reduced by 98 percent. Wal-Mart achieved higher productivity and competitiveness, and there were fewer disputes and delays.

At GE's Capital Mortgage Corporation, employees fielded some 300,000 telephone calls a year from customers, using voice-mail and callbacks when a person was not available. To GE, the system seemed satisfactory, since all calls were answered, but there was one major problem: by the time a GE employee called a particular customer back, that customer was often talking to another company, resulting in lost opportunities and lost sales. Now that was a problem!

A master black belt team was assigned the task of solving this daunting problem. The team learned that one of the corporation's forty-two branches had no such problem; nearly all calls were answered the first time around. Why was that? Analyzing its system, along with process flow, equipment, and physical layout and staffing, the team found the answer and then adapted it to the other forty-one branches. Customers who had found the Mortgage Corporation employees inaccessible nearly 24 percent of the time now had a 99 percent chance of speaking to a GE person on the very first try; and since 40 percent of their calls resulted in business, the return for GE amounted to millions of dollars.

At GE Plastics, polycarbonates met the extremely high purity standards that GE had set, internal standards that the majority of the industry felt was satisfactory. But the Plastics business still could not meet

Sony's performance requirements for its new higher-density CD-ROMs and music CDs. Accordingly, two Asian suppliers took all of Sony's business. GE Plastics got none of it.

A black belt team examined the situation. It was not interested in GE's standards, only Sony's. Once it was clear what Sony expected, the team devised a filtration method for the business's production process that permitted the polycarbonate to perform precisely as Sony wanted. GE Plastics eventually took away all the business from those Asian suppliers.

NBC entered the quality fray in the summer of 1997 when it appointed a quality officer, choosing the person deemed to have the highest potential in the company (a "high pot" in GE's phrase), excluding the head of sports, programming, and entertainment. That person was John Eck, head of finance for NBC's international business, an operations troubleshooter. Wright told Eck not to start with the news division, but to work on projects that could be more easily measured via six sigma standards. Wright felt that the news division would be suspicious of the quality initiative, so he asked Eck to begin with the eleven owned and operated stations at NBC, selecting eleven different projects. Two people would be taken from each station and assigned full-time to improve quality in areas that had significant economic impact on the stations. The goal was to develop uniform software for all the stations.

At Power Systems, GE had focused on delivering equipment on time, but little attention was paid to other critical quality standards defined by customers. A six sigma process revealed that customers felt the documents GE produced to explain the equipment—documents that were crucial for their compliance with the agencies that regulate them—were far too complicated, wasted too much time, and were too costly. A black belt team studied the situation, simplified the documents, and saved GE's utility customers over $1 million a year. It also saved GE several hundred thousand dollars.

In each of these cases not much money was involved—a few hundred thousand to a million dollars—but the quality effort was replicated in tens of thousands of other examples around the company.

Gary Reiner, the man in charge of GE's quality program, describes a companywide problem, the process by which GE customers fill out order forms for products. It constituted one of the greatest drags on quality at GE. The order forms often confused customers and GE personnel alike. It was difficult for both sides to agree on what it was the customer really wanted. Reiner acknowledges that the order forms were only at one sigma quality. "We get it half right, half wrong," he admits.

The solution was to create new software, called configurators, that could spew out forms that were far easier for both sides of the sale. "The software gives you a picture of exactly what you ordered," says Reiner. "And you have a feedback loop so that a copy of that picture is sent to the customer at once. There is no opportunity for defects. Many of our businesses that sell complex products and services are doing this now."

Quality problems existed with billing as well. Gary Wendt cites an example from GE Capital's Rewards credit card: "We got more productive, and faster, and our cost per credit card went down when we undertook the quality initiative. And all the measurements were down, but the number of errors when the customer got a bill was the same. We thought it was important to get the card to the customer faster than ever before; but we never asked the customer what he or she thought was important. It turned out that the customer thought speed was important, but getting the bill right was also very important. If the bill was wrong, the customer had to call GE and ask for it to be straightened out. Then someone at GE had to investigate. We discovered we were spending a lot of money on investigation. Now we provide bills with much higher quality."

GE Plastics: From a "Cocktail Commitment" to Six Sigma

The quality program began at GE Plastics in August 1995. In time it became one of the leading-edge examples of GE's six sigma program.

Gary J. Powell, the quality leader at GE Plastics, remembered what the attitude was toward quality at Plastics in the old days: "It was routine to say quality's everybody's job. GE Plastics had been through two initiatives on quality dating back to the early 1970s. Each time we got smarter, but we plateaued. There wasn't the continuous-improvement philosophy that most were seeking in quality. We didn't get the level of business or customer impact needed to set us apart from customers."

Powell had left GE for a while and became a customer of GE Plastics. He bought from GE's competitors as well. From that experience he learned that GE was viewed as having good, but not world-class quality.

The company was still not leveraging quality as a competitive advantage. Powell called GE's attitude toward quality a "cocktail commitment." In other words, GE people "were saying the right thing over cocktails, but the leadership wasn't really committed to improving quality and changing the way we worked."

The business had slipped into some bad habits. Employees asked customers to take shipments the customers didn't really want. Testing was done on products, but results didn't always predict how the product would perform in a customer's application. Says Powell: "We never questioned a positive result."

In earlier days, GE Plastics dealt with fairly simple applications, so there wasn't as much pressure for high quality. Under GE's Work-Out program, the idea was to leverage the knowledge of employees closest to the work. It became fashionable to launch assaults against bureaucracy. But the bureaucracy had been erected in many cases to help impose discipline that assured the quality of products and processes. All too often, the assault on bureaucracy had the effect of getting rid of some of that discipline.

GE Plastics executives noted that Welch's strategy of delayering—getting rid of layers of management—had the benefit of reducing bureaucracy. But with fewer layers of management, it was easy to argue, as GE personnel did, that quality was everyone's business, not just senior executives. So, in the name of delayering, GE Plastics canceled its total quality organization. Accordingly, after its demise, some of the monitoring effort that provided discipline diminished as well.

Welch's emphasis on speed also had an unintended, but nonetheless negative effect on quality. Some tests of products required 24 hours. Once GE began to put the stress on speed, people began to question whether the 24-hour test was really required. Couldn't another test be found that took less time? Other shorter tests were done, but that resulted in more wasted time on the reworking of products. When GE personnel realized this, they began telling senior management that something had to be done.

Don't Do This to Me

With the decision to forge ahead with the quality initiative in October 1995, Gary L. Rogers, the president and CEO of GE Plastics, told Gary

Powell that he wanted him to lead the quality effort at Plastics. Until then, Powell had been doing environmental health and safety for GE Plastics. Powell's response was typical: "Don't do this to me. Anything but a quality staff job." (Powell said later, "This was the most challenging and rewarding opportunity of my career.")

Rogers said Powell's first task was to fill thirty slots from GE Plastics for a class that would train people to become master black belts at Crotonville, starting December 4. Mikel Harry from the Six Sigma Academy was brought in to Crotonville to teach the course, which provided two weeks of training, one in December, the other in February.

Powell sought people out to attend the class, but the response was often, "Why should I do this? I have a great career. I don't want to go into quality." Despite the indifference he encountered, Powell knew he had been challenged to get the very best leaders for the class. After all, Welch had said he wanted the movers and shakers of each business to get involved, and that was that. The thirty who took Harry's course became the first master black belts at GE Plastics. And, Welch kept in close touch with the senior managers who ran the quality program at Plastics.

On a Thursday in March 1996, the chairman got in touch with all GE officers, asking them to provide him with written documentation that would help him decide how large their bonuses would be. In essence, Welch was asking the managers to justify their bonuses by demonstrating the strides they were making in the quality program. He let it be known that 40 percent of their bonuses would be based on their work in this area.

The chairman gave them until Monday to hand in their responses, by which time he had their answers in hand. He was disappointed by the results. Some officers at Plastics had made the error of replying vaguely that they planned to train as many black belts as possible. But Welch wanted specifics. *How many?* Some said, with equal vagueness, that they expected benefits to flow from the quality program. The chairman again decried the lack of specifics: *How large would the benefits be?*

By Tuesday an exasperated Welch fired back notes to the officers. "This isn't even close," he told them. He demanded more aggressive commitments from his executives. The chairman's stinging retort got the manager's attention. "There was panic in the leadership team," Gary Powell recalled. "Few understood the level of change the CEO wanted from them. Even fewer appreciated the power of the six sigma process to change the way we worked. But they worked hard and came up with acceptable answers."

A lot of people at GE Plastics wondered whether the quality initiative would work. With Welch prodding them, the quality leaders set some pretty aggressive goals, reaching $20 million in benefits in the first year of 1996 ($20.5 million was in fact achieved). They had also committed themselves to putting 300 staffers in the program by the end of 1996.

GE Plastics had "only" 13,000 employees. Adding 300 in that short a period seemed daunting. Because Welch expected only the best employees to be among the 300, that caused some friction in the ranks. Some vice presidents were opposed to freeing their best people to take on quality responsibilities. But the CEO lit a fire under Gary Powell and the others. As Powell recalled, "Before, we never fully had the leadership's commitment; we had only a cocktail commitment. And we had never really resourced a quality initiative. This was an opportunity to do it right and to drive results. We had to get off to a quick start."

Putting additional pressure on GE Plastic's resources was the edict that in order to get promoted by January 1, 1998, people had to have green belt training.

Six Sigma, Year 2000

In August 1996, GE Plastics called in 260 people from around the globe and brought them to Florida to do a critical assessment of the quality program thus far. It had been working at such a maddening pace to train and get people into projects, that some felt it was time to take a measure of where the program was going. This "global time-out" meeting became a model for other such efforts around GE.

GE Plastics became so enthusiastic about the initiative that in May 1997 it held a six sigma tournament in which ten GE Plastics teams from the Asia-Pacific region competed against one another for the best quality project.

The winning Singapore team, which began measuring quality in July 1996 and calling its project "color for money," triumphed for reducing minor differences in color between plastic products. Color variance between each product unit was considered inferior quality.

The "color for money" project, which raised quality from 2 sigma to 4.9 sigma, took four months and saved GE $400,000 a year for one plant. The team's efforts also made it easier for customers to use plastic parts in their production work. The Singapore team hopes to get the colors on its products up to six sigma standards by the year 2000. When the team appeared before a GE audience as the acknowledged winners, the team enthusiastically explained how the project had unfolded and then team members standing on the stage shouted with unbridled enthusiasm, "*Six Sigma! Year 2000!*"

For 1997, GE Plastics was expecting upward of $70 million in net benefits. It hoped to get $1.4 billion in incremental benefits by the year 2000.

Even the Critics Approve

What's been the reaction to GE's six sigma program?

In February 1997, Morgan Stanley, Dean Witter, Discover & Co., reported on the conclusions of a study on General Electric's quality initiative. It stated that GE had reached a level that no one would have believed possible for a company.

Here's what Jennifer Pokrzywinski, a Morgan Stanley financial analyst, wrote in an April 1997 company update:

> **How do you know the difference between Six Sigma and GE's plain old "productivity"? There is admittedly plenty of gray area—if there is a production problem, someone usually knows it, and GE probably would have addressed it less capably with existing tools. The important difference with Six Sigma is that the project doesn't count until its "black belt" proves that the problem stayed fixed. Too often in the past, GE has fixed the problem, but it slowly reverts over time, so that this year's "productivity" represents the latest solution of the same problems GE "fixed" two years ago. Or GE decided to fix the problem with more inspection, so it eliminated the problem at a huge cost. Also, Six Sigma savings don't count until a finance staffer says so, to keep the black belts honest and to keep the system as objective as possible.**

In the spring, Welch attended a meeting of analysts and congratulated Pokrzywinski on her February report, telling her that she had seen further ahead than he had:

> **Jennifer, I was pleased to get the nice report. I've got to have you stand up. Because in January [1997] when you were saying all these wonderful results I was getting on quality because you had been around to other companies, I said I was pleased to get the nice report, but I wasn't sure we were going to get what you said. I had no idea. . . . The facts are: it's the only program I've ever seen customers win by, employees are engaged in and satisfied by. Shareholders will be. Everyone that touches it.**

Pokrzywinski explained why she has become such a big fan of the GE program: "Everyone has their cost-cutting program. I was a believer that there were cold hard reasons why six sigma was a different approach. And I understood it was a demanding approach. Culturally, not every company is ready to adopt it. If you understood the power of six sigma and knew GE—how culturally aggressive and confident and open they are as an organization—the combination of the two was compelling."

Welch was clearly thrilled. "All our managers are showing incredible dedication to the program. This program is like wildfire." And in the summer of 1997, Welch added that six sigma was "about seven thousand million times bigger and faster, better than my wildest dreams."

GE was getting praise from other analysts as well. Merrill Lynch financial analysts Jeanne G. Terrile and Carol Sabbagha wrote in May 1997 that GE's six sigma effort

> **. . . has the potential to produce hundreds of millions of dollars in earnings annually from better utilization of capacity, labor and raw materials. . . . The interesting thing to us about Six Sigma . . . is that it goes beyond the efficiency of the factory floor. GE's management has said publicly that they erred in the past by measuring themselves against their competitors because many of their competitors had such poor margins (in appliances, for**

example, GE's margins pre-Six Sigma were already twice those of their competitors). We do think that a hidden value in the Six Sigma process is that it measures performance against absolutes, not the relatives of the competition. It also forces greater focus on the needs of customers, a handy thing as GE grows its service businesses.

Some at GE admitted to having doubts at first about six sigma. CFO Dennis Dammerman was one: "It was a little bit scary at first because of its statistical nature but [the initiative had] an ability to rise above the statistics. Quickly we latched onto the control step, of making sure a problem was fixed. The emphasis on getting the facts first was what really differentiated this program from others in the past."

In the past, GE personnel felt that they knew what was important to the customer. But then six sigma revealed that the personnel really hadn't known what the customers wanted. That impressed Dennis Dammerman.

A big plus of the quality initiative has been in getting GE closer to the customer. Gary Wendt told how one of his businesses that finances commercial equipment improved its customer relations through six sigma. Employees noted that a certain customer had done a lot of business with them in 1995, but none in 1996. Why was that? A query form was sent to the customer group asking what GE had done wrong. The answer came back: GE had done nothing wrong.

So then why no business? No one asked us, was the customer's response.

A lesson was learned, as Wendt noted: "Get back to every customer on a constant basis and make sure you have enough salespeople to do that job."

Right now, the quality program focuses almost entirely on improving business processes in order to make its customers more productive. Welch hopes that GE will focus 75 percent on process and the other 25 percent on what he calls DFSS—design for six sigma. (In some GE businesses, the DFSS percentage might be even higher than 25 percent.) Eventually, as the process aspect is improved, Welch hopes the DFSS portion will rise beyond 25 percent. Designing for six sigma means that new products are designed from their very inception with six sigma tools. GE cannot fix products that it is currently making using six sigma tools because it's not possible to reengineer existing products to achieve six sigma standards. That can only be done through using six sigma tools on new products.

Jack Welch has great hopes, dreams, and plans for the quality program. While he likes what has happened so far, he knows there's still much work to be done. Up to this point, GE has been concentrating on improving business processes—with great results. Now Welch will turn his efforts—and the vast resources of GE—to improving the quality of GE's products. But his next goal is to incorporate six sigma thinking and standards into every new GE product. He knows the company will save time, money, and effort. Even though GE has made remarkable progress in the first two years, he still views six sigma as a program in its infancy.

PART
VII

The Toughest Boss/Most Admired Manager in America

"I don't get involved in pricing. I'm more of a coach."

Jack Welch
Deals with Adversity

"We have no police force, no jails.
We must rely on the integrity of our people
as our first defense."

IT IS NO ACCIDENT that the word "integrity" is among the first words to appear in the company's official version of its corporate values. Unfortunately for Jack Welch and GE, ethical lapses among General Electric employees constitute one of the chairman's most perplexing and difficult challenges.

Welch is all too aware that breaches have occurred far too often—and he concedes that they will probably occur in the future. For all of GE's bottom-line success (some say, *because* of that success) few other major American firms have had to suffer through as many ethical lapses as GE.

No Excuses

Yet, Welch has never tried to defend or offer excuses for the lapses, although he does suggest that in any community the size of GE, such violations are unavoidable. After all, he notes, all communities of GE's size have police forces for the simple reason that they are necessary. No one has yet to figure out how to eradicate crime completely.

Given the amount of scandal at GE, one might be left wondering how Jack Welch has remained unscathed. Why hasn't the controversy, which often adorned the front pages of countless newspapers, including *The Wall Street Journal*, hurt Welch's standing as the nation's most admired CEO?

By this time, the answer should shock no one: whenever scandal surfaced, he applied his vintage no-nonsense, no-time-to-lose management style to quell the problem. Welch's response took on a certain pattern. First, he moved quickly to rid GE of the transgressors. Next, he made it crystal clear that future transgressors would automatically be dismissed. And last, he made sure everyone knew he personally had nothing to do with the integrity violation in question.

If such ethical lapses occurred at other firms, the CEO would certainly be in hot water. In fact, he would probably be in distinct jeopardy of losing his job. Yet, not once has anyone ever suggested that Jack Welch should step down as a result of a GE scandal. It is testament to his business acumen (and perhaps his communications staff) that he has always managed to avoid the fray, leaving his golden-boy image intact to live another day. Although it may not fit the usual management paradigm as neatly as "face reality" or "fix, close, or sell," surely one of Welch's gifts is his unswerving ability to remain aloof from the company's ethical troubles. It is not a secret one proudly boasts about, but it is part of Welch's business intelligence nonetheless. And there are valuable lessons to be gleaned from how GE's chairman has dealt with the company's integrity troubles. Here, then, is a brief look at some of those troubles and how Jack Welch coped with them.

Trouble with Time Cards

On March 26, 1985, nearly four years after he took over as chairman and CEO of General Electric, the company suffered one of the worst blows of his tenure. On that fateful day, GE was indicted by a federal grand jury on two sets of charges: one set contended that GE's aerospace business had filed $800,000 in incorrect costs on employee time cards; the second set contended that GE had lied to the government about work it had carried out on a nuclear warhead system. GE's work on the nuclear warhead system was the result of a $40.9 million contract that the U.S. Air Force had awarded the company to overhaul fuses on intercontinental ballistic missiles.

Three days after the indictment, Welch wrote a letter that was distributed to every General Electric employee, hoping to put the front-page scandal into some perspective. He noted that 100 of the 108 counts of the indictment related to 100 time cards, which represented a relatively small portion of the 100,000 time cards filed during that period. "While it is entirely possible," he wrote, "that, during the course of performing several multimillion-dollar contracts, charging errors did occur, there was no criminal wrongdoing on the part of the Company or its employees. The Company has not been convicted of any crime." When other misdeeds occurred in future years, the CEO would use the same argument quite effectively, that the transgression was the act of a few rotten apples and that the company overall was not involved.

As Welch observed after the aerospace indictments, "In any large organization—and GE with its 330,000 total employees is a very large organization—people may make errors in judgment. These must be viewed in relation to the extremely good reputation of our company and its people." After a low-level employee confessed, GE pleaded guilty to the aerospace charges and was fined $1.04 million.

Other infractions followed:

- In 1989, GE settled four civil suits that were brought by whistle-blowers who had alleged that General Electric had cheated the government of millions of dollars by issuing faulty time cards. GE paid $3.5 million.
- In 1990, GE was convicted of defrauding the Defense Department as a result of overcharging the U.S. Army for a battlefield computer system. GE paid $30 million in penalties for that infraction and other defense contracting overcharges.
- In 1992, GE pleaded guilty to defrauding the Pentagon out of more than $30 million in the sale of military jet engines to Israel when an employee took bribes. GE paid $69 million in fines.
- In 1993, GE's NBC News unit staged a misleading simulated crash test, which led to the unit's on-air apology to General

Motors. NBC also agreed to pay GM an estimated $1 million in legal and investigation expenses.

- In 1994, in one of the most embarrassing and most widely publicized scandals of that year, head government T-bond trader Joseph Jett of Kidder Peabody (GE's brokerage unit) concocted $350 million in phony profits over a twenty-nine-month period before being fired in April of that year. As a result, GE was forced to take a $210 million charge against its first-quarter earnings in 1994.
- The SEC was due to rule on the Jett case in the spring of 1998. GE sold a majority of assets of Kidder Peabody to PaineWebber in 1994.

The pertinent question posed by the press—and perhaps by folks at countless water coolers across the country—is this: Is Welch personally responsible for these incidents? *Fortune* magazine certainly thought so: "Most troubling is that [Joseph] Jett's misdeeds, if true, are not an isolated case at GE. When you put the Kidder scandal together with other transgressions that have sullied GE's reputation over the past decade . . . you begin to get a sense that somewhere in the highly successful and celebrated GE culture something is not right." The corollary to the magazine's claim is that, in putting great pressure on his managers to perform, Welch encourages them to look after their self-interests at the expense of company loyalty. Put another way, if you encourage the winning-is-everything mentality, don't play ostrich or run for cover when things hit the fan.

What Can One Do?

To Welch's chagrin, other than take a tough stand against transgressors, he has discovered there is precious little a CEO can do *in advance* to ward off such integrity lapses. One step he did take in 1987 was to issue companywide guidelines, an eighty-page booklet called *Integrity: The Spirit and the Letter of Our Commitment.* Every new employee was required to read the booklet and sign a card found in the booklet (or answer by e-mail) that they had read it. And all other employees had to do the same once a year. In that booklet, Welch wrote in his Statement of Integrity:

Integrity is the rock upon which we build our business success—and our quality products and services, our forthright relations with customers and suppliers, and ultimately, our winning competitive record. GE's quest for competitive excellence begins and ends with our commitments to ethical conduct.

He then urged all GE employees to make a personal commitment to follow GE's code of conduct, to obey applicable laws and regulations, to avoid all conflicts of interest, to be honest and fair and trustworthy.

The Jack Welch Defense

Welch testified before the Subcommittee on Oversight and Investigations of the House Committee on Energy and Commerce, in Washington, D.C., on July 29, 1992. He refused to make excuses for GE's misdeeds: "Theft of a dollar is theft and fraud is fraud," he told the committee. He also refuted the notion that his aggressive management style led to the integrity violations:

There is now a nascent view that goes something like this: An atmosphere where excellence and performance are always in demand is an atmosphere that encourages breaking the rules. . . . At the Olympics we've heard people talking about steroids and suspicions. And we hear people wondering whether the pressures of competition are driving people to cheat. Those isolated violations cast their shadows on the real champions.

What's the solution? Tell athletes to run slower, jump lower, so they'll be above suspicion? Our view, put in those terms, is that you must run as fast as you can, and jump as high as you can, but if you break the rules, your medals are gone and you're out of the game for good. That's our view of competitiveness and integrity, and every leader in our company is striving to get that message across. Competitive results must be written on a blackboard of integrity. Our competitiveness is not just compatible with integrity. It's built on integrity.

Can anyone seriously contend that excellence and competitiveness are incompatible with honesty and integrity?

Welch went on to point out that there are no second chances for those who violate the ethical code:

No one at GE loses a job because of a missed quarter . . . a missed year . . . or a mistake. That's nonsense and everyone knows it. A company would be paralyzed in an atmosphere like that. People get second chances. Many get thirds and fourths, along with training, help, even different jobs. There is only one performance failure where there is no second chance. That's a clear integrity violation. If you commit one of those, you're out. . . .

We have an employee population that would rank with St. Paul or Tampa if it were an American city. We have no police force, no jails. We must rely on the integrity of our people as our first defense, in addition to what many agree are the most rigorous standards and policies of any company in America for monitoring our dealings with the government: hotlines, ombudsmen, voluntary disclosure policies, and constant leadership emphasis.

We are not so arrogant as to believe our personnel processes are so selective, so perfect, that they can screen every virus out of the company's bloodstream. The occasional betrayal of our company by an individual—despite our passionate commitment to stop it— can happen again.

But I take great pride that 99+ percent of our 275,000 people get up every morning all over the world and compete with passion and absolute integrity. They don't need a policeman, or a judge. They only need their consciences as they face the mirror each morning.

They see no conflict between taking on the world's best, every day, all over the globe, giving 110 percent and more—to compete and win and grow—and at the same time maintaining an instinctive, unbendable commitment to absolute integrity in everything we do.

One Violation, and You're Out

In December 1997, in an interview with the author, Welch talked at length about his handling of the integrity issue at GE. He began by recalling an internal GE meeting he had recently attended at which an NBC intern asked him if he could guarantee that GE would never have a "Texaco incident." (The intern was referring to the 1996 incident in which Texaco officials were caught on tape making racist remarks; the officials had to pay $115 million in reparations.) Welch said no, he couldn't make such an ironclad guarantee:

> I can't guarantee anyone in this room that you're not a thief. That you haven't stolen something. Or robbed somebody this morning. All I know is that if I knew that, you wouldn't be on the payroll. We have a code of conduct here that anybody we know who's doing something won't be on this payroll for an hour.

When asked how he had managed to cope with GE's scandals and remain unscathed, he replied:

> Look, that would be the most overstatement one could have, that I've figured out how to deal with this. I've figured out one thing: I figured out that I cannot personally police perfect behavior of this organization. I can, though, have a set of values. Integrity. We have talked about it at every meeting. A violation of integrity. There's no discussion. You are *gone*. And we have example after example where people are just taken right out the door.

Immediately? he is asked:

> Immediately. They get a hearing. But they're gone. There is never a corner to be cut—a wink, we use the word "wink." No winks on any type of behavior.

Isn't it one of the most difficult parts of management?

No, I don't think so at all. I find it very clear, very clear. This is not a hard issue. We're going to be the most competitive—and the most ethical—company on earth, and if we're not, we're going to find out why, who did it, why they did it, and take action.

Yet, Welch is asked, does he feel he puts too much pressure on his managers who in turn feel forced to commit transgressions in order to achieve? He answers by offering an example from scholastic life. Some students get A's, some get C's. Who cheats more, the A students or the C's? Welch asks:

I don't think there's a higher percentage of A's that steal, cheat, and do other things in school versus those who are C's. I don't think that the bottom ten have a better record on ethics than the top ten. I just don't buy it.

Perhaps the real reason Welch has gone unscathed over the years has to do with the subject Welch hates to talk about—the numbers. The fact is that GE's numbers—its revenues and earnings—have been nothing short of remarkable, and have rarely been affected by the scandals. Since no harm has come to the company, there has been little motivation for anyone to hold the chairman's feet to the fire. In addition, Welch has persuaded everyone—justifiably—that he is above the fray, that he has not been personally involved with any of the ethical lapses that have plagued GE.

So the real lesson here is that if you're running a company, particularly a good-sized one, some sort of ethical breach is probably inevitable. In order to keep matters from getting out of hand, you may want to deal with the problem head on: fire the violator, let others know that any similar breach will be treated the same way, and if you're not personally involved, let the world know that as soon as possible. That's the Jack Welch Way. For him and for GE, it has been an uncannily effective method of dealing with adversity and scandal.

Jack Welch Deals with the Next Generation

"The ability to energize is the ingredient that counts."

*F*ORTUNE MAGAZINE calls General Electric's management institute at Crotonville "the Harvard of Corporate America," and with good reason. It is the place where the company's junior and senior managers discuss, debate, create, and recreate GE's vaunted management style and techniques. A 50-acre campus nestled in the Hudson Valley of New York, it is a brainstorming center for GE's senior managers and a center of education for junior managers. The world's first major corporate business school, Crotonville has something of a split personality: to an outsider, it feels like something between a fraternityless college campus and a superluxurious army training center.

A Boot Camp for Executives

General Electric purchased the property, which was first a farm and then an artist's colony, in the 1950s. To the people at General Electric, Crotonville is far more than some obscure location on a New York State map. The openness of the place and the ever-present discourse that takes place within its halls make it a metaphor for the company itself: a multifaceted boot camp for GE executives who engage in a continuous debate on everything from good management technique to the ever-changing state of the competitive global arena. GE executives make the point that Crotonville is unique. While the majority of other businesses routinely summon senior executives from the United States—and around the world—to seminars and retreats like Crotonville, far fewer companies summon junior executives and provide them with such extensive coursework; fewer still provide such lengthy and constant exposure to the bosses and senior management.

While Crotonville does offers courses, it is not the typical old-style classroom technique in which students sit upright, busily scribbling notes as some self-absorbed lecturer delivers two-hour monologues. The key word at Crotonville is "confrontation." The whole idea of the place is to get open, candid interaction going between and among GE personnel. Senior executives, when they show up at Crotonville, expect to be subjected to close scrutiny. Junior executives are given the oppor-tunity—and responsibility, as it is a badge of courage—to point out all sorts of things to their bosses that could improve the company. That's why stiff formality is nowhere in evidence at Crotonville. Jack Welch wants to keep the place as boundaryless as possible so that people at all levels of the hierarchy can mix, mingle, cajole, exchange ideas, and ulti-mately learn from one another.

Crotonville is certainly not restricted to the American GE staffers, and it is not unusual to find Asian, European, and many other non-U.S. managers in a single Crotonville course. The informal, confrontational style that defines Crotonville is hardest on them, since most come from cultures that discourage junior members of a business from speaking out. They are taught to keep their noses to the grindstone, take orders from the bosses, and keep their mouths shut. That's a far cry from the GE training center, which encourages, even demands, that staffers come prepared to take on conventional wisdom and their bosses at the same time. But after a short while, even they get the point, and ulti-mately contribute to the combative intellectual discussion that is the key to Crotonville.

Jack Welch loves Crotonville. He loves everything about it—the openness of the place, the confrontational style of debate, and most of all, the glimpse it gives him into what is really going on inside the company. Crotonville provides Welch with the perfect forum for imparting his business insights to large numbers of employees. So it's really no surprise that the chairman of the world's most valuable company visits its training nucleus some twelve times a year. During his monthly visits he speaks to employees both in and out of the classroom, but he far prefers the more informal postlecture receptions that afford him the chance to rub elbows one-on-one with the staff.

He feels more at home at Crotonville than at any other GE location, including the confines of his office at Fairfield headquarters. Since he's always eager to interact with GE personnel, and even more eager to deliver talks on his business strategies and philosophies, Crotonville is tailor-made for Welch's "eyeball-to-eyeball" approach. Somehow GE's more traditional office buildings aren't nearly as conducive to that open, no-holds-barred approach.

Since Welch welcomes confrontation and debate, he can hardly take exception when an employee hurls a tough question his way. After all, he wrote the book on facing reality, so he doesn't mind when the occasional eager beaver throws cold water in his face with a particularly tough or embarrassing question. The GE chairman gives as good as he gets, and he looks forward to mixing it up with the staff during those Crotonville visits and talks.

But he's not going to Crotonville simply to lecture and deliver sermons on his business philosophies. Sure, that's a big part of it. But, he also goes there to learn as well. Walter Wriston, a longtime GE board member, once told Welch something that he never forgot: that as chairman and CEO, Welch will always be the last to know when something is going on in the company. Welch thinks of Crotonville as the perfect place to prove Wriston wrong.

A Family Secret

With so much candid talk and free-flowing dialogue at Crotonville, Welch tries to keep the place something of a family secret. He is perfectly willing to talk about it, and sometimes goes on about the place for long stretches at a time, but that's where he draws the line. He has shrouded the place in secrecy and forbids outsiders such as journalists and authors from entering its hallowed halls—for good reason. He wants GE employees to feel uninhibited at Crotonville. He wants them to be confident that their candid talk won't end up in the next day's newspapers.

So while journalists and authors have had access to most other parts of GE, Welch has kept Crotonville largely out of bounds. He did make a rare exception in 1991, taking this author along with him to observe a class he was teaching. He made a second exception, allowing the same author to tag along when he visited Crotonville in the fall of 1997. The same set of rigid conditions laid down for the first visit were still in effect for this second one. No tape recorder or laptop computer allowed. Otherwise, the class would discover that a writer was in their midst. Taking notes longhand was permitted, however.

On this day, September 24, Welch would be talking for three hours to a group of seventy senior executives who had been identified as "high pots": candidates with high potential for even bigger jobs at GE.

They were attending the three-week course in manager develop-ment where they would acquire skills that would enable them to run one of GE's businesses. According to the syllabus, "Participants develop executive skills in relation to key business issues, such as developing business strategy, competing globally, diversity and globalization, lead-ing teams and change, and advancing customer satisfaction."

The visit to Crotonville begins in the lobby of GE's main building at Fairfield headquarters at precisely 1:40 P.M. Joyce Hergenhan, the vice president for corporate public relations, would be accompanying Welch and the author on the helicopter ride to Crotonville. While we are waiting for Welch in the lobby, she adds to the previously announced list of ground rules: There can be no mention in the book of any coun-tries or GE customers referred to by Welch in his presentation.

Precisely at 1:45 P.M. Welch appears in the lobby carrying a small attaché case containing the slides he planned to use in his teaching stint. Wearing a coat and tie, he almost apologizes for his formal attire by mentioning that he has just come from a series of meetings. He is friendly and warm and ducks quickly into the waiting car. We join the chairman in the sedan and minutes later arrive at another part of GE headquarters, the company's helipad.

At precisely 1:50 P.M. the helicopter lifts off. Airplane-size bags of pretzels and snacks are on the seat across from Welch. He removes the items from the seat, indicating that I should sit there. The entire heli-copter ride lasts no more than fifteen minutes (by car, it takes a bit over an hour), and we are able to take in some spectacular fall scenery en route.

Welch seems genuinely excited by the upcoming visit. In his early days as CEO, he could have closed Crotonville. He could have deemed it irrelevant, a costly relic of the past. But, like his predecessors, he understood that it had the same potential for spreading his message. Even as he was downsizing the company in the early 1980s, he invested heavily in the place. (GE still spends $800 million a year on its various training and educational programs at Crotonville and elsewhere.)

Shouting above the din of the helicopter engine, I ask Welch if it might have been better if Crotonville were closer to Fairfield, given how important the Leadership Development Center is to GE. No, he said without a moment's hesitation, "I like it some distance from us. It's much better." He chose not to explain himself, but I assume he meant, At Fairfield, we run the company. I wouldn't want to mix that with *thinking about* how to run the company as effectively as possible.

The chairman peppers me with questions. Who had I seen at GE thus far? In what ways did the company seem different to me from six years ago? He listens intently to my answers, which I purposely kept short. I wanted to get back to interviewing *him*.

Into the Pit

The helicopter touches down at 2:05 P.M. A car awaits us, and we are driven the few hundred yards to the building where the GE chairman will give his class. Joyce Hergenhan whispers in my ear: "He's Professor Welch today. Dr. Welch. Not Chairman Welch." (Welch actually is a "Dr." He has an undergraduate degree in chemical engineering from the University of Massachusetts, and a master's and a doctorate from the University of Illinois in the same field.)

Welch greets Steve Kerr cheerfully; Kerr is the man in charge of Crotonville. Welch is especially proud of having selected Kerr for the job: he views the former head of the USC Business School as the perfect man to run the Leadership Development Center.

The greetings take only a minute. Welch walks briskly into the main auditorium, more commonly known as The Pit. With its five horseshoe-shaped rows stacked one on top of the other, it has been carefully designed to evoke a certain mood. You sense only that this looks like thousands of other classrooms—with no suggestion of the confrontations that go on in this room all the time. Indeed, GE personnel have dubbed the room "The Pit" to indicate that whoever stands in front of an audience here is likely to face tough questioning. But does that include Jack Welch?

As Welch moved toward the bottom of The Pit, where a lectern and a white screen had been set up, I took a seat in the back of the room. I had been advised to dress casually—no coat or tie—and meld into the crowd.

The room is pretty sparse. No gaudy GE logos. No large pictures of Chairman Welch hanging from the walls. No cult of personality here—not even a portrait of Edison. Just a clock on the back wall and a world map on another.

The crowd grows quiet. You can practically feel the butterflies in the participants' stomachs. This is, after all, the day the boss is showing up—the man who makes the promotions and signs the paychecks. One-on-one with Jack Welch. Some are openly terrified; others try to pretend that they're not. How will the day turn out? Will the CEO lob missiles into the crowd—or will he be as gentle as a lamb? These are the questions gnawing at the seventy people anxiously waiting for the chairman to enter the room. He may be temporarily donning the mantle of professor, but everyone knows that he's the Chairman.

Two items have been placed next to each attendee: a bottle of mineral water and a large white card with the person's first name etched in big block letters (last name in smaller letters). Just the names. No titles. No way of telling if Jim or Jane is from GE Plastics or GE Medical Systems. Welch will soon find out.

The audience—middle-level executives with GE for roughly ten years, one-quarter of them women, nearly half non-Americans—is a key target group for Welch. Conveying his message to the senior executives has been a far easier task than getting the word out to junior-level managers. He doesn't give three-hour lectures to his business leaders. At least, not anymore. But he does come to Crotonville as many as twelve times a year to reach deep inside the company.

Let's Get Acquainted

Welch takes off his jacket, but keeps his tie on. He takes a seat in the second row off to the right side of the room. He announces that he wants to get to know everyone so when he calls on someone, he's going to ask for their names and what GE business they're in.

The first person he turns to gives his name and place of work.

Welch asks a question about the business.

A second person introduces himself.

This time Welch says simply, "Congratulations." An obvious reference to how well that person's business has performed in the last year.

A third person, a woman, says hello.

Welch asks the person if she knows so-and-so, who is a more senior executive at her business. Yes, she says, with a smile, a bit embarrassed at the mention of her boss.

A fourth person volunteers name and place of business.

Welch shifts uncomfortably in his chair. He seems to be hesitating about whether to say something. Then he speaks.

"Have you shipped a few?"

The reference is to some product the business makes.

"Not as many as we would have liked."

Well, at least he gets candor from the guy.

Another woman introduces herself.

Welch's eyes show a sparkle.

He notes that in a few weeks he'll be off to Asia for another one of his three-week jaunts to a host of countries, and he'll be stopping in to see a certain executive with whom GE does business.

Welch asks the person, "What's he [the executive] going to hit me with?" In other words, what sort of questions will he put to Welch?

A brief dialogue ensues, the woman indicates what issues the executive will likely want to discuss with the chairman.

Welch feels the meeting is progressing satisfactorily.

Sometimes a Welch comment evokes huge laughter from the audience. A nervous kind of laughter. The kind you express in relief when you realize that the boss won't bite after all.

One member of the audience, who works in purchasing at GE Plastics, is caught off guard when the chairman asks him "Has benzene gone up?"

Welch is asking if the price of this raw material used at Plastics had risen lately.

"I don't know."

More candor.

"You've been down here too long."

Candor greeted by the Welch wit.

The chairman urges the class to be as candid as possible with him. He tells them that if they don't talk honestly to him during the next three hours, he might as well go home now. And he seems to mean it. A few times during the afternoon he repeats, "I hope I'm not offending anyone. We're trying to have a straight discussion here."

Someone introduces himself as working in Public Affairs at a certain GE business.

Welch grows impatient.

"We don't need public affairs, we need sales."

"Amen," says the Public Affairs man. "You're preaching to the choir."

The crowd laughs. Welch's remark, had it been made by some other business leader, might have seemed harsh, brutal. Coming from Welch, it is merely . . . candid.

Another man introduces himself as playing a major role in GE's new quality initiative.

Welch shows enormous interest in him. He fires question after question at him. How are you doing? What are the savings you're reaping from the program? It's clear that Jack Welch is zealous to the point of obsession with the current quality initiative.

One after another, the CEO of General Electric speaks to the audience. Never patronizing. Never belittling. He exhibits enormous patience with everyone. For their part, no one in the audience seems intimidated by him. They treat him with respect, but not awe, not undue reverence. He creates an informal atmosphere, and the audience picks up on that quickly. They call him Jack. Never Mr. Welch.

He seems genuinely interested in what they have to say, and they respond positively to that. But they understand that he has not come to listen to them lecture. Their comments are brief and to the point.

When Welch asks them tough questions about their businesses, they reply candidly, "Things are going well" or "Things are not going well." Once, after Welch has mentioned one of his patented business strategies, he elicits more candor than he bargained for: one person explains why that particular strategy won't work in his business. Welch doesn't get defensive or bark out some canned response. Instead, he listens and stares at the person. He has not come to argue. He has come to give his opinions and to explain his thoughts. It is OK to disagree.

When he hears good news, he takes obvious pride. When he hears bad news, he makes sure to convey the impression that he accepts the bad with the good. That's facing reality. He can't let the audience feel that he doesn't want to hear bad news.

He wants to be encouraging.

A woman introduces herself and Welch asks, "Did you take so-and-so's [he mentions the person's name] job?"

"Yes," answers the employee, stunned that Welch actually knows her predecessor.

"Congratulations. It's a tough job. Are you getting a lot of support?"

"Yes."

When someone mentions a certain GE business, Welch talks about the new leaders coming into that business. "You'll find him [one of the new leaders] to be extremely appealing and smart as hell," he says. Of another new appointment, he says with obvious affection for the man, "Now he's going to be tested. We'll see how he does."

Finally, Welch wraps up the opening phase of the class. He's been in the room thirty minutes and hasn't even begun his main presentation. But he's met everyone and had at least one conversation with almost everyone. He's demonstrated a vast working knowledge of the business, but at the same time makes it clear that he wants to learn even more about GE from the audience. His approach is friendly, and he seems genuinely pleased to have this direct, personal contact with GE personnel.

The mood in the room has shifted: fewer butterflies, more self-confidence, and even some laughter.

Who would have guessed?

Becoming a Leader

Welch moves over to the slide projector, places the first slide on it, looks at the white screen behind him, and laughs. "I could have written that same chart seventeen years ago." The room erupts in laughter.

He's there to tell the audience what leadership is all about. No other subject in business is closer to Jack Welch's heart. He has given much thought to the concept of leadership for decades. For the last sixteen years, he's had the chance to put many of his leadership ideas to the test, and the bottom-line results have been remarkable. The public's reaction to Welch and his leadership has been extraordinary. He is routinely described as one of the country's most powerful and impressive leaders. So the GE chairman believes, quite correctly, that he has something meaningful to say about what makes a good business leader—and what does not.

He informs the audience that recently he's made the same presentation both to the GE board and to a group of financial analysts. He's proud of that, proud that he delivers the same message to whatever audience he's addressing. Welch doesn't like to dwell on numbers; he prefers to talk values. If the company gets the values right, the numbers will follow. Yet, for someone that doesn't like numbers, he certainly loves charts. He knows he has to spend some time on numbers, and the charts help him to simplify the numbers. The charts show how incredibly well GE is doing. It's no wonder that Welch loves charts.

It's time for the main feature, the Welch lecture, and right from the start, it's obvious that Welch is going to play cheerleader and coach. He's there not just to teach leadership, but to turn the audience into better GE leaders.

During the introductory period some in the audience had discussed the problems that exist in the businesses back home; Welch seemed perturbed that the tone had become too gloomy. "You may have individual problems," he says to the audience, "but together you're on a helluva team. The ball is moving." He holds a pencil in his hand. He occasionally takes a sip of water. "The growth shouldn't be in your mind. As a company, we're growing like hell. You should be able to talk about this [growth] even as you struggle in your own world." In other words, I want you to become cheerleaders for the company when you get back home.

He then launches into a discussion of how GE grows. He notes proudly that GE recently acquired Woodchester Investments of Ireland for $862 million in the largest corporate takeover in Irish history. Woodchester is one of Ireland's biggest financial services companies and specializes in auto and equipment leasing, installment credit, and other businesses in Ireland and Britain. While the acquisition gives GE an additional $862 million in revenues, Welch doesn't want the audience to think that the company should rely exclusively on acquisitions to achieve growth. It's up to GE's businesses to run themselves better, he says, and not just acquire new businesses to get earnings. Still, acquisitions can play an important role in the GE growth formula.

As he speaks there's not a peep in the audience. Everyone's eyes are glued to the speaker. No one shuffles restlessly in his or her seat. No one glances at a watch. After all, the chairman is speaking.

He brings up the fact that GE is evolving into more of a service-oriented company. But he's careful to warn that "we're not getting out of manufacturing. If we don't have good products, we won't have good services."

Since this is a class in leadership development, the class has prepared some questions in advance for their "leader" to answer. These seemed to be tough questions that participants had wrestled with, but couldn't answer.

Someone throws out the first question: How do we blend the need for employee mobility with long-term customer relationships? Put another way (as I did in my mind), How do we keep customers happy when their GE contacts keep moving on to different parts of the company?

Welch doesn't love the question, and thinks even less of the person's assumption. He doesn't feel that the way to keep customers is to develop close relationships with them.

As for employee mobility, he definitely favors the idea. "Do you want to be in the same job forever?" he asks the audience.

"No," the crowd roars.

"It's a crazy question," Welch says. "It's a lifelong problem. I don't have a solution. Does anyone have a solution?"

Amazingly, someone in the audience raises his hand. "You're a great example," he says to Welch. "How long have you been in the same job?"

The answer is sixteen years, of course. But then, everyone in the room knew that.

"I topped out early," Welch quips, getting a huge laugh, not answering the question, but lightening the mood.

Then, more seriously, Welch sums up: "When you've got people in a job for fifteen years, they get stale. They're dead. Only they don't know it." By now, Welch is shouting.

There are other questions put to Welch. As GE globalizes, is it optimizing specific country knowledge across the boundaries? How could transitions in job changes be made more smoothly?

As for the first question, the chairman has few specifics to offer. On the second, he indicates that it is his responsibility to take care of the transitions at the top. "But it's up to you to handle the transitions at your level. I can't do beans about that." The topic of his own succession—which is some three years away—comes up. He obviously isn't going to dwell on that topic. All he would say is, "If we do it right, you won't see a blip."

Welch spends most of the remaining time defining what makes a good business leader. First of all, a business leader has to be able to make solid judgments about personnel. "My whole job," Welch tells the audience, "is people. I can't design an engine. I have to bet on people. I'm not like Andy Grove at Intel. He knows how to make a chip. I know I couldn't add anything to a refrigerator. The CEOs of car companies are car guys, so they do product reviews. . . . I don't get involved in appliances, plastics pricing. I'm more of a coach. I'll get involved in acquisitions a great deal, and people. I probably meddle in NBC more than I should." That last remark about NBC is made in an offhand way, but, if pressed, Welch would probably say that his "meddling" had been necessary: NBC had to cut costs and expand into other areas, so that explains his interfering in network affairs.

Welch next addresses the issue of stock options. He's proud that so many in the company (27,000 at last count) are receiving stock options. The GE executive who owns stock options is more likely to care about the company as a whole, since his or her financial future is linked directly to the company's financial future.

He openly admits that stock options are one of his greatest "weapons": by distributing them selectively to certain managers and leaders, he can be sure that his ideas will be carried out. He doesn't believe in handing out options as if they were Christmas candy. He much prefers giving them to those who are helping to advance his favorite management initiative, currently, the companywide quality program.

Keep the A's, Nurture the B's, Discard the C's

For the next half-hour, Welch works with the class to define the characteristics of a great business leader.

"The most important job you have is 'growing' your people, giving them a chance to reach their dreams. Your problem is that you won't face the decision to get A's around you all the time." Welch divides leaders into A's, B's, and C's: A's he wants to keep; B's he wants to nurture; C's he wants to get rid of.

Welch says that a leader has to have a vision, has to be able to articulate that vision and drive its implementation throughout the organization. Being able to articulate the vision "is where energy comes in. You cannot say your vision enough times. You have to bore yourself silly." Many managers do everything but drive the implementation. "This is where the edge comes in. Edge is all about making a decision. You may have had a great vision, but you need the courage to have the edge.

"If people have the right values, you give them a second chance. This is a numbers culture. That's the stamp of approval. That gets you another look. This is a performance-driven culture. The great leader without managerial skills runs into trouble. A lot of it is in recycling. There is nothing worse than a manager who sits on his butt counting nickels and dimes and catching people doing things.

"You don't say 'I hope to do this.' You *do* things. You *make it happen.* It's becoming clear that the ability to energize is the ingredient that counts."

It's 5 P.M. and Welch is finishing up. He's demonstrated great stamina, and at the same time has dished out plenty of wisdom. He seems to be thrilled with his performance. He never seemed to grow weary, despite the open-heart surgery of two and a half years earlier. When the three-hour talk ends, he announces that he plans to stay on and have dinner with the group: Professor Welch may be through for the day, but Chairman Welch is ready to keep talking. The seventy members of the audience gather with Welch for a reception in the foyer just outside The Pit. Welch finds the organizer and says he prefers to have drinks outside, and as the group makes its way to the outside terrace, Joyce Hergenhan speculates that Welch will never get to dinner. Everyone will want a five-minute one-on-one with the chairman, so the reception will just go on and on.

What are we to learn from our day with Professor Welch? It is clear that he regards honest, open, even confrontational debate as an essential ingredient of every good organization. He also believes that the folks closest to the businesses—and closest to the customers—can teach the leader a great deal about the business. One fact is abundantly clear: Jack Welch and GE place a great deal of value on training, and back that commitment up by investing heavily in its vital function. The class that I observed was part of a three-week course; that means those executives would be away from their businesses for almost a month. Now, that's commitment, and it's only the tip of the iceberg.

So if you're a manager in an organization, think about the last time your company sent you or a colleague away for three straight weeks of training. If you are the leader of an organization, think about what your company can do to better train and inculcate the values of the company into the hearts and minds of your troops. It doesn't have to be a lavish, three-week affair, and you don't even need a helicopter to inject a bit of the GE Way into your organization. In fact, you may want to start off smaller and simpler, with some honest-to-goodness open dialogue.

Jack Welch's Vision for the Millennium

"People always overestimate how complex business is. This isn't rocket science."

Bolstering General Electric

"I want GE to develop a big-company body in a small-company soul."

F OR THE LAST SEVENTEEN YEARS, one man has charted the course of General Electric and left his indelible mark on the House That Edison Built. Jack Welch *is* General Electric, and so much of what the company is about is due to him. But what will GE become when Jack Welch retires in two years? What will the company's goals and values be in five years? In a decade?

While no one could have predicted how much GE would change when Welch took the reins in 1981, there is every reason to believe that a post-Welch General Electric will resemble the present company in many important ways. For one thing, the Chairman will likely choose a successor who shares his vision and subscribes to the same business values as he does. To most GE watchers this comes as no surprise, since the CEO has made his value system required reading for his business leaders.

Is it safe to assume, then, that the new chairman and CEO will be a Jack Welch clone? In many ways, yes. One can expect the new leader to share the present CEO's desire for an open, candid, boundaryless company, one that promotes a learning culture. Yet things will undoubtedly be different. Welch himself warns that a new chairman will inevitably take steps that he would not have taken. What both Welch and his successor will inevitably share is a conviction that GE must not stand still:

> **The last sixteen years of revenue and earnings growth are already history. We have no interest in what has already passed. It is impossible for a company to always stay still. It must always expand or decline. We invest our management resources in fields where we can expect growth and we strive for expansion. Growth is the engine of the future.**

Welch has increased the value of GE by more than $200 billion. Would it be possible to do just as well during the next decade? "Absolutely," he says. "Much better. Our growth rate is accelerating. Take a look at the figures for GE Plastics in Europe—an average of 27 percent annual growth since 1993—and at the height of the European recession! So just imagine, if the governments inject money to relaunch their economies, the trend will be even higher.

No Limits to Growth?

But are there no limits in GE's growth? Welch says emphatically there are none: "As early as the eighties people used to say to me again and again that I had finally squeezed the lemon dry. Look at where we are today. My people grow with their responsibilities. Jack Welch grows every day, the whole company is growing because we have such a productive atmosphere. There are no limits to productivity; we will never run out of ideas!"

Might GE enter new businesses and exit present ones while Welch is still running the show? Newspaper articles in early 1998 predicted that Welch planned to launch a $2 billion restructuring drive later in the year, but the GE chairman was silent on the subject.

He was sure of one thing about the future of GE, however, and was not afraid to talk about it. He would not be taking the company into the field of telecommunications, even though it has been one of the hottest fields of the 1990s. Says Welch: "Remember that we don't just manage twelve business divisions. GE Capital alone has twenty-seven different sectors. In total, we control more than fifty. Additionally, it makes it easier for the Annual Report, but you've still got to manage it all. As for telecommunications, it's not for me. Far too many large players already have a stake. The sector's much too crowded."

No matter which direction a new GE takes, Welch insists that it must stay intact. Spinning off businesses is simply out of the question. In the 1995 Annual Report, Welch had noted that one of the hot trends of the moment was rushing to break up multibusiness companies and "spin off" their components. The theory was that the cumbersome size of a megacorporation—as well as its diversity—inhibited the company's competitiveness. With GE as the world's largest multibusiness company, many asked when GE would begin to spin off businesses. The CEO's reply was sharp and to the point: "The short answer is that we're not. We've spent more than a decade getting bigger and faster and more competitive, and we intend to continue. Breaking up is the right answer for some big companies. For us it is the wrong answer."

Judging by GE's trajectory in the late 1990s, it's likely that it will resemble a service business in the new millennium, not a manufacturing company. At the start of the 1990s, the company's profits and revenues relied largely on hardware sales (turbines, electrical transformers, plastic hardware, aircraft engines, etc.). But by the year 2000, 80 percent of profits and 70 percent of revenues should come from services. GE Capital is sure to play the leading role in the company's shift to a service-oriented organization, but all other businesses will be making a contribution.

It seems likely that GE Capital will continue to represent a large share of overall profits. In fact, its growth potential is nothing short of remarkable; it may grow from producing 38 percent of GE's total profits in 1996 to producing more than half by the year 2000.

And globalization will continue to make its mark on the company. Even if GE's overseas businesses do not yet enjoy the standing of other large American firms such as Coca-Cola and IBM, overseas sales are soon likely to account for half of GE's revenues—compared to only 23 percent in the summer of 1987.

Make Things Simpler

For his remaining time in the CEO's chair, Welch strives to make everything within GE's businesses simpler. He explains:

For the next couple of years, we'll be focusing very hard on simplifying. On getting simpler with communication with each other. With presentations. With products. We'll concentrate on products that have fewer parts and simpler designs. Business tends to overcomplicate things—most of life tends to overcomplicate things. So we're going to be driving across our three values— boundaryless, speed, and stretch—a genuine pressure and challenge to simplify. We think simplification is the next goal in making our revolution work.

He gave some examples. In 1993, the Toshiba camcorder had 1,000 parts, but by 1995 it had reduced that number to half. GE's current washing machines had 60 percent fewer parts than earlier models; making such items simpler meant less maintenance and more use of standard parts.

Welch wants business presentations to become simpler as well:

Too often they're too complicated. Everyone wants to put all the data that they can think of on a page. My idea is, simplify it. Enrich the language; that carries the day, not the paper. There's no tradeoff in terms of the information content, not for me, because I can't do anything with all the information. It doesn't help most people at the next level to have all that data. What they need to know is, What are the strategic questions I have to answer? What are the variables?

Welch wants GE to keep stressing high involvement for its personnel:

I want GE to be a company where everyone is involved. It's an ever-increasing and intensely global world today. The only way you're going to win is by involving everyone in the enterprise. The challenge of management today is to ensure that no one comes to work in a dull, mindless endeavor.

My challenge is to make GE the most exciting place, for people to fight to get in the door, to stay as long as possible, and to be a high-spirited, exciting place for people to hang around. So that every university graduate wants to get there. So that there's an

atmosphere where cronyism doesn't apply; where only the best make it on their merits.

As Welch expressed it in 1994, he wants GE to develop "a big-company body and a small-company soul." One that had the financial muscle and speed to deal with global competition.

GE in the Year 2020

When asked whether GE would look like it does today in twenty to thirty years, Welch said, "I doubt it. I hope it will be the greatest learning institution in the world. I hope it will always look outside. I want it to have curiosity. I want it to have soul. I think that's important. The soul of an informed organization, searching for a better idea everywhere, everyday, is the heart of what this is all about. Now you can add quality to it; you can add services to it. The soul of it is that idea. People searching for better ideas every day and being encouraged, to be cheered on by it; rewarded by it."

Paolo Fresco believes that Welch's greatest legacy will be the openness and boundarylessness that will continue to permeate GE down through the years. "What we call the ability to instill the spirit of small companies in the body of a giant. Jack has done two things: he has been able to keep the youthfulness, the creativity, the intellectual stimuli that are typical of entrepreneurial organizations. And he has been able through the sharing of best practices to get the best out of being big. It's this combination that has remained the best model for large, multiline companies."

Unquestionably, quality will be the key strategic initiative at GE for the next five to ten years, thanks to Welch. As he noted in his January 1997 speech to the operating managers, he expects all of GE's leadership to be black belt–trained by the year 2000. And GE planned to hire only black belt–trained personnel. He described the quality program as GE's central activity, its future.

In the late 1990s the GE workforce is expanding once again. This is in stark contrast to the early Welch period of the 1980s, when the chairman laid off 100,000 people as part of his overall company restructuring. Years later, Welch has no regrets. In 1994 he told a reporter:

Cutting people is the lousiest part of the job. I became "Neutron Jack" in the early 1980s, like the bomb that destroys people but leaves the buildings intact, because I was the first one to do it. And now IBM is laying off 150,000 people and they're being applauded.

Every day you read in the paper that someone's laying off 6,000 or 8,000, or 10,000. We did that ten years ago. So what we have here today are mostly survivors of a difficult battle. If I talked to the people who were laid off, I'd get a different story. But healthy companies are good for society. Fat, sloppy institutions add nothing to a society. Growth, eliminating waste, continuing to make things better—*that's* what's good for a country."

The questioner noted that Japanese executives often say, "GE can do things its way and we'll do things our way because we're different." "I don't think we're all that different," Welch responded. "But some executives still think of their old businesses as shrines. What I mean by that is that a business that may be number five or six in the market can be weak and some executives are still holding onto the shrine. That's an issue facing Japanese manufacturing. What do you think the employees feel like in a subsidiary that's number six in the market? They're not excited. Holding on to number six is just holding on to the past."

A reporter noted in July 1997 that "as the number of employees was halved, the share price of GE increased almost twentyfold." He then asked whether the wallets of the shareholders were more important to Welch than the families of his former employees.

"When we started restructuring General Electric it was easy for everyone to find a new job," said Welch. "If we had waited, it would have been worse for everyone. In a global economy you cannot manage a company in a paternalistic way just because it feels better. If you don't sort things out in good time they will eventually explode in your face. Then you have to become brutal and cruel. . . . Because we started [downsizing] in good time, we have never slipped into the red. Today we are employing again. In the last two years we have taken on as many as 30,000."

Quality and Service

Quality and service are taking center stage at General Electric as it nears the millennium. And financial analysts are quite pleased that a company of GE's size was making the effort to reinvent itself. Here, for example, is what Lehman Brothers analyst Robert T. Cornell wrote in late 1997:

> **What has to be truly amazing to GE watchers is how quickly GE can install such an in-depth system as Six Sigma. In our view, the fact that GE is getting this done is as much the story as Six Sigma itself. The scary thing for competition is that GE's culture can continue to make major changes. This is a key reason why we have to come to believe EPS growth can be sustained at 14–15 percent per year. Also at work is the go-global initiative that is a culture changer. Next up is the services initiative, which we view as GE's vehicle for premium growth past the year 2000. In Power Generation, for example, GE notes that its definition of the served market has expanded from $19 billion to $700 billion, with the expanded served markets mostly in value-added services. In an increasingly competitive world, GE notes that not only is the global value-added service market huge, but that a competitive advantage in services is more sustainable.**

Other analysts were equally respectful of GE's growth potential. Nicholas P. Heymann at NatWest Securities noted in a report he wrote in mid-1997:

> **We continue to strongly believe GE will prove to be one of the best-performing large-capitalization equities for the rest of this decade, and believe it remains especially prudent to hold at least a market weighting in GE's share. Rarely have we seen the momentum of a corporation of any size build the way GE's currently has caught fire.**
>
> **The dynamics driving the acceleration of GE's growth are very evident today: six sigma, a rapid shift to higher-margin, higher-growth aftermarket service and support revenues, accelerating**

international growth, and an all-out race through 2000 by all GE's operating managers to become the company's next chairman.

And Now for the $64,000 Question . . .

It is hard to avoid the subject of Welch's successor. People at GE know that the succession race is on. They know that in a few years the company might be a very different one, if only because the CEO won't be at the helm.

Welch will have a large say in choosing his successor. Chances of his staying on beyond November 2000 seem remote. The GE board might have good reason to ask him to stay on, but both the board and Welch appear firm in their resolve to adhere to the GE practice that a chairman and CEO retire at age sixty-five. Still, every once in a while, Welch shows a bit of ambivalence on the question of his departure, as this 1995 interview in *Business Today* showed: "There should be no reason for me to go home for chronological reasons," said Welch. "I have as much energy as anyone else. The fact that anybody goes home should be because they've run out of ideas. I'll go home in the next five years, yes, but I should go home when I'm still generating ideas. The day I go home, I'll disappear from that place and the person who comes in will do it their way."

Welch's comment is intriguing; it reveals something about Welch's love for the thrill of the game. Welch talks like the president of a country nearing the end of his term. It's obvious that Welch is not looking forward to stepping down. While these comments are telling, they have gotten lost in the shuffle, perhaps because the article was published so far from home; or maybe because no one believes the chairman would actually stick around beyond 2000.

When asked what he was looking for in a successor. Welch replied that while he couldn't say beforehand *whom* he would select, he thinks he knows *what kind of person* he will choose:

I want somebody with incredible energy who can excite others, who can define their vision, who finds change fun and doesn't get paralyzed by it. I want somebody who feels comfortable in Delhi or Denver. I mean, somebody who *really* feels comfortable and can talk to all kinds of people. I don't know what the world's

going to be; all I know is it's going to be nothing like it is today. It's going to be faster; information's going to be everywhere. I've seen our jobs—my job is three times as fast as it was.

The Obsession

Welch admits that the question of succession is constantly on his mind:

It's like an obsession. I'm always talking about it with Paolo Fresco, even when we go out for a drink. What's so-and-so like, can he take a balanced view of things or to what extent does he bring in new ideas? It's on my mind constantly, and finding the right person is the most important thing I can do for my group at the moment.

Has he made his choice?

I'm not going to tell you. . . . No, of course not. But it's not just up to me. I will make a recommendation. In any case, an external solution is out of the question. You've seen all the talent I've got at my fingertips. Why should I look around for someone elsewhere?

Is he worried about GE splitting up?

If my successor breaks the company up, I will have chosen a real son of a bitch! Okay? I will have made a huge error. It's true, GE Capital could survive on its own, like GE Plastics and the others. But if someone did that, they obviously wouldn't have appreciated the enormous advantages to be gained from this group. We have a vast laboratory. I know that it's not the trend in the United States, but some of these breakups are stupid and nonsensical. The amount of talent you can develop in a group like ours is staggering. Everyone tells me about the disadvantages of conglomerates, but when are they going to understand that the strength of our organization lies in mutual development?

I have just spent a week listening to all my European managers. And, next week we will be devoting four days to rallying the best

of the ideas to all the group's divisions. But this can only work if you break down the barriers, and I can tell you that this is not the case in the majority of large firms. I can assure you that my successor will build something even bigger and better.

Choosing a successor is perplexing because Welch has to assure that there will be no mass exodus by the losing candidates. He expressed confidence that everyone would remain at GE:

Generally they're pretty good friends. There is a real collegial atmosphere here. People help each other. I hope whatever I do doesn't destroy that. I hope they have enough trust that the decision will be taken with the best of intentions. I have so many terrific people in this company, all of whom I like. I have a unique team of wonderful people.

When his predecessor, Reg Jones, was in charge, losing candidates became so embittered at not being selected that they left the company. Because bonuses were not tied to the company's overall performance back then, they had little incentive to increase the company's bottom line. With no stock options and with GE's stock lethargic, business leaders only had incentive to care about their individual performance. Now, says Welch:

I come with a group of people who are used to getting along, who are used to liking each other, who are used to supporting each other. Who are used to helping each other. It doesn't mean they don't have ambition personally. Reg had warring factions because the system was set up to encourage warring factions. There was no encouragement. There was no motivation to be supportive of the total. It was run as a decentralized company. And all you had to do was to take care of your own numbers.

What do we know about a post-Welch General Electric? We know it will be led by a GE veteran; Welch is adamant about not bringing in an outsider.

We know that the new CEO will possess many of Jack Welch's qualities, but he will be different too. He will be younger, for one thing (yes, it will be a man), and less experienced. But eager, oh so eager, to prove that he is capable of filling the shoes of John Francis Welch.

We know that the new leader will be cautious at the outset—just as Jack Welch was when he took over in 1981. And with good reason. If Jack Welch was assailed in his day for tampering with "a good thing," his successor will be raked over the coals for tampering too much with the House That Jack Built.

Yet, we can be reasonably certain that the new leader, once he gains some self-confidence, will begin to wonder, What should I change here? What's really happening out there in the business environment? He probably won't ask, What would Jack do? He'll know that the question is pointless. No one could say what Jack would do. Instead, the new leader will ask, What do we have to do to keep this place the most competitive enterprise on earth?

Advice for Other Companies

"Focus on innovation. Produce more for less through intellectual capital."

P EOPLE NATURALLY HOPE that Jack Welch will provide a road map for the future of American business. This is the man, after all, who seems to read the signs along the competitive landscape as well as anyone. He is the CEO who correctly identified the Japanese storm clouds gathering over the American horizon. And he was the one man who realized how vital it was to revamp his company, when all others wanted to stand pat. This is someone who has a great deal to say about issues that are relevant to *every* part of corporate America.

He never comes out and says it directly, but Jack Welch appears to believe that other companies would be smart to emulate his style and business strategies.

So most of the advice he gives to other companies will sound familiar.

Just as he favors increasing productivity at GE, he is a firm believer in other enterprises concentrating on productivity. Welch asserts that the key to survival for other companies will be their ability to boost productivity well beyond the traditional levels of the past. Annual productivity increases of 6 percent will not be enough. To remain truly competitive, companies will have to see increases of 8 to 9 percent a year. (GE's productivity growth rate was running in the 6 percent range at the end of the 1980s; in 1997 it was a bit over 4 percent.)

Not surprisingly, Jack Welch believes that other companies can benefit from speeding up their business processes. Toward the end of 1996, he said:

> **In today's world, moderation and obsessions with the past lead to massive losses. Americans' impatience in getting results quickly was a disadvantage in the 1970s, but it's now a plus.**

> **The world is becoming more information-intensive, and decision-making and quick responses are indispensable weapons. In the twenty-first century, change will be even quicker. The old advantages of patience, paternalism, and respect for tradition are now hurdles in a world that is rapidly changing. . . .**

> **There are no signs of inflation in the United States even though we've continued to grow over the past five years. New employment opportunities with high wages have emerged, and the unemployment rate is at a historical low. But I insist that we need even higher growth. That's because only growth can solve all kinds of problems.**

> **The United States is amid an intensive information revolution. Some old jobs may disappear in the process. That's why we need even higher growth, not just 2 percent or 2.5 percent.**

America and the World

Toward the end of 1997, I was able to spend nearly two hours with Jack Welch. That talk was the final interview in the series I had conducted with him for this book. He had begun the day in Crotonville, talking to GE managers. Originally, he had planned to take the helicopter to Fairfield headquarters in time for our meeting, but owing to the inclement weather, he was forced to make the trip from Crotonville by car, so our meeting was put off an hour. An hour into the interview, Welch excused himself to hold a pre-Christmas luncheon with members of the corporate executive office. We resumed in the afternoon for another hour or so. During one part of the interview I asked Welch what advice he would impart to other companies hoping to remain competitive in the decades to come.

I must confess that his answers surprised me. He didn't give me the usual Welchisms, such as "aim for simplicity" or "go for the quantum leap." Instead, Welch chose to answer with a broad view of the international economic scene. Specifically, he discussed the effects of currency shifts and their effect on the current state of world economies. This was about as far from "don't focus on the numbers" as one could get, and as I sat there, desperately hoping that the tape recorder would not run off its spool, I was reminded of something that is sometimes easy to forget when talking to Jack Welch. This man leads the most valuable company on earth, a $90 billion juggernaut whose annual sales exceeds the gross national product of many nations. GE has operations in dozens of countries, and currency shifts would certainly play an important role in determining the success of a particular GE business. But Welch views the role of currencies as even more important to the bigger economic picture:

I think these things come in waves and currencies are great equalizers. For example, in the eighties and the early nineties a lot of America's recovery was currency-driven. A lot of it was structure-driven by leveraged buyouts and financial markets that took out fat, and companies got a lot more productive and a lot better. But currency played an enormous role.

Don't forget the German deutsche mark went from 2.60 to 1.40. The Japanese yen went from 300, 290, to 90. Currencies are a great equalizer. Look at Europe today. Everyone was talking about Europe a year ago like it was the U.S. in the eighties. Remember the eighties? It was all going to be Germany and Japan—there was nothing left in America. That was the eighties thing.

The nineties thing is that it's all American. And the Germans are dead. Everyone's dead over there. Now the deutsche mark this morning was 1.81, up from 1.40. You know what that is? That's 30 percent less in labor costs and some materials than they cost nine months ago.

Then it was a matter of luck?

After sharing his thoughts on the effects of currency fluctuation, Welch shifted ground and returned to more familiar territory. It is apparent that Chairman Welch (or perhaps this was Dr. Welch) has particularly strong feelings about the value of education:

> **You have just got to constantly focus on innovation. And more competitors. You've got to constantly produce more for less through intellectual capital. I sat with our union workers, the United Auto Workers in Evandale, Ohio. I had roundtables with them when I went around to all the plants. And one guy looked at me and said, "Jack, I'm worried as hell about my son. Will my son have my job?" And I said, "I don't know if your job will be here." "Well, what should I tell my son?" I said, "You've got to get him a helluva education. And if I were you I'd get him involved in information technology. And I would be sure he got to college. And I would be sure he got good grades. I wouldn't be aiming him for your job because your job may or may not be here. But if your kid has the intellectual capital to play in this changing world—and you know one thing's for sure, there's going to be more information faster [then he'll do well]."**

> **My job today is ten times faster than it was five years ago. A hundred times. The pace is enormously quicker because of technology. So everyone has to be gearing themselves to a faster pace, to more competitiveness, to more intellectual capital. That's the game.**

> **Now the fundamentals have got to be more education. More information knowledge, faster speeds, more technology across the board. Those are the fundamentals. But Europe's not going to disappear. The U.S. isn't going to disappear. Asia isn't going to disappear.**

More Computers, Please

American companies, Welch believes, should also step up their investment in information technology:

During the sixties and seventies, the information function was often the abode of failed financial executives and was frequently mired down in the finance organization. . . . In the eighties things improved a bit. . . . Today information is understood as a competitive necessity, from resolving internal organizational issues to addressing market-based competitive realities.

Today in our company—and probably yours—information management is at the heart of everything we do! . . . Today, with advanced information systems and flat organizational structures, everyone has simultaneous access to the same information; everyone can be part of the game. We believe there is nothing more important in winning in today's global marketplace than getting everyone involved and using every brain in the organization.

Should the United States become less manufacturing-oriented, Welch was asked? No, he said. More service-oriented? Again his response was in the negative:

It's got to be a big combination. Andy Grove [CEO of Intel] is creating knowledge every day at Intel with faster chips. And he's creating hardware with massive intellectual capital. Bill Gates is creating intellectual capital with software every single day. You can call one service. You can call *both* services. But in the end manufacturing is what Andy Grove does. He makes chips. He spends billions of dollars on wafer factories. But it's all intellectual capital that's going into that manufacturing. When we're servicing a new engine on the wing of a plane and monitoring it in flight when it flies from Vancouver to New York, those are services. But if we weren't doing the engine and the advanced diagnostics and all that, we couldn't do the services.

People shouldn't ask, "Are you going to be out of manufacturing and into services?" If you are, you're dead. If you are going to be all services and no manufacturing, you're dead. If Bill Gates didn't have cooperation with Intel, his system wouldn't work on their chips. It's an integrated game.

A Word about Japan

Welch commented on the Japanese, noting how good they are in business:

> No other country in the world could take a currency penalty like Japan has paid for its success and survive. I call this a currency penalty. And you're still surviving. It's amazing how good Japan is. A lot of things are being said about Japan's difficulties, but the competition from other countries would evaporate overnight if you put the yen at 360 to the dollar. The idea of American companies becoming more competitive and Japanese companies becoming less competitive is wrong. If you change the currency rate, the situation changes overnight. Its success has brought Japan the need to improve.

But exchange rates won't change so easily, his questioner suggested:

> Yes, they will. If you can't fix your issues, the currency will weaken. A strong yen rate means you've demonstrated an ability to export and have a very positive current account. The yen will fall if you can't export anymore.
>
> Currency's a great equalizer. A lot of papers are saying how American companies and manufacturers are more competitive now. Yes, we're a lot better than we were, but we got a tremendous break through currencies. There's plenty of room for improvement.

And Welch explains why he believes that Germany's economic future is bright:

> Just you wait and see. Germany's industry is about to become unbelievably competitive once again. For me the Europe of today can be likened to the United States of the mid-eighties. At that time the newspapers were full of stories prophesying a gloomy end to America and a golden future for Europe and Japan. Just another five years, they said, then all is over and done with in the U.S.A.

But let me tell you that in five, seven, or ten years' time they will be writing stories about how powerful Europe is. You can already see how the deutsche mark is weakening, exports are growing, and companies are once again becoming profitable. . . . Europe has an enormous amount of well-educated, intelligent people. It has a survival instinct that has driven its people through the centuries. And it is so much older than America. The Europeans have suffered all kinds of wars and revolutions, and they will also survive this crisis. We have doubled our turnover in Europe in the last five years, right in the middle of the recessions. We have tripled our profit. What more do you want?

Are the Socialists a Problem?

Do the new socialists, Prime Minister Tony Blair in England and Prime Minister Lionel Jospin in France, bother him? Welch replies:

Politicians come and go. A flexible company like General Electric has to come to terms with that. What matters to us is what the country will be like in a few decades. And therefore it doesn't really matter whether the prime minister in 1997 was John Major or Tony Blair.

But couldn't socialist parties make life difficult for GE by demanding higher minimum wages?

There has, of course, been a shift to the left in Europe and this trend will continue. But nowhere do we have a government that is antibusiness. [Italian Prime Minister] Romano Prodi, for example, is doing an excellent job. And look at how the French stock exchange reacted after the election. Share prices went up.

Once, Welch complained that Germany was overregulated and inflexible. Yet, now he was buying up one German firm after the other. Has his view of Germany changed?

Germany is changing. Companies are restructuring all over the place, just as we did a few years ago. That presents a lot of good buying opportunities for us.

Don't the talks about creating a new currency for all of Europe worry Welch?

I don't know whether anything will come of it or not. The euro would, of course, make life easy for us because we would no longer have to protect ourselves from all kinds of exchange rate risks. But, basically, it doesn't matter one way or the other to us; we have done very well without the euro and I believe we will also do very well with it.

How does Welch explain the healthy state of the American economy?

This is a phenomenon that dates back ten years. There are two reasons: the weakness of the dollar, which helped us considerably; and the restructuring of the industry geared toward increased productivity and less bureaucracy. France and Germany are about to reap the same benefits. Thanks to their currency, they are able to increase their exports. In any case, the euro is not a threat to the United States. On the group level it will simplify local operations. But this was already part of our strategy. We have never been focused on the national markets. We've always considered Europe to be a single market.

In all of his remarks about the American and the world economy, Jack Welch had exercised a good deal of caution. He was careful not to proclaim excessive optimism about the future; however, he wasn't mired in gloom either. To truly improve itself, to increase its profitability, American business must get more productive and restructure when necessary. That, in a nutshell, was Welch's message. But it is important to note that Welch delivered these remarks against a backdrop of an American economy that was doing very well. As such, he did not seem overly alarmed. Soon, however, his tone would change. Soon he would look at the ominous international economic landscape and declare that General Electric, and the rest of the American economy, faced an enormous, new challenge that might well slow growth. What had changed so suddenly, and with such force? What had brought Jack Welch to express such warnings?

Epilogue

"You wouldn't want to field a Super Bowl team that didn't have the best athletes."

IT WAS EARLY JANUARY 1998. The 500 senior managers of General Electric had gathered for their annual two-day conference in Boca Raton, Florida. The highlight of the conference has always been Jack Welch's assessment of the company and his views of the challenges on GE's horizon. While the chairman has used the conference as a platform for launching new ideas, he views the meeting as an opportunity to energize his troops, get them on the right path, and make them aware of new economic realities. Presiding over GE's unprecedented era of growth, Welch usually sounded buoyant, uplifted by the previous year and optimistic about the next one. But this year was different. This time the chairman had some bad news for his managers: not about GE's financial performance, since as usual, that had been outstanding. In 1997, GE's revenues, profits, and income per share had shattered all records by racking up double-digit increases. GE's stock had soared by a phenomenal 48 percent in 1997; for the third straight year, it had increased by more than 40 percent.

Welch's message was about a new economic reality, one that had surfaced with little warning. For the past few months, the chairman had been reading the mounting warning signs of this inevitable new reality:

the major slide in commodity prices (copper, for example); falling bond interest rates; and perhaps most significantly, the growing crisis that was catching the attention of Federal Reserve chairman Alan Greenspan.

By late 1997 it had become clear to GE's chairman that the international economy was in trouble. It was entering a period of deflation, characterized by overcapacity and falling prices.

Not since the early 1980s, when he correctly called the rising wave of foreign competition, had Welch assessed the economic situation so ominously. But he was ready to tackle the issue head on, relying on his tried-and-true business doctrine that had served him well for over seventeen years.

In recognizing that deflation would become a major economic issue for GE in 1998, Welch was taking a dose of his own medicine and facing reality. Taking stock of the new business environment, Welch was convinced that he would have to take dramatic steps to deal with the looming crisis. Although the situation was serious, Welch wasn't panicked. He embraced change, knowing that it was sometimes essential so that GE could stay one step ahead of the problem. Having identified the new economic reality, Welch was ready to act decisively.

However sanguine Jack Welch had been about the American and European economies earlier in the 1990s, he was now convinced that the combination of the United States' new deflationary period and the 1997 Asian economic collapse represented a dire situation. As usual, Welch was not afraid to communicate the new reality to his managers when he proclaimed the economic situation "the most difficult scenario that most of us have ever faced."

While many theories existed about why the Asian economies had unraveled, Welch thought the most significant catalyst had been China's 1994 devaluation of its currency, which, he said, altered the international competitive landscape. While most of the news was bad, one small benefit accrued to GE immediately: It could export lightbulbs it produced in China more cheaply.

Whatever the actual cause of the collapse, the effect on GE and the rest of the American economy was clear: excessive capacity. "About everyone is producing more than they are consuming," he told his managers. "That's not a good situation." With the collapse of the Asian economies, currency values in Europe and Japan declined. The net result for the world economy, as Welch described it to his managers, was that the dollar was strengthening vis-à-vis industrialized Asia. Germany and Japan were becoming greater global exporters; with excess capacity, selling prices were coming under more and more pressure. Hence, Welch predicted low inflation rates and slower growth for the American economy. With the American market now the most attractive country for the increasingly competitive low-currency countries, the United States would come under tremendous import pressure. The implication for industry, and specifically for GE, were as follows:

Price-share management has never been more important. Never. Productivity is critical to counteract this enormous price pressure. Assets are going to be worth less, rather than more. So the asset efficiency, inventory turns, receivable turns have got to improve. P and E [plant and equipment expenditure] has got to be more carefully managed. . . . And we've got to expand the global niches like Europe, places where we can win.

With the rise in imports to the United States, everyone at GE will be under greater pressure, Welch predicted. This was not a time to be adding new costs. He urged his managers to consolidate their new acquisitions quickly.

Indicating how seriously he interpreted the Asian collapse and its worldwide economic effects, Welch ordered his managers to rip up the budgets they had composed only three months earlier, in order to take the new deflationary environment into account. Welch's decree showed how quickly GE could—and did—respond to the external environment. He asked for one page ("We don't need a book.") by the end of January. Net income would stay the same, but he wanted "different geography" as to how the managers would arrive at those figures, one "reflecting plans that reflect today's reality. Not the reality of three months ago when you put the [budgets] together. The test for us is not identifying deflation as an issue a couple of months ahead of everybody else. . . . The test is how fast can we do something about it. This is not an intellectual economic exercise. This is taking this data and jumping on it and [getting] ahead of the ball game."

With GE in uncharted waters, entering the toughest economic climate in a decade, Welch insisted that his managers work harder to meet their financial commitments:

> The one unacceptable comment from a GE leader in 1998 will be: "Prices are lower than we thought and we couldn't get costs out fast enough to make our commitments." Unacceptable. Unacceptable behavior—because prices *will* be lower than you're planning, so you better start taking action this week. We have a lot going for us. Our European strength will be a big help in 1998. Our services and acquisitions will give us real growth in 1998 and six sigma quality will be the way to overcome some of the pressures. Six sigma must define everything we do. Just as we wouldn't knowingly hire someone who was not boundaryless and we removed leaders who weren't boundaryless in the early nineties, the same will be true about quality in the future. Anyone not committed totally to six sigma, anyone not deeply into the quality commitment, won't be here as we enter the next century.

The Asian crisis wasn't the only item on the chairman's agenda that day in Boca Raton. He also felt it important to address the issue of integrity. For Welch and other GE officials, the less said or written about the company's problems with integrity, the better. So it was significant that the chairman included a discussion of the integrity issue, making a fresh plea to his managers to make sure that everyone behaved honestly:

> With our number one global reputation, [GE] is a perfect target. We've made numerous acquisitions of late. Tens of thousands of new employees are with us. They come from different backgrounds and different cultures. You must set the example. There's a new bar for you with these new acquisitions with lots of people. No winks. No looking the other way. You've got to be out in the front. We've got a new competitive environment that makes things tougher. There's excessive capacity in every industry, so the pressures are greater and we've got new employees— all ingredients that could cause us a problem, and for those of you with all these new employees, you've got to go out even further to get ahead of this particular issue.

Sparking Welch's comments on integrity in part was a new focus among attorneys on "consumer compliance" laws, which govern transactions between companies and customers, including advertising claims, product warranties, and truth-in-lending requirements. An increasing number of lawyers have been bringing lawsuits against companies like GE for failure to comply with these laws. Accordingly, Welch wanted to drive home the point that GE, in all of its businesses, had to scrupulously abide by both the letter and spirit of these laws. He wanted to avoid all the negatives that occur when GE people are found to be less than honest:

> **The press runs with it. The attorneys general run with it. What appears to be the norm, what appears to be standard practice, comes upon you as a bolt of lighting, a brutal shock to the system, to see the devastation that occurs from seemingly innocent people who are basically innocent, but the issues run away from them, and [to] see businesses potentially crater, careers crater, families injured, reputations soured. You just can't let it happen, and this wave of consumer compliance that's out there now, this enormous pressure is going to come down on every single business. We're not here to police you. We're here to go right to the core of your values—to be sure every one of you doesn't stain the person sitting beside you because you ended up with a violation of an issue of integrity.**

Welch concluded the two days of meetings in Florida with some tough talk on the art of leadership. In earlier years at lectures such as this one, he would take the time to expound on his definition of effective leadership. Managing less is managing more. Create a vision and spread it through your business. Avoid bureaucracy. Get boundaryless. Empower your workers. And so on. But Welch seemed to feel that his managers were beyond that, that they didn't need another talk brimming with management generalities. Instead, Welch opted to tackle a more specific aspect of leadership.

It was a subject that he felt strongly about, and one that he deemed vital to GE's future. It is interesting to note that Welch, when faced with a serious crisis, chose not to talk about one of his vintage strategies such as "fix, close, or sell," but instead selected a topic he felt was even more critical to GE: the quality of the GE workforce. When push comes to shove, he wanted his managers to have the courage—and the will—to hire and keep only the best performers, those motivated individuals capable of delivering Super Bowl results each and every day on the job.

The chairman knew that he was delivering this critical message to the right audience. Seated before him were the men and women who had the fates of thousands upon thousands of GE employees in their hands. They possessed the power to be career makers or career killers. Welch wanted them not to shy away from such power and responsibility, but to use it judiciously and effectively. He wanted them to turn themselves loose on all those who were performing below the lofty standards he had set for the company.

For weeks the business press had been speculating that something big was about to happen at GE: the Master of Restructuring was at it again, and another round of downsizing was imminent. Yet, until Welch spoke to his 500 managers that day in Boca Raton, it was not clear if there was any truth to the reports or what was behind the latest Welch initiative. Now, having identified the new economic reality, the CEO clearly felt that having his managers rewrite their budgets was simply not enough.

The reality of the situation was too daunting, and if GE was to maintain its competitive edge, it would need to have the very best people in place to order to compete effectively in this new, turbulent economy. Therefore, Welch urged all of his managers to make sure that GE had only the best performers in its ranks, and to jettison those who could not live up to Welch's standards.

The Jack Welch who showed up in Boca Raton on that sunny January morning was not the same man who had sized up his company all through 1997. It was as if he had made a New Year's resolution: I've got to get tougher. The environment out there is lousy, and it's going to stay that way for a while. I've got to look at this company with a fresh eye. I've got to make sure I've got the best team possible.

So he implored his managers to take a cold, hard look at their employees, and make some cold, hard decisions:

> **I want to remind you what I believe management leadership is all about. It's all about people. All about getting the very best. You wouldn't want to field a gymnastic team, a volleyball team, or a Super Bowl team that didn't have the best athletes. The same is**

true about business teams. The market is rewarding you like
Super Bowl winners or Olympic gold medalists. I know I have
such athletes reporting to me. I have no C's. And over the years
I've had some. Today none. Can you all say the same thing? Can
you put your team against my team? Are you proud of everyone
who reports to you. if you [aren't] you can't win. You can't win the
game. You can't be a winning engineering manager with B and C
engineers riding it out, not reeducating themselves, not being
current. You can't be a winning sales manager. . . . You can't survive as a manufacturing manager with B and C players who can't
improve asset turns, who can't get capacity from six sigma, who
can't put the intellectual capital into their business. Everyone of
you must leave Boca committed to only having the best athletes
on their teams, only A's, with a few B's, but no C's.

Several thousand GE employees had noted that the company's leadership did not deal with marginal performers fast enough, said Welch:

Let's commit ourselves to fixing that perception. Take risks. Give
people a chance to stretch. Give black belts big jobs. The world
we will face will require each of you to keep raising the performance bar. As you move on today's C's, new ones will emerge
because the bar will move. You must be more demanding than
ever before. Many of today's B's will be tomorrow's C's. They
won't make it as you raise the bar. You need to press everyone to
find those high-energy, high-intellect winning athletes. . . .
[You've got] to have the guts to remove those fairly and kindly
who aren't the very best. You've got to have the courage to hire
only the best and the brightest and take risks on high-potential
people.

Soon after the January senior manager's meeting, Welch was back at
GE headquarters, devising a strategy to deal with the less than pleasant
economic climate he had so carefully defined and analyzed in Boca
Raton. In late January and early February, Welch toiled through draft
after draft of his all-important 1997 Letter to Share Owners. He knew
that few documents were as carefully scrutinized as his letter, and recognized the fact that business enthusiasts and the popular press anx-

iously awaited its arrival in the hopes of culling more information about the company. Since Welch is usually tight-lipped throughout the year, the letter is often the outside world's best chance to get a rare glimpse of what is going on both inside the company, and inside the mind of the most successful CEO in the nation.

By the time he penned the final version of his letter, it was apparent that GE's chairman was slightly less gloomy about the company's prospects for coping with the Asian economic crisis. Here's what he wrote in that letter, which was published in March 1998:

> **The uncertainly brought about by the Asian economic difficulties creates both challenges and opportunities. For GE, Asia represents about 9 percent of our revenues (about half in Japan)— exposure that is by no means insignificant, but certainly manageable—and we are confident that we can minimize any impact on our existing operations.**
>
> **It has been our repeated experience that business uncertainty is inevitably accompanied by opportunity. The Asian situation should be no exception; it should provide us with a unique opportunity to make the strategic moves that will increase our presence and our participation in what we know will be one of the world's great markets of the 21st Century.**

In a slight departure from his custom, Welch turned to the past to provide some insight into the future. He did so as a way of offering proof that GE was making the right moves to deal with the Asian crisis. In his letter he suggested that the challenge posed to GE by the Asian crisis was reminiscent of another challenge put to the company in the early 1980s—the American recession. At that time, the pundits expressed doubt that American manufacturers, including GE, would be able to remain unscarred. But, wrote Welch, GE found a way to confound the pundits, by investing in a broad restructuring and in new businesses. As a result, the company became more competitive and productive.

Dealing with crisis is nothing new to GE. The company employed the same daring strategy when Europe suffered through its downturn in the early 1990s. Though many wrote off Europe at the time, GE invested heavily in the continent, purchasing new companies and expanding its presence in the region. When Europe recovered, "GE Europe," Welch proudly reported, experienced double-digit growth, to its present lofty $20+ billion level. Revenues doubled in the three years since 1994, and net income tripled during that same period, to over $1.5 billion. Rather than wait for better economic times in Mexico, GE applied the same aggressive techniques to that country when it moved through stormy economic waters in the mid-1990s: the company acquired ten companies and invested over $1 billion in new and existing operations. As a result, GE enjoyed a 60 percent increase in earnings in 1996 and a 100 percent increase in earnings in 1997. General Electric, Welch asserted, planned to deal with the Asian problem by employing the same aggressive tactics it had employed in dealing with crises in the United States, Europe, and Mexico. "Globalization," he wrote in the 1997 letter, "is one of the engines of GE growth, now and well into the next century. There will be dislocations and speed bumps on the road to prosperity in all the world's critical markets, but one cannot afford to write off any region in difficulty. . . . The path to greatness in Asia is irreversible, and GE will be there."

All the news in the 1997 letter was not as chilling as the Asian situation, and the optimistic Welch couldn't wait to discuss GE's accomplishments. Welch was particularly proud of the strides GE had made in the service side of the business. He happily announced that 1997 had marked GE's second straight year of double-digit growth in product service revenues, as well as continued improvement in net operating margin. He expected that in 1998 more than two-thirds of the company's revenues would come from financial, information, and product services. And he predicted that GE's growing capability in the service realm, much of it related to information technology, would help the company to increase its revenues from product service by over 30 percent to $13 billion in 1998.

While topics like globalization and services are certainly on the mind of the chairman, it is a much different topic that seems to occupy his soul. In fact, Welch couldn't wait to wrap up his discussion of those other topics so that he could devote the lion's share of the letter to his favorite subject—the six sigma quality initiative. Indeed, most of the 1997 Letter to Share Owners focused on that initiative: "the centerpiece of our dreams and aspirations for this great company," in the chairman's words. Welch attributed the speed and ease with which GE launched the quality program to the company's openness to change and its eagerness to find and integrate new ideas. As he noted, "finding the better way, the best idea, from whomever will share it with us, has become our central focus."

Welch was downright ebullient. Not only had GE integrated six sigma into the company far faster than original predictions, but its impact on the bottom line exceeded even Welch's grandiose expectations:

> **Operating margin, a critical measure of business efficiency and profitability, hovered around the 10 percent level at GE for decades. With Six Sigma embedding itself deeper into Company operations, GE in 1997 went through the "impossible" 15 percent level—approaching 16 percent—and we're optimistic about the upside.**

Welch reported that six sigma had delivered more than $300 million to GE's 1997 operating income, and that was only the tip of the iceberg. Six sigma would add an astounding $600 million to GE's bottom line in 1998—twice the already impressive 1997 figure. With results like that, it was no wonder that the most sought-after candidates for senior-leadership slots were the black belts and master black belts who were finishing six sigma assignments. They had become the new role models for leadership at GE:

> **In the early 1990s, after we had finished defining ourselves as a company of boundaryless people with a thirst for learning and a compulsion to share, it became *unthinkable* for any of us to tolerate—much less hire or promote or tolerate—those who cannot, or will not, commit to this way of work. It is simply too important to our future. . . . The reality is, we simply cannot afford to field anything but teams of A players.**

The six sigma quality initiative, Welch concluded, was moving GE closer to what had always been the company's goal: "a more than hundred-billion-dollar global enterprise with the agility, customer focus, and fire in the belly of a small company."

Once again, as he has done numerous times in the past, Welch used the occasion of the 1997 Letter to Share Owners to define the kind of business leaders he wanted to help run GE—people he called A players:

> **At the leadership level, an A is a man or woman with a vision and the ability to articulate that vision to the team, so vividly and powerfully that it also becomes their vision.**
>
> **An A leader has enormous personal energy and, beyond that, the ability to energize others and draw out their best, usually on a global basis.**
>
> **An A leader has "edge" as well: the instinct and the courage to make the tough calls—decisively, but with fairness and absolute integrity.**

As GE moved toward the twenty-first century, Welch pledged that there would be nothing but A's in every leadership position at the company:

> **They will be the best in the world, and they will act to field teams consisting of nothing but A players. The best leaders—the A's— are really coaches. What coach, with any instinct or passion for winning, would field an Olympic swimming or gymnastics team, or a Super Bowl team, that wasn't made up of the absolute best available? In the same vein, what business leader worthy of the name would even consider fielding a team with anything other than the very best, the A players?**

What are A players like?

> **In finance, for example, A's will be people whose talents include, but transcend, traditional controllership. The bigger role is one of full-fledged participant in driving the business to win in the market- place—a role far bigger than the dreary and and wasteful budget "drills" and bean counting that once defined and limited the job.**

Leaders in engineering . . .

are those who embrace the methodology of Design for Six Sigma. A engineers can't stand the thought of "riding it out" in the lab, but rather relish the rapid pace of technological change and continually reeducate themselves to stay on top of it.

In manufacturing, A players are those immersed in six sigma technology . . .

who consider inventory an embarrassment, especially with a whiff of deflation in the air—people who understand how to drive asset turns and reduce inventory while at the same time increasing our readiness to serve the customer.

Finally, in sales, A players use the enormous customer value that the six sigma quality initiative was generating to differentiate GE from the competition, to find new accounts, and to refresh and expand old ones. They are totally unlike C's . . .

whose days are spent visiting "friends" on the "milk-run" circuit of customer calls.

Welch concluded this section of the letter by indicating that the business of GE was to make sure it had A products and A services, which were delivered by A players around the globe.

As Welch's letter was going to press, General Electric got another terrific boost: For the first time ever, it was voted by *Fortune* the "most admired company in America." The chief ingredient in achieving this honor was the leadership at the top. In the insightful words of superinvestor Warren Buffett, "People are voting for the artist, not the painting." In *Fortune*'s words, GE won the prize this year because of admiration for Welch, "who has rewritten the book on management while keeping GE huge, nimble, and immensely profitable. Welch and GE get credit not only for what they have accomplished during his almost 17 years at the helm but also for what they have avoided. Since 1981 nearly every other corporate behemoth—AT&T, Exxon, Ford, GM, Sears, IBM, Philip Morris, Prudential—has collided with serious trouble: one-time arch-rival Westinghouse has deconstructed and then morphed into a broadcast outfit. GE has stayed its industrial course and keeps getting better." Again, Buffet was quoted: "People admire Jack for what he has done at GE more than they would if he had been at IBM and merely maintained it at the top. Before Jack, we thought GE was big and good, but not big and great."

In the spring of 1998, Welch went from strength to strength, heading not only the most powerful business enterprise, but also the most admired. As he wrestled with the new, tough issue of deflation, as he sought to improve GE's standing with customers by improving the quality of its products and processes, it was no accident that he turned to his arsenal of business secrets to guide him through these latest thickets. To cope with deflation, he invoked the secret of "embrace change, don't fear it." To improve customer relations, he embarked on the quality exercise in one more demonstration of GE's capacity for adapting and integrating ideas, part of Welch's dogged determination to create a learning culture at the company.

Although no one knows what the future will bring, Jack Welch isn't worried. His management secrets had served him well for almost two decades, and he was confident that they would serve him well in the future. After all, business is simple. Or, to phrase it as Jack Welch would, People always overestimate how complex business is. This isn't rocket science.

Acknowledgments

In June 1991, when I first approached the people at General Electric about writing a book about their chairman and chief executive officer, Jack Welch, I was told two things: one, he would prefer that no one write a book about him; but two, if I was absolutely determined to undertake the project, he would cooperate with me. Thanks to Welch's cooperation, I was able to put together an in-depth profile of his first decade (1981–1991) at GE's helm: *The New GE: How Jack Welch Revived an American Institution* (Business One Irwin, 1992). I spent many hours with GE's chairman and had access to all GE personnel. And I became the first outsider to visit the Crotonville Leadership Development Center.

The New GE described how the nation's most successful CEO transformed his company into a business powerhouse. When it became apparent that people wanted to know more about Jack Welch's management techniques, I wrote a second book, this one called *Get Better or Get Beaten! 31 Leadership Secrets from GE's Jack Welch* (Irwin Professional Publishing, 1994).

When editors at McGraw-Hill suggested that I write a third book on Welch, he was as friendly and cooperative as ever, making himself available for two long interviews and inviting me once again to be his guest at Crotonville. Because the purpose of this new book was to update the second one, I spoke also to many of Welch's senior colleagues, including most of the heads of GE's twelve businesses. I am grateful to Jack Welch and to everyone else at GE who spoke with me.

My year of research for this book—from the spring of 1997 to the spring of 1998—coincided with another record-breaking financial period for GE. But it was also a period when exciting new initiatives were springing up at the company. Welch's two-year-old quality exercise—known to everyone around GE as six sigma—was hitting its stride in 1997. His program boosting the company's service segment was beginning to have a strong impact on the bottom line. As for the chairman, he seemed fully recovered from his open-heart surgery in 1995. But he was due to retire in November 2000, and GE personnel were quite willing to discuss (off the record, of course) the most sensitive, and most fascinating, question around GE: Who will succeed Jack Welch?

In so many ways, as I traveled around GE, I saw a company going through major transformation. In other companies, such upheaval might have been an ominous sign. Not at Jack Welch's General Electric. He loves change and believes change is vital for a business if it is not to stagnate. With so many new developments, a third book on Jack Welch and General Electric made perfect sense. Much of Welch's more traditional business philosophies are still very much in evidence around the company, and the main purpose of *Jack Welch and the GE Way: Management Insights and Leadership Secrets of the Legendary CEO.* is to explore how those secrets have fared through the years, to find out whether they survived intact or whether Welch modified them to accommodate new realities.

In doing my research for this book, I had a strong anchor at General Electric in the person of Joyce Hergenhan, who heads up corporate public relations at GE. As has been the case since my original research on GE in 1991, Joyce was always gracious, helpful, and incredibly efficient in responding to my numerous requests. As with my other GE books, this project was independent and I did not show a copy of the manuscript to *any* GE employee in advance of publication.

A word of appreciation about my editor, Jeffrey Krames. He and I have worked together on and off for the past fourteen years. In every case, including this one, he has given me the greatest gift an editor can bestow on an author—his unconditional enthusiasm for the project. He has labored hard to make sure this is the best book we could produce together, and I have benefited at every step in this exercise from his wisdom.

I also want to thank some other prominent members of the McGraw-Hill team, including Philip Ruppel, publisher of Business McGraw-Hill, Lynda Luppino, and Claudia Riemer-Boutote. I also want to thank my agent, Chris Calhoun, at Sterling Lord Literistic, and Jean Max.

Thanks also to those members of my family who have supported me and my book projects unstintingly and with smiles on their faces as I traveled around the United States, dropping in on them occasionally. I especially want to thank Roslyn and Judd Winick, Jack and Bea Slater, Michael and Bobbi Winick, Judith Resnik, and Dennis Curtis.

Finally, I am ever mindful of the important role my immediate family plays in helping me see a book project like this one through to publication. I thank them above all for their encouragement and love—my wife, Elinor; my children, Miriam, Shimi, Adam, and Rachel; and my grandchildren, Edo and Maya.

Endnotes

Introduction

3   "I take absolutely no comfort in where we are today," Jack Welch, interview, December 12, 1997.

6   "The excitement comes from within him . . . ," W. James McNerney, Jr., interview, September 26, 1997.

7   ". . . the advertising manager of our company.," Jack Welch, interview, "Roberto Goizueta and Jack Welch: The Wealth Builders," *Fortune* magazine, December 11, 1995.

12   "What sets (GE) apart . . . ," Jack Welch, speech, General Electric Annual Meeting, Charlotte, North Carolina, April 23, 1997.

Chapter 1

18   "As a result, you are. . . . ," W. James McNerney, Jr., interview, September 26, 1997.

19   "Jack is quick to sense . . . ," Robert Wright, interview, July 24, 1997.

20   "It was a reminder . . . ," "Jack Welch quoted in "Robert Goizueta and Jack Welch: The Wealth Builders."

22   "I could see a lot of . . . ," Jack Welch, interview, July 8, 1991.

25   "We want to be more . . . ," Jack Welch, speech to the General Electric Annual Meeting, Charlottesville, Virginia, April 24, 1996.

Chapter 2

28   ". . . controls rather than facilitates . . . ," Jack Welch, speech, July 15, 1991, after accepting the National Management Association's Manager of the Year award.

28   "They equate (managing) with . . . ," Interview with Jack Welch, *Monogram*, Fall 1989, pp. 2–5.

29   ". . . inspire with clear visions . . . ," Ibid.

29   "We've chosen one of the world's . . . ," "Speed, Simplicity, Self-Confidence," Noel Tichy and Ram Charan, *Harvard Business Review*, September–October 1989, pp. 112–120.

29   ". . . very rarely on a quantitative . . . ," "Face to Face: Jack Welch," *FOCUS*, the Journal of Egon Zehnder International, January 1997, pp. 3–12.

29   "You can quantify it . . . ," Ibid.

30   "Managing is knowing . . . ," David Calhoun, interview, September 25, 1997.

31   "My job is to put . . . ," Jack Welch, interview, October 22, 1991.

31   "I have no idea how . . . ," Jack Welch, interview, *Der Spiegel*, July 14, 1997.

31   "They are the job killers . . . ," Jack Welch quoted in *Washington Post*, February 27, 1994.

31   "So organizations constantly . . . ," Jack Welch quoted in *Industry Week*, May 2, 1994.

31   ". . . I don't run . . . ," Ibid.

31   "It's silly. I can't . . . ," Ibid.

32   "I don't set them . . . ," Jack Welch quoted in *Nikkei Business*, February 21, 1994.

32   "The thing I've noticed . . . ," Jack Welch, interview December 12, 1997.

Chapter 3

36   "But this person won't talk. . . . ," Jack Welch quoted in *Nikkei Business*, February 21, 1994.

37   "What we are looking for . . . ," Jack Welch, Letter to Share Owners in 1993 General Electric Annual Report.

38   "Too many of you work. . . . ," Jack Welch, speech, Operating Managers meeting, Boca Raton Resort and Club, Boca Raton, Florida, January 5–7, 1997.

39   "The younger people really want . . . ," Patrick Dupuis, interview, September 25, 1997.

40   "We have in the U.S. . . . ," Jack Welch, interview, December 12, 1997.

40   "That is a total . . . ," Ibid.

41   "The biggest advice I give . . . ," Ibid.

41   "A lot of them don't . . . ," Ibid.

41   "What happens is . . . ," Ibid.

42   "Today's CEO in 1997. . . . ," Jack Welch quoted in *Washington Post*, March 23, 1997.

42   "I've got all 'As' . . . ," Jack Welch, interview, September 24, 1997.

Chapter 4

47   "In the twenty-first century . . . ," Jim Baughman, interview June 20, 1991.

47   "Our strengths were lost . . . ," Joyce Hergenhan, interview, June 17, 1991.

48   "Unfortunately, it is still possible . . . ," Jack Welch, Letter to Share Owners in 1991 General Electric Annual Report.

49   "I would have liked . . . ," Jack Welch, interview, *L'Expansion*, "The Secrets of the Finest Company in the World," July 10–24, 1997, pp. 26–39.

49   "One of the truly . . . ," Dennis Dammerman, interview, July 28, 1997.

Chapter 5

51   "Somebody runs the . . . ," Jack Welch quoted in *Washington Post*, March 27, 1997.

52   ". . . relentless consistency, a . . . ," Ibid.

53   "There isn't a human being . . . ," "Face to Face: Jack Welch."

53   "If a leader wants to drive . . . ," Jeffrey R. Immelt, interview, September 26, 1997.

54   "I don't say one thing . . . ," Jack Welch, talk at Crotonville, Croton-on-Hudson, New York, September 24, 1997.

54   "It's not that I changed . . . ," *Control Your Destiny or Someone Else Will*, Noel M. Tichy and Stratford Sherman, New York, Doubleday, 1993, pp. 64–65.

54   "I haven't changed a thing! . . . ," Ibid., p. 210.

55   "The most remarkable thing . . . ," David Calhoun, interview, September 25, 1997.

55   "Change ideas," Jack Welch, interview, December 12, 1997.

Chapter 6

59   "I had the luxury . . . ," Jack Welch quoted in Roberto Goizueta and Jack Welch: The Wealth Builders.

60   "the winners would . . . ," "Face to Face: Jack Welch."

61   "When you're number four or five . . . ," Jack Welch, interview, *Business Today*, February 7–21, 1995.

62   "These are the businesses . . . ," Jim Baughman, interview June 20, 1991.

64   "I have never 'laid off . . . ," Jack Welch, interview, *Nikkei Business*, November 18, 1996, pp. 144–47.

65   "Jack never tried . . . ," interview, Gary C. Wendt, July 31, 1997.

66   "We wouldn't even think . . . ," Jack Welch, interview, December 12, 1997.

66   "The notion behind being number one . . . ," Steven Kerr, interview, July 29, 1997.

Chapter 7

71   "GE people were engineers and accountants . . . ," Tom Brokaw, interview, August 8, 1997.

75   "We are very much in danger . . . ," Robert Wright, interview, October 23, 1991.

Chapter 8

78   "People try to mythologize . . . ," Don Ohlmeyer quoted in "How GE Made NBC No. 1," *Fortune*, February 3, 1997.

79   "He's generally if not always . . . ," Robert Wright, quoted in "How GE Made NBC No. 1."

79   "There's a lot of Don . . . ," Jack Welch quoted in "How GE Made NBC No. 1."

79   "I talked about the integrity . . . ," Tom Brokaw, interview, August 8, 1997.

80   "Making small calls," Jack Welch, interview, December 12, 1997.

83   "Bob Wright is like . . . ," Ibid.

84   "People, say, Jack, how can you . . . ," Jack Welch quoted in "How GE Made NBC No. 1."

86   "There was no one . . . ," Tom Brokaw, interview, August 8, 1997.

86   "Don't forget, after a decade . . . ," Jack Welch, interview, December 12, 1997.

Chapter 9

90   "Numbers aren't the vision . . . ," Jack Welch, interview, *Industry Week*, May 2, 1994.

93   "Even senior people . . . ," "Face to Face: Jack Welch."

93   "I'll never get it there . . . ," Jack Welch, interview, December 12, 1997.

Chapter 10

95   "We soon discovered . . . ," "Face to Face: Jack Welch."

96   "Historically, at GE . . . ," Dennis Dammerman, interview, July 28, 1997.

96   "Elimination of boundaries . . . ," Jack Welch, Letter to Share Owners in General Electric 1990 Annual Report.

96   "Integrated diversity . . . ," Ibid.

97   This boundaryless learning . . . ," Jack Welch, speech, General Electric Annual Meeting, Charlotte, North Carolina, April 23, 1997.

97   ". . . The quality of an idea . . . ," Jack Welch, interview, *Industry Week*, May 2, 1994.

98   "Among the values . . . ," The Secrets of the Finest Company in the World.

98   "So Welch says moving . . . ," Steven Kerr, interview, July 29, 1997.

98   "I'm very proud of. . . . ," Jack Welch, speech, General Electric Operating Managers Meeting, Boca Raton, Florida, January 5–6, 1998.

102 "It's almost like . . . ," Robert L. Nordell, interview, September 28, 1997.

103 "We have been exposed to all . . . ," "Face to Face: Jack Welch."

103 "Sometimes these leaders have said . . . ," Steven Kerr, interview, July 29, 1997.

103 "In some organizations . . . ," W. James McNerney, Jr., interview, September 26, 1997.

104 "It starts with Jack . . . ," Jeffrey R. Immelt, interview, September 26, 1997.

104 "It's a more fun . . . ," David L. Calhoun, interview, September 25, 1997.

104 "People today look . . . ," Jack Welch, interview, July 22, 1997.

104 "That's a number beyond . . . ," Ibid.

104 "Now that was their energizing . . . ," Ibid.

105 "That's because their organizations . . . ," Jack Welch, interview, *Nikkei Business*, February 21, 1994.

106 "GE Appliances was doing . . . ," Patrick Dupuis, interview September 25, 1997.

106 "We have often observed . . . ," Merrill Lynch analysts, Jeanne G. Terrile, First Vice President, and Carol Sabbagha, Assistant Vice President, report, May 15, 1997.

Chapter 11

113 "Today, people sort of get . . . ," Jack Welch, interview, *Industry Week*, May 2, 1994.

113 "The world is moving at . . . ," Jack Welch, interview, July 8, 1991.

113 "We had a Green Beret . . . Reuben Gutoff quoted in Roberto Goizueta and Jack Welch: The Wealth Builders.

114 "Big corporations are filled . . . ," Jack Welch, interview, July 8, 1991.

115 "By the time you get . . . ," Jack Welch, Crotonville talk, September 24, 1997.

Chapter 12

117 "We (have) to find a way . . . ," Jack Welch, interview, July 8, 1991.

118 "The new arrangement has . . . ," Jack Welch, Letter to Share Owners in 1988 General Electric Annual Report.

119 "For one, they communicate . . . ," Jack Welch, speech, General Electric Annual Meeting, Waukesha, Wisconsin, April 27, 1988.

119 "To get people focused . . . ," Robert L. Nardelli, interview, September 28, 1997.

120 ". . . is the indispensable . . . ," Jack Welch, speech, The New England Council, Boston, Massachusetts, November 11, 1992.

120 "There is something about . . . ," Jack Welch, Letter to Share Owners in 1991 General Electric Annual Report.

120 "This is particularly true . . . ," Ibid.

120 "We begin to erect layers . . . ," Jack Welch, speech, The New England Council, Boston, Massachusetts, November 11, 1992.

120 "If you're not fast . . . ," Jack Welch, quoted in *USA Today*, July 26, 1993.

121 "Most small companies are uncluttered . . . ," Jack Welch, Letter to Share Owners in 1992 General Electric Annual Report.

122 "At USC . . . ," Steven Kerr, interview, July 29, 1997.

122 "Speed is the product . . . ," "Face to Face: Jack Welch."

Chapter 13

126 ". . . limited our ability . . . ," Jack Welch, Letter to Share Owners in 1996 General Electric Annual Report.

126 "Productivity is not the squeezing . . . ," Jack Welch, interview, *Industry Week*, May 2, 1994.

126 "There was no horizontal . . . ," Jim Baughman, interview, June 20, 1991.

127 "The pace of change . . . ," Jack Welch, quoted in "Today's Leaders Look to Tomorrow," *Fortune*, March, 26, 1990, pp. 30–31.

128 "Boundarylessness was necessary to . . . ," Gary Wendt, interview, July 31, 1997.

129 "We teach that when someone . . . ," Steven Kerr, interview, July 29, 1997.

130 "Boundaryless behavior is how . . . ," Jack Welch, talk, Crotonville, September 24, 1997.

130 "And he believed in calling . . . ," Paolo Fresco, interview July 22, 1997.

131 "It is an enormous opportunity . . . ," David Calhoun, interview, September 25, 1997.

131 ". . . we involve suppliers as . . . ," Jack Welch, Letter to Share Owners in 1991 General Electric Annual Report.

Chapter 14

136 "The complacent and timid . . . ," Jack Welch, speech, The Bay Area Council, San Francisco, California, September 6, 1989.

136 ". . . the competitive world of . . . ," Ibid.

139 "To an engineer . . . ," Ibid.

139 "The leader's unending . . . ," Ibid.

139 ". . . overarching message—something big . . . , *Control Your Destiny Or Someone Else Will*, p. 246.

139 "Simple messages travel faster . . . ," Jack Welch, Letter to Share Owners in 1995 General Electric Annual Report.

140 "Some people get it . . . ," Jack Welch, Letter to Share Owners in 1990 General Electric Annual Report.

140 "Self-confidence does not grow . . . ," Jack Welch, speech, The Bay Area Council, San Francisco, California, September 6 1989.

140 "Self-confident people are open . . . ," Jack Welch, Letter to Share Owners in 1995 General Electric Annual Report.

141 ". . . a work ethic . . . ," Jack Welch, speech, The Bay Area Council, San Francisco, California, September 6 1989.

141 "If you don't have . . . ," Jack Welch, interview, *Industry Week*, May 2, 1994.

Chapter 15

144 "The way to get faster . . . ," Jack Welch, speech, The New England Council, November 11, 1992.

145 "We generally used to tell . . . ," Jack Welch, quoted in *USA Today*, July 26, 1993.

145 "Can you put in . . . ," Steven Kerr, interview, July 29, 1997.

145 "That doesn't mean abdication . . . ," Jack Welch, interview, *Industry Week*, May 2, 1994.

146 ". . . would have produced . . . ," Jack Welch, interview, October 22, 1991.

147 "We have to create . . . ," Jack Welch, quoted by Jim Baughman, interview, June 20, 1991.

148 "We complain, on occasion . . . ," Jack Welch, speech, General Electric Annual Meeting, Greenville, South Carolina, April 26, 1989.

148 "If you are controlling . . . ," Jack Welch, interview, *Nikkei Business*, February 21, 1994.

Chapter 16

150 "Wrestling with the boundaries . . . ," Jack Welch, speech, General Electric Annual Meeting, Decatur, Alabama, April 24, 1991.

Chapter 17

159 "When you've been told . . . ," An anonymous electrician quoted in "How Jack Welch Keeps the Ideas Coming at GE," *Fortune*, August 12, 1991, p. 43.

161 "Don't ever tell me . . . ," Jack Welch, interview, July 8, 1991.

163 "As we took down much . . . ," Jack Welch, speech, General Electric Annual Meeting, Florence, South Carolina, April 22, 1992.

163 "The most important thing . . . ," Jack Welch, interview, July 22, 1997.

Chapter 18

165 "We have found that . . . ," Jack Welch, speech, Annual Meeting, Charlottesville, Virginia, April 24, 1996.

166 "People work for a month . . . ," Jack Welch, interview, "Face to Face: Jack Welch."

166 "Rigorous budgeting alone . . . ," Ibid.

167 "You've got to think . . . ," Jack Welch, interview, *Industry Week*, May 2, 1994.

167 "Allows people to constantly . . . ," Jack Welch, interview, *Business Today*, February 7–21, 1995.

167 "Stretch is a concept that . . . ," Jack Welch, Letter to Share Owners in 1993 General Electric Annual Report.

168 "We used to timidly . . . ," Ibid.

168 "Decimal points are nonsense . . . ," Jack Welch, interview, *Industry Week*, May 2, 1994.

169 "I don't think we . . . ," Paolo Fresco, interview, July 22, 1997.

169 ". . . replaces a grim, heads-down . . . ," Jack Welch, Letter to Share Owners in 1994 General Electric Annual Report.

170 "But in stretching for these 'impossible' . . . ," Jack Welch, Letter to Share Owners in 1995 General Electric Annual Report.

170 "If they don't have the team . . . ," Jack Welch, interview, *Nikkei Business*, February 21, 1994.

170 "If we look at . . . ," Eugene F. Murphy, interview, September 24, 1997.

171 "Stretch means really challenging . . . ," Robert Nardelli, interview, September 28, 1997.

171 "You can abuse stretch . . . ," David Calhoun, interview, September 26, 1997.

172 "We don't know how to live . . . ," Patrick Dupuis, interview, September 25, 1997.

172 "If you have a lousy relationship . . . ," Jack Welch, interview, December 12, 1997.

172 "You'll never succeed . . . ," Jeffrey Immelt, interview, September 26, 1997.

Chapter 19

175   "The opportunity for growth . . . ," Jack Welch. Letter to Share Owners in 1997 General Electric Annual Report.
178   "All these things . . . ," Jack Welch, interview, July 22, 1997.
179   "That asset had been underwhelmed . . . ," W. James McNerney, Jr. interview, September 26, 1997.
181   "The service business is an eye-opening . . . ," David Calhoun, interview, September 26, 1996.
181   "We know the technology . . . ," Ibid.
181   "Where the temptation is . . . ," W. James McNerney, Jr., interview, September 26, 1997.
182   "Now we think servicing. . . . ," Paolo Fresco, interview, July 22, 1997.
182   "We offer them . . . ," The Secrets of the Finest Company in the World.
183   "I would be concerned . . . ," Paolo Fresco, interview, July 22, 1997.
183   "The problem is to convince . . . ," Ibid.

Chapter 20

187   "You know how . . . ," Gary Wendt, interview, July 31, 1997.
188   "According to one magazine . . . ," *People*, December 22, 1997, "Woman's Work," p. 72.
188   "He is not saying, 'You weren't . . . ," Cathy Callegari quoted in *Woman's Work*.
188   "The judge," said Lorna, "has found that . . . ," Ibid.
188   "He brought home the bacon . . . ," Lorna Wendt quoted in *Time*, December 29, 1997–January 5, 1998.
188   "The old idea was that you shouldn't pay . . . ," Nicholas Heyman quoted in "GE Capital: Jack Welch's Secret Weapon, *Fortune*, November 10, 1997, pp. 116–134.
190   "You can't make money . . . ," Gary Wendt quoted in "Jack's Encore," *Business Week*," October 28, 1996.

Chapter 21

194   "It's very difficult to jump . . . ," Paolo Fresco, interview, July 22, 1997.
195   "Plastics eventually emerged . . . ," "Face to Face: Jack Welch."
195   "Jack's perception of the world . . . ," Gary Wendt, interview, July 31, 1997.
195   ". . . don't mean a thing . . . ," The Secrets of the Finest Company in the World.
196   "There's one GE . . . ," Ibid.
197   "The classic global . . . ," Jack Welch, interview, July 22, 1997.
198   "There's almost no expansion . . . ," Jack Welch, interview, *Industry Week*, May 2, 1994.
198   ". . . The constant sharing of business . . . ," Jack Welch, Letter to Share Owners in 1996 General Electric Annual Report.

199 "... you know, people say ...," Jack Welch, interview, *Industry Week*, May 2, 1994.

199 "Today we like India ...," Paolo Fresco, interview, July 22, 1997.

200 "Overall, we were impressed ...," from report written by Lehman Brothers analyst Robert T. Cornell, May 30, 1997.

Chapter 22

205 "As Boundaryless Learning has defined ...," Jack Welch, speech, General Electric Annual Meeting, Charlotte, North Carolina, April 23, 1997

206 "... in the eye of the Asian competitive hurricane." Jack Welch, speech, General Electric Annual Meeting, Charlottesville, Virginia, April 24, 1996.

207 "It's gotten better with ...," Jack Welch, Ibid.

207 "So many of us grew ...," Dennis Dammerman, interview, July 28, 1997.

208 "One of the things ...," Paolo Fresco, interview July 22, 1997.

208 "When we say a lack ...," Ibid.

208 "Jack always thought....," Robert Wright, interview, July 24, 1997.

209 "We want to be more ...," Jack Welch, speech, General Electric Annual Meeting, Charlottesville, Virginia, April 24, 1996.

211 "... had a real ring of substance ...," Dennis Dammerman, interview, July 28, 1997.

212 "Six sigma had a systems ...," Robert Wright, interview, July 24, 1997.

212 "This is not a slogan ...," Jack Welch, interview, July 22, 1997.

212 "We felt like we ...," Gary J. Powell, interview, August 6, 1997.

212 "You could see the sparkle ...," Ibid.

213 "When GE decides to do ...," Paolo Fresco, interview, July 22, 1997.

213 "What we learned....," Gary M. Reiner, interview, July 30, 1997.

213 "By increasing your quality....," Paolo Fresco, interview, July 22, 1997.

Chapter 23

216 "Very little of this requires invention," Jack Welch, speech, General Electric Annual Meeting, Charlottesville, Virginia, April 24, 1996.

216 "... There is no company....," Ibid.

217 "1.) Enormous energy....," letter sent by Jack Welch on July 19, 1997, to all Corporate Executive Council attendees.

218 "Simply put, quality must be ..." Jack, Welch, speech, General Electric Operating Managers Meeting, Boca Raton Resort and Club, Boca Raton, Florida, January 5–7, 1997.

219 "The methodologies of six sigma....," Jack Welch, Letter to Share Owners in 1996 General Electric Annual Report.

220 "In the next century ...," Jack Welch, speech, General Electric Annual Meeting, Charlotte, North Carolina, April 23, 1997.

220 "Does this look like ...," Jack Welch, interview, *Der Spiegel*, July 14, 1997.

221 "There are people who would ..., Dennis Dammerman, interview, July 28, 1997.

221 "Quality is the next act ...," Jack Welch, interview, July 22, 1997.

221 "... is both a top-line ...," Ibid.

222 "It was a totally different . . . ," Ibid.
222 "Job security. Enhanced . . . ," Ibid.
222 "We only have meetings . . . ," Ibid.
223 "Six sigma has gone . . . ," Jack Welch, speech, General Electric Annual Meeting, Charlotte, North Carolina, April 23, 1997.

Chapter 24

229 "The snowball is growing . . . ," Jack Welch, speech, General Electric Annual Meeting, Charlotte North Carolina, April 23, 1997.
232 "We get it half . . . ," Gary Reiner, interview, July 30, 1997.
232 "The software gives you . . . ," Ibid.,
232 "We got more productive . . . ," Gary C. Wendt, interview, July 31, 1997.
232 "It was routine to say . . . ," Gary Powell, interview, August 6, 1997.
233 ". . . cocktail commitment . . . ," Ibid.
233 "We never questioned . . . ," Ibid.
234 "Don't do this to me . . . ," Ibid.
234 "This isn't even close . . . ," Ibid.
235 "Before, we never fully . . . ," Ibid.
236 ". . . How do you know the difference . . . ," Jennifer Pokrzywinski, report, "General Electric: Beating Six Sigma Targets . . . ," April 3, 1997.
237 "Everyone has their cost-cutting . . . ," Jennifer Pokrzywinski, interview, August 20, 1997.
237 "All our managers . . . ," The Secrets of the Finest Company in the World.
237 "About seven thousand . . . ," Jack Welch, interview, July 22, 1997.
237 ". . . has the potential . . . ," Jeanne G. Terrile and Carol Sabbagha, report, "Are you Worried about GE's Multiple?", May 15, 1997.
238 "It was a little bit scary . . . ," Dennis Dammerman, interview, July 28, 1997.
238 "Get back to every . . . ," Gary Wendt, interview, July 31, 1997.

Chapter 25

245 "While it is entirely possible . . . ," quoted in letter from Jack Welch letter to GE employees, March 29, 1995.
245 "In any large organization . . . ," Ibid.
246 "Most troubling is that . . . ," "Jack Welch's Nightmare on Wall Street," *Fortune*, September 5, 1994, pp. 50–55.
247 "Integrity is the rock . . . ," Welch in his Statement of Integrity in "Integrity: The Spirit & Letter of Our Commitment," 1987, booklet produced by General Electric.
247 "There is now a nascent . . . ," Jack Welch to the Subcommittee on Oversight and Investigations of the House Committee on Energy and Commerce, in Washington, D.C., July 29, 1992.
249 "I can't guarantee anyone. . . . ," Jack Welch, interview, December 12, 1997.
249 "Look, that would be . . . ," Ibid.
249 "Immediately. They get a . . . ," Ibid.
250 "No. I don't think so . . . ," Ibid.
250 I don't think there's a . . . ," Ibid.

Chapter 26

251 "The Harvard of Corporate . . . ," How Jack Welch Keeps the Ideas Coming at GE," *Fortune*, August 12, 1991.

257 "Have you shipped a few?" This and all subsequent Jack Welch quotes in this chapter are from his appearance at Crotonville, September 24, 1997.

Chapter 27

268 "The last 16 years . . . ," Jack Welch, interview, *Nikkei Business*, November 18, 1996.

268 "Absolutely. Much better . . . ," Jack Welch, interview, The Secrets of the Finest Company in the World.

268 "As early as the eighties . . . ," Jack Welch, interview, *Der Spiegel.*

268 "Remember that we don't . . . ," Jack Welch, interview, The Secrets of the Finest Company in the World.

269 "The short answer is that . . . ," Jack Welch, Letter to Share Owners in 1993 General Electric Annual Report.

270 For the next couple . . . ," Jack Welch, interview, *Business Today*, February 7–21, 1995.

270 "Too often they're too . . . ," Welch, Ibid.

270 "I want GE to be . . . ," Welch, Ibid.

271 ". . . a big company body . . . ," Jack Welch, quoted in *Washington Post*, February 27, 1994.

271 "I doubt it. . . . ," Jack Welch, interview, July 22, 1997.

271 "What we call the ability . . . ," Paolo Fresco, interview, July 22, 1997.

272 "Cutting people is the . . . ," Jack Welch, interview, *Nikkei Business.* February 7–21, 1995.

272 "I don't think we're . . . ," Ibid.

272 "When we started restructuring . . . ," Jack Welch, interview, *Der Spiegel*, July 14, 1997.

273 "What has to be truly amazing . . . ," Robert T. Cornell, report, November 3, 1997.

273 "We continue to strongly . . . ," Nicholas P. Heymann, report, May 12, 1997.

274 "There should be no reason . . . ," Jack Welch, interview, *Business Today*, February 7–21, 1995.

274 "I want somebody with incredible . . . ," Jack Welch, interview, *Der Spiegel*, July 14, 1997.

275 "It's like an obsession . . . ," Jack Welch, interview, The Secrets of the Finest Company in the World.

275 "I'm not going to tell you . . . ," Ibid.

275 "If my successor breaks . . . ," Ibid.

275 "Generally, they're pretty . . . ," Jack Welch, interview, December 12, 1997.

275 "I come with a . . . ," Ibid.

Chapter 28

280 "In today's world . . . ," Jack Welch, interview, *Nikkei Business*, November 18, 1996.

281 "I think these things . . . ," Jack Welch, interview, July 22, 1997.
283 "During the sixties and seventies, the . . . ," Jack Welch, speech, The World Economic Forum, Davos, Switzerland, January 30, 1997.
283 "It's got to be a big . . . ," Jack Welch, interview, July 22, 1997.
284 "No other country . . . ," Jack Welch, interview, *Nikkei Business*, February 21, 1994.
284 "Yes they will . . . ," Ibid.
284 "Just you wait and . . . ," Jack Welch, interview, *Der Spiegel*, July 14, 1997.
285 "Politicians come and . . . ," Ibid.
285 "There has, of course . . . ," Ibid.
285 "Germany is changing . . . ," Ibid.
286 "I don't know . . . ," Ibid.
286 "This is a phenomenon . . . ," The Secrets of the Finest Company in the World.

Epilogue

288 to 293   "About everyone was producing more . . . ," Jack Welch, speech, General Electric Operating Managers Meeting, Boca Raton, Florida, January 5–6, 1998. All Jack Welch quotes on these pages are from the same meeting.
294 "The uncertainty brought about . . . ," Jack Welch, Letter to Share Owners in General Electric 1997 Annual Report.
295 "Globalization is one of the engines . . . ," Ibid.
295 ". . . the centerpiece of our dreams . . . ," Ibid.
296 ". . . finding the better way . . . ," Ibid.
296 "Operating margin, a critical measure . . . ," Ibid.
296 "In the early 1990s . . . ," Ibid.
296 "more than a hundred-billion-dollar . . . ," Ibid.
297 "At the leadership level, an A is a man . . . ," Ibid.
297 "They will be the best in the world . . . ," Ibid.
297 "In finance, for example, A's will be people . . . ," Ibid.
298 ". . . are those who embrace . . . ," Ibid.
298 ". . . who consider inventory an embarrassment . . . ," Ibid.
298 ". . . whose days are spent. . . . ," Ibid.
298 "People are voting . . . ," Warren Buffet, quoted in "America's Most Admired Companies," *Fortune*, March 2, 1998, pp. 70–87.
299 "People admire Jack for . . . ," Ibid.

Index